THROUGH THE TIGER'S EYES

THROUGH

STANLEY BREEDEN AND BELINDA WRIGHT

THE TIGER'S EYES

A CHRONICLE OF INDIA'S WILDLIFE

TEN SPEED PRESS

BERKELEY, CALIFORNIA

Maps on pages xiii, 80, and 100 by Virender Kumar.

Photos on pages xi, xii (left), xiv, 32 (top left), 52, 61, 65, 68 (bottom), 74, 118, 151, and 164 copyright National Geographic Society.

Photographs by Belinda Wright with some additional photography by Stanley Breeden, except for the following: photos on pages 134 and 135, used by permission of Dr. Ullas Karanth; photo on page 138 by Tariq Aziz, copyright WPSI; photos on pages 130 and 169 by F. Memon; photos on page 167 (top left and bottom right) by Andrew Dennis.

A Kirsty Melville book

Ten Speed Press
P.O. Box 7123
Berkeley, CA 94707

Distributed in Australia by E.J. Dwyer Pty Ltd; in Canada by Publishers Group West; in New Zealand by Tandem Press; in South Africa by Real Books; and in the United Kingdom and Europe by Airlift Books.

Text and cover design by Nancy Austin
Printed in Singapore

Library of Congress Cataloging-in-Publication Data on file with publisher.

1 2 3 4 5 — 00 99 98 97 96

Preceding pages: A tigress surveys Ranthambhore National Park from the ruins of a fort (page i). Barasingha, or swamp deer, stags on the meadows of Kanha National Park at daybreak (pages ii–iii).

To Salim Ali—
A dear friend and uncompromising champion of India's wildlife.
We miss him greatly.

ACKNOWLEDGMENTS

Belinda's mother, Anne, who has been a courageous conservationist since the late 1960s, has given us unstinting support, encouragement, and advice. Nothing is ever too much trouble for her. Over the years, both Anne and Belinda's father, Bob, have helped us in many ways. We would also like to thank Rashid Ali and Jan Molony for their cheerful company at Kipling Camp.

In our travels throughout India we have made many friends who went out of their way to assist us and often generously shared their homes. To all these people we extend our thanks.

We are especially grateful to Billy Arjan Singh, not only for his friendship but also for his unflagging efforts in trying to save the tiger; to Fateh Singh Rathore for his friendship, encouragement, and the use of his Jeep while we were working in Ranthambhore; to Dave Ferguson and the U.S. Fish and Wildlife Service for their long-term support, particularly for our work in Keoladeo; to Bholu Khan for sharing his deep knowledge of Keoladeo, his unfailing cheerfulness, and his friendship; to Ullas Karanth, John Wakefield, and Shekar Dattatri for their hospitality and company at Nagarahole; to Brijendra Singh for his warm friendship over the years and his hospitality at Corbett National Park; to Manju Barua for making our visit to Kaziranga so comfortable and so stimulating; to Cliff and Dawn Frith for their friendship and their constructive comments on the text.

We also thank the National Geographic Society for allowing us to use the photographs published in their magazine and for generously supporting so much of our work—photography, writing, and filmmaking—over the years.

We are indebted to Elva Castino for deciphering Stan's handwriting and turning it into an immaculate manuscript, and for transcribing many hours of taped interviews.

Since the birth of the Wildlife Protection Society of India in late 1994, Belinda's work has been backed by a dedicated team including an extraordinary band of intrepid informers who must remain nameless. WPSI's Governing Board, led by Lalit Mohan Thapar, has supported the Society through all its teething problems. No one has been more generous than Samir Thapar. Particular thanks must go to Ashok Kumar, WPSI's vice president, who since 1993 has patiently, tirelessly, and with great good humor advised Belinda on her work every step of the way. Ashok also shouldered the day-to-day running of WPSI, without a murmur of protest, while Belinda worked on this book. Belinda's colleagues in the IUCN Cat Specialist Group have constantly offered support and advice.

We are also grateful to Kamal Nath, for it was he who first believed the horror stories of tiger poaching and the tiger bone trade and in his capacity as the minister for the environment took extraordinary steps to try and solve the problem.

Our acknowledgment would not be complete without mention of the pioneers of the Indian tiger conservation movement, including the late Mrs. Indira Gandhi, Dr. Karan Singh, Dr. Ranjitsinh, and Anne Wright. To them we offer our deepest respect for their courage and foresight.

CONTENTS

VI. THE LAST GREAT JUNGLES

Nilgiri tahr race down a hill.

Banseri was almost invisible in the undergrowth. She now turns and walks directly toward us. Her stripes, borne through the bamboo by her sinuous gait, are mesmerizing. When she is about ten meters away, she stares fiercely at us before melting away again. She is the very spirit of the forest.

—From our diaries

PREFACE

Kanha National Park, Central India—
27 May 1983

Usually we call the tigers we come to know well after the tree under which we first find them, using the Hindi name. We first saw this tigress lying under a canopy of bamboo, but we thought *bans* a little mundane. So we called her Banseri, which is a bamboo flute and also a girl's name. Banseri was never very friendly but neither did she avoid us by running away—as some others did—when we approached riding our elephants. She would stare at us and occasionally curl her lip in a half-snarl or bare her perfectly white, large canines.

Ten days ago we had the first clear view of Banseri with her two cubs. She lay on her side on a large, flat rock in front of the cave where the cubs were born, and until now had been hidden. We judged the cubs to be between two and three months old. They ran and played around their mother. One sat on top of Banseri and was knocked down gently with a soft swipe of its mother's paw. Banseri then licked its face, seeming to wrap the small head in her pink tongue.

Today has been hot, 45 degrees Celsius, but now, near sunset, the air has cooled a little. Dry, fallen leaves crackle under the feet of the elephants we are riding, as we slowly climb the small plateau to Banseri's cave. The plateau's more or less level top is ringed with large granite boulders. Banseri lies draped over one of these, her soft coat and bright color contrasting with the harsh, black rock. Only after several minutes of looking carefully around do we see the two cubs lying side by side in the space between two boulders. They look intently at us and the elephants. Their eyes have an orange tinge to them, quite different from Banseri's yellow-green eyes. We back off a little, not wanting to intimidate the cubs. Banseri gets up and walks out into a clearing. She lies down, but with her paws out in front of her, her head up. Far from being intimidated, the cubs rush out and chase each other through the dry leaves, making as much noise as they can. One stands in front of my elephant and stares at it. The elephant fidgets. The cubs sharpen their claws on the bark of a tree, then run up to their mother. One rubs itself languorously and sinuously under Banseri's chin while the other pounces on her twitching tail. They mew softly at her and nuzzle her side. Banseri remains as she is, alert, head raised. The cubs lie down about ten meters from her. The sun goes down and the lingering orange glow enhances the tigers' colors and that of the warm brown and yellow leaflitter. A fantailed flycatcher, a small gray bird with white eyebrows and spots, catches small insects in midair around Banseri's head. A crested hawk-eagle, perched low in a kulu tree, cries "kee-kee, kee-kee" in a rising crescendo. Finally Banseri relents. She lies on her side. Slowly the cubs walk over to their mother and, lying side by side, they suckle. They drink without quarreling,

Two cubs suckle Banseri as night descends on the jungle.

Opposite: Banseri in March 1991, nearly ten years after we first saw her.

heads touching, paws on Banseri's flank so that they rise and fall with her breathing. The cubs suckle for thirty-five minutes. When they have had enough, Banseri rolls onto her back, paws in the air, stretches luxuriantly, and yawns. She then sits up again and cleans herself thoroughly, washing her face like any domestic cat.

Without warning, in one fluid motion, Banseri gets up and walks off, passing within a few meters of our two elephants. The cubs stalk her, then, falling over each other, "attack" her around her throat. Banseri gives them a few playful cuffs. It is almost dark as the three descend the plateau to drink from the pool at its base. The two cubs, one on each side, press so close to their mother that she must be careful not to trip over them.

Banseri and one of her cubs.

Belinda and I look at each other, nod, and smile. There is no need for words. Rarely, if ever, has a wild tigress been observed suckling her cubs. When the young are this small they are usually well-hidden and their lair vigorously defended. Today's experience is an indication of the extent to which Banseri has accepted our presence. But seeing a probable "first" in tiger behavior is insignificant compared to other feelings that assail us. What we have just witnessed is a culmination of tracking and observing Banseri for more than a year. It was an extraordinarily affecting moment.

★ ★ ★

Out of experiences like these, and with other animals such as rhinos, elephants, monkeys, and many kinds of birds, grew our insights into, and our deep attachment to, Indian wildlife. These are the reasons why we spent twenty years observing the plants and animals in the jungles.★ They are also the reasons why Belinda, at the cost of great physical peril and mental anguish, has decided to devote her life to trying to save the tiger and other threatened Indian animals. The great joys that wildlife provides can no longer be separated from the potent forces determined to destroy it. In this book we will primarily examine the joys, but we must also consider the despair.

Banseri mates with the tiger we called Langra.

★The word *jungle* is derived from the Sanskrit word *jangala*, meaning dry ground. In India, *jungle* was originally used to denote wasteland or land covered by rank grass and tangled vegetation. In modern Indian usage, *jungle* means any wild vegetated place, be it rain forest, grassland, bamboo thicket, or sparse thorn scrub.

TIGER RESERVES IN INDIA

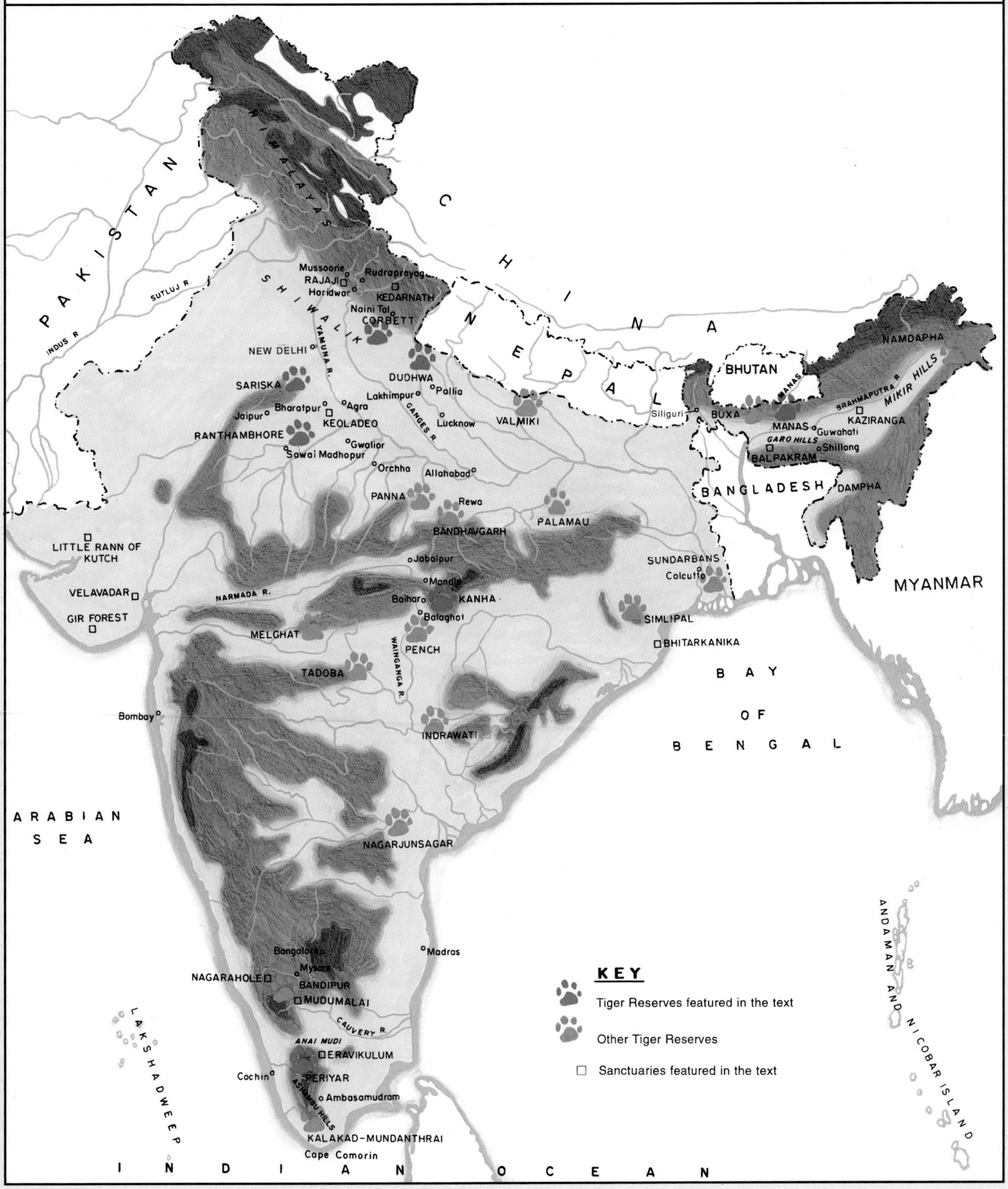

PAKISTAN

CHINA

NEPAL

BHUTAN

BANGLADESH

MYANMAR

HIMALAYAS

SHIWALIK

INDUS R.

SUTLUJ R.

YAMUNA R.

GANGES R.

NARMADA R.

WAINGANGA R.

CAUVERY R.

BRAHMAPUTRA R.

MIKIR HILLS

GARO HILLS

Mussoorie
RAJAJI
Haridwar
Rudraprayag
KEDARNATH
Naini Tal
CORBETT

NEW DELHI

SARISKA
Jaipur
Bharatpur
Agra
KEOLADEO
RANTHAMBHORE
Sowai Madhopur
Gwalior
Orchha

DUDHWA
Lakhimpur
Pallia
Lucknow
VALMIKI

Allahabad

PANNA
Rewa
BANDHAVGARH
Jabalpur
Mandla
Baihar
KANHA
Balaghat
PENCH

PALAMAU

SUNDARBANS
Calcutta

SIMLIPAL
BHITARKANIKA

LITTLE RANN OF
KUTCH

VELAVADAR

GIR FOREST

MELGHAT

TADOBA

Bombay

INDRAWATI

ARABIAN
SEA

BAY
OF
BENGAL

NAGARJUNSAGAR

Siliguri
BUXA
MANAS
MANAS
Guwahati
KAZIRANGA
Shillong
BALPAKRAM
DAMPHA
NAMDAPHA

Bangalore
Mysore
Madras
NAGARAHOLE
BANDIPUR
MUDUMALAI

ANAI MUDI
ERAVIKULUM
Cochin
PERIYAR
ASHAMBU HILLS
Ambasamudram
KALAKAD-MUNDANTHRAI
Cape Comorin

LAKSHADWEEP

ANDAMAN AND NICOBAR ISLAND

INDIAN OCEAN

KEY

Tiger Reserves featured in the text

Other Tiger Reserves

☐ Sanctuaries featured in the text

The external boundary of India as shown in this map is neither authentic nor correct. Not to scale.

PART I

INTO THE JUNGLE

I had never before seen the countries of warm temperature, nor the country of Hindustan. Immediately on reaching them I beheld a new world. The grass was different, the trees different, the wild animals of a different sort, the birds of a different plumage, the manners and customs of the wandering tribes of a different kind. I was struck with astonishment, and indeed there was room for wonder.

The Moghul Emperor Babur in "Babur-nama," AD 1504

[CHAPTER 1]

THROUGH THE TIGER'S EYES

Since our exhilarating days spent watching, photographing, and filming tigers, I have moved to Australia. Belinda still lives in India where, out of necessity, she has become a tough, uncompromising conservationist. Over the years we have kept in close contact. Belinda keeps me informed about the plight of the tiger and her adventures. The following, for example, is a letter she wrote in response to one of my questions.

New Delhi—26 October 1994

You ask me if large-scale tiger poaching has only recently been uncovered but has actually been going on for about twenty years? My answer is: no, absolutely not. It is very interesting, really. The tiger was first protected in 1970. Before that it was still legal to shoot them. For a few years after 1970 poaching continued, but always for skins.

In 1972 the Wildlife Protection Act was passed. The tiger was listed in Schedule I of the Act, which meant they were an endangered species and strictly protected. Under no circumstances, except if they were proven man-eaters, could tigers now be killed. There were heavy fines and even jail terms, on paper anyway. In the India-wide tiger census of 1972 it was discovered that only an estimated 1,800 tigers remained in the wild—a discovery that devastated conservationists, including the then–prime minister, Indira Gandhi. I think that this single fact ignited the conservation movement in India: it was a watershed. Before that everyone was convinced that there were still plenty of tigers out there in the jungle. After all, it was thought that at the turn of the century there were 40,000 tigers in India.

Project Tiger was started on 1 April 1973 as a direct result of the census. Nine sanctuaries and national parks were made Project Tiger reserves, including Manas, Ranthambhore, and Kanha. These reserves,

which had an estimated 268 tigers between them, received special funding, staffing, and other considerations from the central government, thereby lightening the financial burden of the states. There are now twenty-three Project Tiger reserves.

The beauty of Project Tiger was that it began just as the market for tiger and other cat skins began to wane. It not only became unfashionable to wear animal-skin coats but also socially unacceptable. For the first time ever, actual tiger habitat was protected. Money was available for radio communications, vehicles, and guns.

Good and efficient people were trained and put into senior positions. Management plans were not only drawn up but actually carried out. The Project reaped incredible dividends. Tiger numbers in India doubled in just over ten years. I don't think the tiger would still be here without Project Tiger. There was some tiger poaching, for skins, but these were nearly always from outside Project Tiger areas.

Once the Project became a success we all sat back and said, "Isn't this marvelous"—and it was, for a time. There were lots of tigers in Kanha, the habitat was improving, and we could actually see tigers during the daytime. It was the golden age for tiger watching. We all became complacent. It was a bit too good to be true.

The first signs that something was wrong, and that there was a change taking place, came in the late 1980s. In 1986, I think it was, there was a seizure of tiger bones near Dudhwa National Park. In 1989, a parcel of tiger bones was seized on a bus going to Jabalpur, near Kanha.

Looking back, I should perhaps also have read danger signs in three consignments of skins seized in Calcutta between June and September 1989. Collectively, the parcels contained the skins of 8 tigers, 13 leopards, 231 leopard cats, and 1 marbled cat. No bones were included. The policeman involved in the seizure of one package from Howrah Railway Station was a charming man and genuinely concerned about what was happening to the tiger. He said to me, "At the rate these tigers are being discontinued, they will soon be instinct [sic]." But what should have

---

Preceding pages: A Hanuman langur lopes across a forest clearing.

rung alarm bells, more than it did, was that the person on whose information the parcels were confiscated was beaten to death a few days later. It was one of the first large-scale seizures and also a clear indication of what savage and ruthless people were involved. Gangs of criminals, in fact.

But it was not until 1992 and 1993 that two events took place that shocked us into a realization of what was really going on. These were key events, as was the tiger census of 1972. These discoveries also turned my life upside down.

The first inkling I had that all was not well in Ranthambhore Reserve came in Calcutta in early 1992, at a cocktail party, of all places—I'm afraid cocktail parties are inescapable when I stay with my parents. I met a friend there who had just returned from Ranthambhore. He said that his guide and his driver had told him that tigers were being killed in the park. He questioned them closely and offered them money for specific information that could be acted upon. My friend also commented that few tigers were being seen. Badhiya, the main tiger tracker, had died under suspicious circumstances and it was rumored that he'd been killed by an organized gang of poachers.

Belinda holding the skull of a tiger killed by poachers. The skull is believed to be that of a male she photographed in Kanha National Park in the early nineties (pictured on the front cover of this book). Belinda, the third generation of her family to be involved with Kanha's tigers, was largely instrumental in uncovering poaching and trading rings operating around the national park. Tigers everywhere are now at critically low numbers.

Alarmed by this information, I rang my friend Ashok Kumar, who was an adviser to the Minister for the Environment at the central government in New Delhi. Ashok said there was no report of poaching in Ranthambhore, but he arranged to send someone to investigate the rumors. He could find nothing. The ministry's categorical statement was, "There is no poaching at Ranthambhore." I was not convinced.

There was another warning sign. In the tiger census of May 1992, only seventeen tigers were counted in Ranthambhore, where a few years before there had been forty-five. The Forest Department, alarmed by this figure, hastily withdrew it and said that there had been a mistake; there were really still forty-four tigers in Ranthambhore.

I decided to talk to Fateh Singh, who is, as you know, the field director and "creator" of modern Ranthambhore. He had lost his political patronage and his many enemies had connived to have him removed from Ranthambhore. He was now field director at Sariska Tiger Reserve. Unbeknown to me, Fateh had also received word of tiger poaching and had strong suspicions. I went back to Ashok Kumar and badgered him to send a low-profile person to just dig around locally, asking questions around the bazaars of Sawai Madhopur, the nearest town, and in villages. The investigator came back with the information that tiger

poaching was indeed going on in Ranthambhore. Pressure was brought to bear on the local police. Raids were made in June 1992 and one tiger skin and some bones were seized. A local butcher was implicated and it was discovered that tiger **bones**, not skins, were the main prize. The poachers admitted to killing seven tigers. The police estimated, from intelligence gathered from villages around the park, that twenty tigers had been killed in Ranthambhore since 1989. This case, like all the others, is still pending in court.

This discovery was a severe blow for the tiger, and one with far-reaching implications. Ranthambhore was one of the best-known and, until Fateh Singh was removed as field director, one of the best-managed tiger reserves. Tigers and their prey species were flourishing in completely rehabilitated habitats. It was well-known within India and throughout the world as a place where you could see tigers in an unparalleled setting. A nongovernment organization, the Ranthambhore Foundation, was trying to address the problems of the villagers living around the reserve, who persistently tried to invade Ranthambhore to graze their cattle, goats, and camels, and to gather wood and collect fodder. The Foundation's idea was to take pressure off the reserve, and the tiger, by providing alternative sources of fodder and fuel for cooking

Anne Wright, Belinda's mother, center, with a large consignment of illegal tiger, leopard, and other cat skins confiscated in Calcutta in 1989. This was one of the first signs that tiger poaching was on the increase. Anne was also a member of the group who set up Project Tiger in 1972. Kanha was among the first nine Project Tiger reserves.

kilograms of tiger bones, the skeletons of at least thirty-three tigers. During negotiations with the traders, when Firoz posed as a buyer, he was offered one thousand kilograms to be delivered within a month. These bones could have come from any part of India.

The exposure of the poaching of tigers in Ranthambhore and the seizure of tiger bones in Delhi, made headlines worldwide and sent Indian conservationists into a state of shock and despair. But here at last was physical evidence that tiger poaching was happening on a large and organized scale. The Ministry of the Environment and Forests at the central government was convinced and ready to act. It gave Firoz and myself support in the sense that it would act on and take seriously information we

fires. It was making good progress. But the reserve was not helped by the Foundation's efforts. The managers of the Foundation, like just about everyone else, were oblivious to the poaching. If such a catastrophe can happen in Ranthambhore, in this well-known, supposedly well-protected reserve, it can happen anywhere, absolutely anywhere, including Kanha.

Over the last few years, there had been a few seizures of tiger skins and bones — made mostly by officials' accidentally bumping into the illicit spoils. In January of 1993, Ashok Kumar set up TRAFFIC-India* and began to study these cases. In August of that year Ashok and a colleague of his from the Middle East, Firoz [not his real name], masterminded an investigation that resulted in the largest seizure of tiger bones ever. They were stockpiled in the back streets of Old Delhi, a tricky and dangerous place. The police eventually seized four hundred

*TRAFFIC stands for Trade Record Analysis of Flora and Fauna in Commerce. It is a joint program of the World Wide Fund for Nature and the International Union for the Conservation of Nature.

passed on. This was not always the case in the states and in the various reserves themselves. Surprisingly the central administration of Project Tiger persisted with the view that the figures had been fiddled and that there were only isolated incidents of poaching, which were of no real concern. Their complacency goaded conservationists into action.

Cairns, Australia to New Delhi, India— 2 and 3 February 1995

In midafternoon I take off from Cairns, in the northeast corner of Australia. Flying westward, the plane dodges between the towering white columns of monsoon clouds. For a while there are views of dense tropical rain forest covering hills and mountains. Inside that forest is my home, sixty hectares bordering on a vast national park.

I am elated and excited to be returning to some of India's wild places. Perhaps I will meet the incomparable tiger again, an animal that played such a large part in our lives. For Belinda the tiger is still central to all she does.

Over the last few years Belinda has gone through a tough and stressful period. She has fought to stop poachers killing rhinos, elephants, and tigers, and to expose politicians bent on destroying the last great breeding colony of the olive ridley turtle. Every day there was another threat to the environment or some species of plant or animal. Because of her efforts, she was harassed by officials and threatened by gangs of criminals. The harassment and the fact that she could trust no one and had to work alone were at times unbearable. Often she had telephoned me in a state of depression, finding it difficult to go on. But she always did. All I could do was offer sympathy and a safe haven if needed, and provide some kind of constant reference point in her life. There were times when I felt pangs of guilt at having abandoned Indian wildlife, and the tiger in particular.

To us, tiger protection is the most urgent—and, because of its symbolism, also the most important—conservation issue facing the world. If we cannot save the tiger, one of the world's most magnificent animals and one that most people regard with awe and admiration, what can we save? And there is no doubt that if the tiger is to survive in the wild, it will be in India, despite its' being one of the most densely populated countries.

Belinda has decided to do whatever it takes to stop the poaching of tigers and the trade in tiger parts. As a result of her investigations during 1994, millions of dollars worth of illegal animal parts, from tigers to jackals, were seized. Scores of traders and poachers were arrested. It is dangerous work. Her life is often under threat and for some periods she has police protection.

I think about this as we leave the rain forest behind. The plane, entering the monsoon clouds, rolls and bucks.

For fifteen years, starting in 1974, Belinda and I crisscrossed the subcontinent, traveling to as wide a variety of habitats as we could. We stood on high alpine meadows in the Himalayas, struggled through the mud of mangrove forests, rode elephants through four-meter-high grass, raced after wild asses over scorching salt flats, stalked tigers from a Jeep through semiarid thorn scrub, craned our necks at rare monkeys in tall rain forest, and walked through dry deciduous forest where we came face to face with tigers. They were extraordinary years, during which we came to know the breadth of Indian wildlife as few people have had the opportunity to do. Some places and some species of animal we were able to understand more

Austin Henry Layard, Anne's father, second from left, was a member of the party that organized a tiger shoot for the Viceroy of India, Lord Reading, seated on left. That was at Mukki on the western end of Kanha during the 1920s. Seven tigers were shot, none by Layard. It was at a time when tigers in the area were not just common but plentiful. Layard was the first of three successive generations—with his daughter Anne and granddaughter Belinda—deeply concerned with tigers and tiger conservation near Kanha.

An Indian roller, one of India's myriad species of brilliantly colored birds, lands on a tree stump.

deeply. We spent months, sometimes years, in such places as the tall grasslands of Kaziranga on the Brahmaputra River, the wetlands of Keoladeo on the Gangetic Plain, and the hills and lakes of Ranthambhore in semiarid Rajasthan. We lived in and around Kanha National Park in central India for several years, and it was there that we first entered the lives of wild tigers. The park's hills, meadows, and forests are to us the quintessential India. Recently Belinda built her perfect jungle home in the forest just outside the park.

Tigers, right from the beginning, captured our imagination; it seemed at times that tigers entered our very spirit. Whether this is the reason why Indian wildlife lodged itself so irrevocably in my consciousness, I cannot say. But the fact remains that Indian jungles stir me more deeply than any other wild places I have been—in Africa, North America, Papua New Guinea, Europe, and even in my homeland of Australia. It is still a puzzle to me, for instance, why the brilliant minivets, jungle fowl, rollers, woodpeckers, orioles, hoopoes, serpent eagles, and peacocks of Kanha transport me to greater delight than the equally brilliant king parrots, golden bowerbirds, cassowaries, wompoo pigeons, white goshawks, and crimson rosellas that I see constantly near my house in the Australian rain forest. Is it simply that these birds are not associated with the tiger? Certainly after my first sighting of the tiger, as it walked mysteriously through a thin ground mist on a moonlit night, it was never far from my thoughts. It was the same for Belinda, who knew tigers before we met.

In every jungle that we went to we were alert to the signs of tigers: their footprints; the alarm calls of monkeys, deer and other prey species; their scent. We would appraise a habitat in terms of tigers and think: this is a good place for a tiger to lie up; that is a perfect spot for an ambush to catch deer; this pool is probably the center of a tiger's territory. Often our deductions were right and would lead us to tigers. We also loved and deeply appreciated the other mammals we saw: elephants, rhinos, leopards, lions, gibbons, bears, langurs, deer, and so many more. In some places like Manas or Keoladeo, birds would induce feelings of pure euphoria. But when we sensed a tiger, heard its roar, or glimpsed its flame through a tracery of bamboo, all those feelings were transcended. We caught our breath and our senses and feelings were engaged to the full. We did indeed see the jungles through the tiger's eyes.

At Delhi airport, I move out into the morning sunshine where I am met by Belinda's mother Anne. Bank mynas, jaunty starlings with glossy black heads and fierce orange eyes, forage centimeters from the rushing feet of porters and passengers and the wheels of taxis and buses. Palm squirrels lie spread-eagled on the trunks of trees, soaking up the sunshine. A hoopoe calls. On the way to Belinda's house we drive through smog-filled crowded streets. Common mynas, sparrows, and pigeons feed on the pavements and ignore the rush, the noise, and the car fumes. Rhesus monkeys sit like heraldic animals on the roof of a school while others try to steal food out of the hands of the students. An elephant ridden by his *mahout* strides majestically through the dusty melee. I am glad to be back in a country where the lives of people and wild animals are intertwined with mutual respect and tolerance. I have stepped back into another life. My Indian life.

★ ★ ★

February is spring in northern India. The large garden around the farmhouse Belinda has rented on the outskirts of the city is dazzling with flowers and with the song and movement of an astonishing variety of birds.

Belinda gives me a warm smile. She looks drawn and tired. With alarm I realize she has taken up smoking again. Belinda has only just moved into the house and is putting the finishing touches to the furnishings. As always the effect is welcoming and tasteful. The tiger motif is everywhere. Large and arresting photographs of some of "our" tigers—Saja, Lakshmi, and Banseri—hang on the walls. Stylish and orderly as the house is, I walk into chaos—an all too familiar kind of chaos I remember from our earlier days.

The tailor is still busy sewing curtains and upholstering chairs. Other guests arrive from overseas and want to chat and be sociable. Belinda's mother is buying land: she has brought two lawyers, and demands that Belinda untangle the complexities for her. A new puppy pees on an exquisite carpet and steals important papers. Phone calls come in about a tiger being deliberately electrocuted in a national park and another being poisoned somewhere else. Faxes report dead elephants in an eastern Indian reserve. Guests will soon arrive for lunch. Belinda has a backlog of reports to write. There is a stream of phone calls from the Wildlife Protection Society of India, an organization Belinda has established. An old friend rings up and says "Please Belinda, you must save Ranthambhore. I have tried for so many years and I have failed. Sometimes I can hardly live with myself for this failure. You must help. I've tried everything else." The news of tigers and elephants being killed visibly disturbs Belinda. By the end of the day she is haggard with stress. For anyone seriously involved in trying to save the tiger, these are traumatic times.

However, I have arrived on a bad day. The crisis passes and life returns to a certain balance. Laughter and small joys return. Belinda, working all night, finishes the most urgent reports and after some sleep regains her humor and her charm. Anne returns to her home in Calcutta. The puppy is slowly getting house-trained. We have time to talk and make plans.

Before heading for the balm and sanity of Belinda's new forest house, Shergarh, and Kanha's jungles, we decide to attend the Tiger Link conference. It has been called by the conservationist Valmik Thapar, an old friend of Belinda's, to try to link the nongovernment organizations and individuals from all over India concerned with tiger conservation. The aim is to join the efforts of like-minded people and so forge a more effective conservation movement. The conference will be a great opportunity for us to gauge the mood about tiger conservation right around the country, and for me to meet old friends, many of whom I have not seen for ten or fifteen years.

The tigress Lakshmi relaxes after having eaten her fill.

[CHAPTER 2]

TIGER LINK

New Delhi—17 February 1995

We are the last to arrive and quickly take our places around the large, circular table where some fifty people are already seated. The room is airy, with the morning sun streaming through tall windows. I return the smiles and waves of recognition from old friends. I take my seat next to Brijendra Singh, Brij to his friends, who gives me a firm handshake and a warm welcome. He has not changed much—there is still a twinkle in his eye and a smile on his friendly, round face. On my other side sits Billy Arjan Singh, the grand old man of tiger conservation. He is in his late seventies but still a powerful-looking man. He had not expected me here and it is wonderful to see his craggy, stern face light up in a welcoming smile. Billy played a major role in Belinda's first encounter with the harsh world of tiger poachers, twenty-four years ago when she was seventeen. Belinda sits opposite me, wearing a bright red Indian-style dress among soberly dressed men. She is one of two women participants.

Valmik Thapar, the meeting's convener, is in the chair and calls the meeting to order. He is a large, somewhat shambling man in his early forties dressed in a jacket, open-necked shirt, and baggy trousers. He has a full, unruly, black beard and a mane of black hair that falls over his forehead. A pair of half glasses balances on his nose. Over them his fierce eyes spark with passion as he eloquently sketches the plight of the tiger and how we are all here to do something about it. He introduces India's Minister for the Environment, who makes the opening address. "I'm here to express my solidarity with you…." On and on he drones.

I cease to listen. Slowly I look around the table and as I do, something stirs in my mind. It is an intuitive rush of feeling: I am witnessing something significant, extraordinary even. A great variety of people sit around the table: nattily dressed lawyers (the reform of conservation laws is a crucial factor in saving the tiger); casually dressed, mostly young people from the field, their faces burnt dark by the sun; urbane, older administrators wearing well-cut suits, smooth men with a pallor and a gloss that suggest they have never been in the field; a scattering of turbaned Sikhs; sandal-wearing, intense social activists. An unsophisticated but honest and dedicated former forest officer sits beside a senior government wildlife official, his face tired and lined after years of dealing with the vicissitudes and inertia of bureaucracies and government policies. Dispassionate scientists of stature and experience look benignly at young idealists setting out uncertainly on their first field study. But unusually in India, all—senior and junior, super sophisticates and people straight from their work in the jungles—are equal. All have things to say. I suppose what I sense is the essence of the gathering—the fire, the intelligence, and the complete dedication and commitment to saving the tiger in most people. But not all. Some have their own agenda and are not in tune with the meeting. You cannot tell this by what they say, for they know the right words and sentiments. It is their manner—conspiratorial, insincere, uneasy—and their lack of commitment that give them away. They are not castigated. They are ignored and most depart before the end of the meeting. The minister's speech grinds to a halt and he leaves.

The proceedings, which are in English, the only common language, now take on a more sober note. People speak about their particular areas—the problems, the trends, and what is needed to save the tiger.

Billy Arjan Singh is the first speaker. He says that the poaching of tigers in Dudhwa Tiger Reserve, near the Nepal border in the north, is going on virtually unchecked. He monitors events from "Tiger Haven," his farm which adjoins the reserve. The authorities do not even want to know about the poaching and maintain it does not go on.

Brij is an honorary wildlife warden in Corbett Tiger Reserve in the sub-Himalayan foothills, also in the north. He spends several months a year there. He says that as far as he knows there is little or no poaching of tigers in Corbett. There are a few murmurs of skepticism.

Imran Khan, a solidly built young man, makes an impressive speech about what is happening in Ranthambhore. There is complete silence as he details the destruction of one of the world's great reserves, one where only ten years ago we filmed tigers in spellbinding closeness. Ranthambhore, he says, is a small island in an ocean of agricultural land. Two hundred thousand people live in towns and villages on its boundary. They have an equal number of grazing animals, about 56 percent of them unproductive. A great many of them feed inside the park. Some 90 percent of its plant growth is consumed by domestic animals. His conclusion is that Ranthambhore cannot survive this onslaught.

The other tiger reserve in Rajasthan, Sariska, is faring no better. Fewer than ten tigers are now believed to survive there

and those may soon disappear. Stone quarries have invaded the edge of the core area.

Devastating as the news from Rajasthan is, worse is to come. One of the first national parks we visited in India, back in 1974, was Manas Tiger Reserve in the far eastern state of Assam, right on the border with the kingdom of Bhutan. It was a place of rain forest–covered hills, river plains, and tall grasslands. As recently as seven years ago it had the greatest diversity of mammals and birds in India and possibly in all of Asia. We went there only once, but the twelve days we spent there live in my memory as few others. I had been aware that there were problems in Manas, but to hear just what has happened from someone who came directly from the area is sobering.

As the speaker put it, Manas is entirely in the hands of "miscreants"—political dissidents. Tigers, rhinos, and elephants are reputedly being killed in large numbers and vast amounts of timber have been removed. No one knows exactly what is happening.

Belinda speaks next about the state of affairs in central India. She begins by saying: "Until recently, habitat loss was

Elephant-mounted guards patrol
Manas Tiger Reserve.

thought to be the biggest single threat to the future of wild tigers in India. It is now clear that the trade in tiger bones and other parts—all of which are destined for use in Oriental medicine outside India's borders—has accelerated this threat and brought the tiger to the brink of extinction." She follows this by a lucid and chilling exposition of the results of a recent investigation that she conducted into tiger poaching and the trade in their parts. She concludes: "The tiger cannot be saved on paper, nor by endless meetings. What is required is action in the field."

A team of three people reports from the southern state of Karnataka, particularly from Nagarahole National Park. This is *the* prime tiger habitat, in terms of cover and available prey

species, left in the world. It may sustain even more tigers per unit area than Kanha or Corbett. The three report there is no significant poaching as far as they know. The leader is the distinguished scientist Ullas Karanth. He treads a fine line between the detachment of a scientist and the passionate involvement of an activist. This gives him both the knowledge and the conviction of why it is important to save the natural environment.

As Valmik summarizes the country-wide reports and re-emphasizes the Tiger Link theme, Brij leans over and, smiling broadly, whispers in my ear, "I hope the tiger is not going to be the missing link in all this."

The meeting is now opened for general discussion. Bittu Sahgal, thin-faced with graying hair and mustache, is the editor of *Sanctuary,* India's principal wildlife and conservation magazine. He makes an impassioned speech about how the people of India are going to save the tiger. "The people will support us," he says. "They now realize that the tiger is part of the soul of India. Even now a group of villagers and activists from Sariska Tiger Reserve is traveling all over India to stop the destruction of our forests and the tiger. They realize that the forests have mothered our culture, our very civilization."

At this, Shomita Mukherjee, a petite young woman studying small cats in Sariska, takes the floor. In a barely audible voice she says, "The people in Sariska and other places may be interested in saving the forests for firewood and other products, but they are not at all interested in saving the tiger. Tigers eat cattle and goats and sometimes people." This leads to various comments around the table about "empty" forests all over India. Many of these are good forests with undergrowth and strong regeneration, but without larger mammals of any kind. In these forests the local people have caught and eaten the deer, antelope, and wild pigs so the tiger and other predators have no prey. It is also now generally agreed that to have "sustainable development" of the forests, and to open them up for the exploitation of minor forest products, has not helped wildlife. The results have been catastrophic.

The final comment on this subject comes from M. K. Ranjitsinh, a man of rare wisdom with a vast experience in wildlife administration and policy-making as well as fieldwork. He speaks quietly about this issue:

The tigress Rela drinks at a pool in the Sulcum River in Kanha.

"One of my favorite places in all of India is the forest surrounding Pachmarhi in Madhya Pradesh. I used to sit at a certain vantage point and just look in wonder at the uninterrupted, untouched forests stretching out in all directions. However, the last time I was there all the forests were on fire. They were crisscrossed by cattle trails. When I saw that I cried. I literally cried. The forest was still there, in a fashion. But the undergrowth had gone and there was no regeneration. All this so people could collect the leaves of tendu trees [for the manufacture of *bidis,* cheap hand-rolled cigarettes] to the value of 26,000 rupees, the price of half a teak log. You want people participation? That is what you will get."

Chital on the Kanha meadows in winter.

By now the late sun slants through the windows. The meeting breaks up. There should be a lot of breast-beating and a feeling of despair. Instead we gather around the coffee and tea urns. Friendships are renewed, old times recounted, details of the last few years filled in. New friends are made. There is laughter and warm feelings. Perhaps the despair comes later, in private moments, and the expressions of friendship help in dealing with the sadness, anger, and feelings of helplessness.

I walk up to Belinda and raising my eyebrows ask, "The tiger cannot be saved on paper, nor by endless meetings?" She gives a wry smile but says this was an unusually important meeting. For the first time an India-wide conservation gathering has acknowledged that poaching is now a major threat, perhaps *the* major threat, to the tiger. Only once this step has been taken can effective countermeasures be initiated. Also for the first time it was realized that trying to get forest-dwelling people on-side in the conservation movement does not automatically safeguard the tiger or its habitat. "And," Belinda adds, "these people are like family to me. I need their support and their warmth and also we all need to be reminded from time to time that we are not alone."

The trends revealed at the meeting are potentially disastrous but Kanha, Corbett, Nagarahole, and their tigers are still there. Kaziranga, in Assam, which I think of as the national park that has everything, has survived against great odds. Keoladeo is as wonderful as ever. There are still rain forests and Himalayan jungles to explore. There are inspiring stories to record of people like Ullas Karanth in Nagarahole, Fateh Singh in Ranthambhore, Brijendra Singh in Corbett, and many others. It is time to leave the city behind, to go into the jungle and see for ourselves what is happening, but also to relate the wonders, the excitements, and the sheer spectacle of the natural India that we have been privileged to witness over the last twenty years.

[CHAPTER 3]

TO THE JUNGLE AND SHERGARH

New Delhi to Shergarh at Kanha Tiger Reserve—14 and 15 March 1995

We decide to drive down to Kanha. The journey, though only 1,000 kilometers long, will take two full and exhausting days. We drive a long, low, underpowered Indian-made car called a Contessa.

On our first day we travel through classic India—and congested India. For an hour or more we move slowly at the pace of grotesquely overloaded trucks that choke the inadequate highway. The air is heavy with exhaust fumes and the pollution of unbroken lines of factories on both sides of the road. Gradually factories are interspersed with villages surrounded by small plots of farmland. Carts pulled by bullocks or water buffaloes at times slow our pace even further. We move so slowly that I have time to identify the birds at village ponds—black-winged stilts, greenshanks, spot-billed ducks, even an avocet. Finally we reach a four-lane highway with a more or less even surface and we can speed along at eighty kilometers per hour. But then trucks and carts going in the wrong direction in our one-way lane of traffic slow us again. We bypass the ancient city of Mathura, birthplace of Krishna and an important center for all of India's main religions. The spires of Hindu temples, Buddhist shrines, and Muslim mosques rise over the city.

We weave in and out through lines of trucks, kilometers long, and eventually

come to a barrier. It is a border crossing between two states. We are waved on by the policeman, but each truck driver has to fill in many, many forms and pay all kinds of taxes. It can take hours. One driver, in frustration perhaps, has painted "Oh God, give me long life" in a neat script on the back of his vehicle. We enter the state of Rajasthan—green irrigated fields, people dressed in brilliant colors, neat villages beneath ancient spreading trees, women filling brass pots at a well, a group of men smoking a hookah, children herding goats and playing between the mud houses.

For several hours I drive through sparsely populated farmland but now we approach the city of Gwalior. The thousand-year-old fort and other ancient structures, built on a sheer-sided mesa, dominate the city. These are some of India's most splendid buildings and sculptures. Belinda has a special genius for driving through heavy city traffic, something that I lack, so she takes over the driving again. Even though we follow a bypass we are soon swallowed up by the maelstrom of vehicles. On either side of a railway crossing lie rusted, twisted railway carriages, the result of a derailment.

Once out of the city, we enter a different realm, where traffic is only sporadic. The occasional truck drivers are more mellow and move over to let us pass, and oncoming vehicles do not try to run us off the road. The sun is setting, a red globe in the dust haze, when we reach Orchha—a small, walled town surrounded by a dazzling complex of ancient temples and palaces. A piece of India from a previous age left behind 400 years ago.

Belinda's house, Shergarh, in the jungle near Kanha.

Part of one palace, perched high on a hillside, has been converted into a hotel. At twilight we sit in the dining room and look over forests, rivers, and temples.

The next day we travel even farther off the beaten track. We pass prosperous-looking villages surrounded by healthy crops of wheat, overtake a colorful religious procession, drive along avenues of old mango trees, cross a barren plateau, and pass through a narrow valley bounded by high rocky cliffs where vultures nest on ledges. We rest for a while in an empty forest. By late afternoon we reach Jabalpur, a city of nearly a million people, all of whom seem to be out on the streets.

Beyond the city the road winds up onto the Deccan Plateau, the heartland of central India's great hardwood forests of teak, sal, and bamboo. Much forest has been cleared. A sign informs us that "Dangerous Curves Need Dexterous Nerves."

At Mandla, the last town before Kanha, Belinda telephones the reserve's field director. She has a long conversation, mostly about the spate of recent arrests of poachers and traders, and the seizure of the bones and skins of tigers and leopards. The arrests were made by the police in villages right around Kanha. The police raids were inspired by the work Belinda did last summer. Local politicians and their strong men were involved in the latest cases. Their stocks were con-

fiscated, which is a major financial setback, and most of the offenders are still in jail. Some of the "miscreants" are from Mocha village—which is only a few hundred meters from Belinda's jungle house. Word is out, the field director says, that Belinda Wright better not turn up in or near the village. He takes that as a veiled death threat. Belinda is unconcerned. She is, however, mortified that tigers and leopards were poached right under her nose, despite her vigilance.

We push on and cross the broad Narmada River, glistening in the moonlight. On a rocky headland stands a large, old bungalow. It is where Belinda's grandfather lived, back in the 1920s, during his first posting as a junior colonial administrator. He subsequently had a long and distinguished career in India, mostly in the then–Central Provinces, now the state of Madhya Pradesh. Belinda's mother spent her childhood in the region.

At long last, after 1,000 kilometers of farmland, villages, cities, towns, and a few empty forests, we drive into the real jungle. The difference is immediately apparent. A small herd of chital—spotted deer—leaps across the road. A chowsingha, a four-horned antelope, stands transfixed in our headlights. A toddy cat, a kind of civet, runs into the undergrowth. Two fiery green reflections from a clump of grass

Flowers of the simul, or silk cotton, tree.

A Hanuman langur eats the flower-buds of a flame of the forest tree.

resolve themselves into the eyes of a leopard, glaring at us. At about midnight we pass through Mocha village. All the houses are shuttered; the street is empty. Just beyond we turn down a dirt track into the jungle and we are at Shergarh, "Tiger House," Belinda's jungle home, shining in the bright moonlight.

Once out of the car, an ineffable feeling of relief, but also one of great love for the jungle, overwhelms us both. For a long time we sit on the verandah, listen to the jungle sounds, and watch the fireflies dance among the trees. We both look forward to the next few weeks to be spent in and around these forests.

Shergarh near Kanha Tiger Reserve— 16 March

I get up when daylight extinguishes the first stars, make myself some tea, and once more sit out on the verandah. A low mist swirls over the stretch of grass and the pond immediately in front of the house. A few flame of the forest trees, covered in clumps of orange flowers, are silhouetted against the pink that begins to color the eastern sky. Coucals, untidy-looking black birds with red-brown wings and crimson eyes, boom their calls from the tree tops. Langur monkeys whoop. A chital stag pauses in his grazing to give his rutting call—a hoarse, throaty and labored "huhh" repeated several times. Brainfever birds scream,

orioles yodel, red jungle fowl crow. Insistent "roo-coo-coos" come from the throats of a hundred doves. They are joined by the rising and falling stutter of a goldenbacked woodpecker, the slow "koor, koor, koor" followed by the rapidly accelerating "chuckoo chuckoo chuckoo" of the barred jungle owlet, and the squeaks and chatter of a pair of Malabar pied hornbills. These far-carrying, mostly distant voices are stitched together by the soft songs, whispers even, of closer, smaller birds—white-eyes, flycatchers, minivets, bulbuls, sunbirds, mynas, and others—into a concert that makes the forest throb. It is a brief symphony, for as the sun rises through the damp haze and spears shafts of yellow light across the small meadow, many birds fall silent.

I skirt around the meadow and walk into the forest. Two jackals trot by, pause to sniff at something, give me a quick sidelong glance, and move on. Already it is warming up. Soon it will be hot. At this dry season many trees shed their leaves and will remain dormant till just before the monsoon sweeps in from the south in mid-June. The jamun is an exception; it is now putting out its new leaves and flowerbuds are ready to burst.

A little farther on, succulent red-pink flowers, nearly the size of my fist, lie scattered over the brown leaflitter. They have fallen from a tall simul, or silk cotton, tree. Its branches, bare of leaves, are crowded with freshly opened flowers. Lime green leaf birds and grayheaded mynas dip into the flowers for nectar. Their heads are dusted with yellow pollen. An oriole and two haircrested drongos join them. A palm squirrel rips into a flower and eats its center. A male purple sunbird, its iridescent plumage reflecting rays of purple, blue, and bronze, is so tiny that it disappears from view, inside the flower, in its search for nectar.

I walk down to the dry stream about half a kilometer from the house. A barred jungle owlet stares down from a

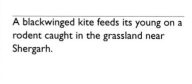

A blackwinged kite feeds its young on a rodent caught in the grassland near Shergarh.

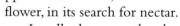

tree hollow through unblinking yellow eyes. The eyes are circled by concentric rings of dark and pale brown, giving the bird a permanently startled look. Above one of the last stagnant pools of water sits a crested serpent eagle, on the lookout perhaps for a water snake slow to abandon the drying pool.

In the past we often saw the pug marks—the footprints—of tigers and leopards in the creek's sand. Only eight months ago Belinda saw a tiger here. The tracks of the resident leopard could be seen almost daily until just a few months ago. Belinda sometimes saw the leopard from her house. The cat was most welcome because it kept the numbers of half-feral village dogs under control. I see no pug marks. Last year's tiger and leopard were almost certainly among the skins and bones seized from Mocha village recently.

Later in the day I sit down at a desk in front of a window without glass to begin writing this narrative. For a long time I am distracted. The parade of animals continues. Orioles and flycatchers come to a birdbath. Members of a troop of langur monkeys chase each other across the tiled roof, sending some of the tiles crashing down. Others press their black faces against small high windows, which have glass, and grimace at me. Among the trees just in front of the house silver-furred

adolescents run about, turn somersaults, and do handstands. The troop's single adult male sits dignified in the middle of the melee, elbows on knees.

In the evening we sit beneath tall trees. An occasional leaf falls, zigzags lazily down, and lands softly. A woodpecker busily hammers some insect out of hard wood directly above us. We make plans and talk about our earliest days. How innocent they now seem as we traveled through the subcontinent absorbing the land, the plants, and the animals with an almost perpetual sense of wonder. Now Belinda has to delve into the ugly, sordid, and corrupt netherworld of large cities to try to save what wildlife remains. A world devoid of innocence and where a sense of wonder is a distraction from your survival instincts, a distraction that can get you killed.

We will spend many hours here at Shergarh as I record Belinda's stories about catching poachers and wildlife traders and other adventures.

But at the moment we are in no mood to go anywhere, to confront anyone. We are at peace with the forest and absorb its power. Leisurely we reminisce about our very first days in the jungle. It all began when we bought a Land Rover in Calcutta in January 1974.

Tiger cubs sun themselves in Kanha National Park. Their mother is Kulu (see page 64).

[PART II]

THROUGH INDIA IN A LAND ROVER: DAYS OF INNOCENCE AND WONDER

Forest is a peculiar organism of unlimited kindness

and benevolence that makes no demand for its sus-

tenance and extends protection to all beings, offer-

ing shade even to the axeman who destroys it...

Gautama Buddha
4th or 5th century BC

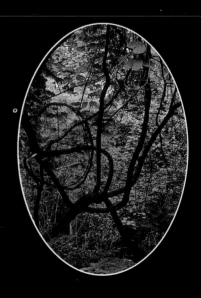

[CHAPTER 4]

GETTING STARTED

Calcutta—20 to 31 January 1974

While I was living and photographing in the Alligator Rivers region of northern Australia, a vast pristine wilderness that had been little explored, I received a message from the National Geographic Society in Washington, D.C. A friend drove all day through uncharted country to deliver it. Would I, National Geographic asked, go to India for a year and photograph endangered wildlife?

Sitting on a sandstone outcrop overlooking intensely green wetlands where a million birds were going about their business, I thought hard about it. The first thought that came to mind was—would there be any wildlife in a country with so many people? But I also recalled my childhood readings of Kipling's *Jungle Book* stories, about the boy Mowgli who was raised by wolves, and about bears, leopards, elephants, deer,

and monkeys. Most of all I thought about tigers, to me perhaps the most spectacular and mysterious animal of all. It did not take long for my imagination to catch fire. I sent a message back saying I would go.

To someone fresh from the wide open spaces of an Australian wilderness, Calcutta is an intense shock. From a place where weeks would go by without seeing another person, I was suddenly bobbing like a forlorn cork in a sea of humanity, my nostrils assailed by alien smells, the air thick with pollution, my ears filled with a language I could not understand, and seeing ways of doing things that left me bemused and bewildered. If it had not been for the safety net provided by Bob and Anne Wright, I would have bolted back to Australia.

National Geographic in their thoroughness had provided me with a short list of people who might be helpful in India. Perhaps intuitively I had chosen to contact the Wrights and they made me very welcome.

★　★　★

Bob and Anne are English, but have lived all their lives in India and, what is even more important, they know well both the jungles and how to deal with India's abstruse bureaucracy. They tell me that their daughter Belinda is also a wildlife photographer. She has traveled widely throughout the subcontinent and speaks several of the languages. I suggest that maybe she would like to join the assignment, National Geographic willing. Belinda is working in Chitwan National Park in Nepal and a message is sent to tell her to come to Calcutta immediately.

Our old Land Rover.
Preceding pages: A herd of elephants on the shore of Periyar Lake in the south Indian jungles.

After several days, Belinda arrives. She is a cheerful, intelligent, and quick-witted twenty-year-old with an engaging manner and an air about her that suggests she is afraid of nothing. To my great relief she agrees to join me. National Geographic has already given their blessing. The four of us have a council of war. It appears that we are trapped in the city as the workers at both the airlines and railways are on strike. We all soon agree that what Belinda and I will need is a vehicle of our own for we will have to travel all over the country and need to be self-sufficient in transport. Easier said than done. In India in 1974 you cannot just go out and buy a vehicle. They are in short supply with long waiting lists for buyers. Bob has an idea. There is a government department that sells cars left behind by diplomats and international agencies. He saw an old Land Rover there, an ex–British Gurkha vehicle, not long ago. We decide to have a look at it.

After winding through seemingly interminable lanes we arrive at a spacious compound. Gleaming cars, sleek and businesslike compared to the battered hulks that clog the city, are neatly aligned. There is no one in sight and no sign of Land Rovers. Finally two boys appear—coated from head to foot with black oil and grease, their teeth extra white by contrast. Bob explains our interest and a few minutes later a senior clerk comes over, rotund, smiling genially, and dressed in immaculate white *kurta* and *dhoti*. He carefully holds his *dhoti* clear of the greasy courtyard. Chattering away he leads us to the back of a large shed and there stand two Land Rovers. My heart sinks. They have stood there, in the open, for eighteen months or more. The canvas hoods are shredded, the seats are torn, they sag on collapsed tires, rust and dust have congealed over everything. Only the Ghurkha insignias of crossed Nepalese knives called *kukris* give them a cheery note. Bob is undaunted. The car will clean up and in this condition it will be cheap. The boy-mechanics promise to have everything

We film a tiger from our friend Fateh Singh Rathore's Jeep. Fateh Singh was for many years the field director of Ranthambhore Tiger Reserve.

greased and ready tomorrow. The very next evening Belinda drives the limping Land Rover to the Wrights' house.

While a somewhat shifty mechanic called Fatty repairs the tires, tunes the engine, has a new canvas top made, and builds some wooden boxes into the back of the vehicle so we can lock our equipment away, Belinda and I do the rounds of the bureaucracies to get our various clearances.

Finally we take delivery of the cleaned, tough-looking Land Rover resplendent with a new green canvas top and sturdy teak-wood boxes. It has a brand new number plate, WBJ 2749. Quickly we pack up and, in the middle of the night to avoid the traffic, we drive out of Calcutta. We are off to Assam—to Kaziranga and Manas—and, I hope, elephants, rhinos, and perhaps even a tiger.

[CHAPTER 5]
MEETING THE LARGE MAMMALS

A low mist, white in the full moon, lies like a blanket over the grass. A tiger "arooms" loudly, close to our forest bungalow. Moments later it appears out of the mist and walks between the bungalow and the small outbuilding where the caretaker is asleep and oblivious of the predator walking silently by his door. The tiger goes as it came, like a striped ghost into the mist. We hear its moaning roar again, near the small lake in front of the bungalow, a call of frustration perhaps as it missed a deer coming to drink.

I am too excited by this ethereal apparition—my very first wild tiger—and by the jungle sounds to go back to sleep. I sit on the verandah and shiver, as much from the cold as from the elation at being in the real Indian jungle at last.

The moon pales and an orange glow lightens the sky. Adjutant storks, their shoulders hunched, stand starkly outlined as they roost in the silk cotton trees towering, here and there, above the tall grass.

The bungalow, called Arimora, is deep inside Kaziranga National Park. For the first time since arriving in India I cannot see or hear another human being. The bungalow is a two-story structure and from the top verandah I have a commanding view of the low, flat landscape. In all directions swathes of grass, as much as five meters tall, stretch to the horizon. Irregularly dotted throughout are the silk cotton trees, deciduous and now without leaves. On one side a small stream winds sluggishly towards the wide Brahmaputra River, a few kilometers away. The stream is bordered by tall trees forming a deep green band of forest that snakes through the paler grass. To the south stand the rain forest–covered Mikir Hills, blue in the early light of sunrise.

This morning I feel as if I have been transported in some kind of time machine to a peaceful natural world of another era. Last night we arrived in the pitch dark after a long journey from Calcutta, so I had seen nothing of the Indian jungles until they unfolded in this morning's sunrise. For the first time in my life I am in a place where large mammals live in the wild, a *real* jungle.

We quickly remove the Land Rover's canvas top and drive off towards the riverine forest. Belinda drives slowly and gingerly for the tracks are still slippery after the rains of two days ago. Mist lingers among the trees. Entering the first patch of forest we dimly see the bulky shapes of a female elephant and her calf standing in the middle of the track. She does not seem alarmed and extends her trunk trying to get our scent, then continues to feed.

We hear the sounds of huge branches being snapped and smashed to the ground. The mother and calf that block our way belong to a large herd. Perhaps as many as fifty of the animals are around us, and yet we see only two of them. A tree is violently shaken, branches break, we hear the crunching sounds of elephants chewing. Emerald doves, plump brown birds with iridescent green wings, strut along the track. A pair of red jungle fowl scratches in a pile of fresh elephant dung. Every so often the cock stops, stretches his neck, and crows. Not quite a barnyard sound, too high-pitched and cut short at the final syllable. I realize these are wild birds, ancestors of all chickens. Leaving a trail of broken branches and piles of droppings, the elephants move deeper into the forest. Already dung beetles are busy at the steaming heaps. The mist rises and the sun is warm.

Slipping and sliding we descend to the rickety bamboo bridge across the Diphlu River, a silt-laden arm of the Brahmaputra. Before attempting to scramble up the opposite, equally slippery bank, we stop on the bridge, which sways and

Wild water buffaloes and swamp deer at a marshy lake known as a *bheel*.

creaks under the weight of the car. The river is alive with huge fish, surfacing and twisting, their silver scales glinting in the sun. Each fish weighs at least seven or eight kilograms—much too big for the otters that are rolling and diving around a small muddy spit. At first the otters ignore us, continuing their games, but as we get out of the car they whistle in alarm and standing upright on their hind legs, stare at us intently. Then they dive into deeper water and swim off, looking repeatedly back over their shoulders. A Gangetic dolphin comes up to breathe almost under our feet, giving us a start as it puffs through its blowhole. The dolphin is almost the same muddy color as the Diphlu. It is impossible for it to find its prey by sight—even the big fishes virtually rubbing fins with it. The dolphin's eyes are only rudimentary, even lacking true lenses. This two-and-a-half-meter-long mammal navigates entirely by sonar and feeds mostly on crustaceans and catfish on the river bottom.

We emerge from the forest. The track winds like a tunnel through four-meter-high grass. A shaggy black sloth bear stands upright on the track, then drops down on all fours and shuffles off. Rhinos lumber along their trails, more often heard than seen. A bull elephant with imposing tusks materializes eerily in front of us, faces us, then equally silently disappears. Every so often there is a break in the wall of grass giving views of swamps and small lakes, surrounded by short grass. Through one such gap we glimpse two wild water buffaloes staring and sniffing at something on the ground. One is a cow with an enormous spread of horns, the other is her three-quarter-grown calf. As I look through binoculars, my heart skips a beat. Lying in the mud right under the larger buffalo's nose is a tiger. All three are motionless. Our first thought is that the tiger may have attempted to kill the calf and was gored to death by the mother. Two rhinos graze a short distance away.

Elephants, buffaloes, a bear, a tiger, rhinos, all within one hour of leaving the bungalow and all fairly close—I am in a daze, a state of shock almost. But we must attend to the business at hand. We debate whether we should try to approach the dead or wounded tiger. We can do it only on foot for the ground is soft and marshy. It is a reckless thing to do with rhinos nearby, an irate buffalo, and a possibly wounded tiger. A second tiger moans and growls somewhere in the tall grass beyond the buffaloes. On the other hand, nothing ventured nothing gained. Carrying a camera with a large and heavy lens and a tripod, we make slow progress slurping and sloshing through the swamp. The rhinos look up then trot off in a surprisingly light and springy gait.

The tiger is not dead. When we are halfway to where he lies, he leaps up, his fur clogged with mud, and runs for cover. The cow buffalo charges after him, head lowered. After a short sprint the tiger vanishes into the safety of the high grass; an undignified exit for the first wild tiger I have seen clearly.

The track meanders on towards slightly higher ground. On a rise overlooking Burra Bheel, meaning "large lake," we stop to watch a handsome male rhino amble out of the elephant grass. He wades through fields of yellow-flowered herbs, and we can smell the plants' aromatic tang as he crushes them underfoot. The rhino comes closer and closer…jungle mynas, the breeze ruffling their small crests, climb all over him searching inside his ears and nostrils and between the folds of his skin for insects, mites, and ticks.

When no more than four meters from the car, the rhino stops, towering over us. With quiet calls of "treloo, treloo" the mynas fly off. We keep taking pictures, a little apprehensively, for another vehicle was charged and badly dented by a rhino in this same place not long ago. Almost brushing the car with his thick hide, the rhino finally walks off, never threatening us. His every detail, the bubbly texture of his skin, the gouge mark down his horn, his shiny toenails, remain indelibly impressed on our memories.

The nasal "aang, aang, aang" of bar-headed geese interrupts the song of skylarks. Flock after flock flies in and lands in the lake. Pale gray spotbilled pelicans in their hundreds drive fish into shallows then scoop them up in competition with an equal number of adjutant storks, who, hunched and lugubrious looking, seem to wait for the pelicans to drive the fish toward them. As soon as the fish come near, the storks dribble to meet them in a moving forest of long legs, and snatch at their prey with heavy beaks. The pelicans take wing and try their luck at another corner of the lake. One by one the huge storks follow them and are again waiting for the pelicans, and the fish, when they near the shore.

By early afternoon it is hot in the sun. Rhinos move to mud pools to cool and to rest. We surprise a small group of water buffaloes in a patch of short grass quietly chewing their cud; the heat does not worry them. As we approach they rise reluctantly; arching their tails and necks, they stretch luxuriously. Remembering that these are not the docile water buffaloes we have seen pulling carts and being bullied by small boys, we approach cautiously on foot, trying for some close, low-angle pictures. The buffaloes lift their noses in the air till their immense horns lie along their backs. These horns are deadly weapons that

Female wild water buffaloes: the females have longer, more slender horns than the males.

they wield with great cunning and accuracy. As we come nearer, the buffaloes begin head-tossing and snorting. A new-born calf suddenly stands up and peers at us inquisitively over the grass tops. Fluffy and almost white, it makes a sharp contrast to the dark gray, rough-textured adults.

In the twilight of late afternoon we almost miss the elephants gathered at the exact place where we saw the tiger-buffalo confrontation this morning. More than eighty of them are standing at the swamp's edge, dousing themselves with black mud. A small group of four females stands apart from the rest. One of the group is agitated and pushes at something on the ground with her trunk and forefoot. The other three females are crowded around her, touching her with their trunks and then touching the bundle in the short grass. The remainder of the herd, having finished their mud baths, turn and, in a wall of dark shapes, vanish into the tall grass. The three attending females reluctantly follow, trumpeting and shaking their heads as they catch up with the herd. Last to leave the clearing is the agitated female. In her trunk she carries the limp body of her small, dead calf. She holds the baby around the neck, its small trunk and legs dragging along the ground. Twice the mother stops, puts her calf down, and prods it. She does not seem to understand that the calf is dead. Still carrying the body she too moves on.

Darkness has set in by the time we leave the marshy lake for the six-kilometer drive back to Arimora. Rhinos, frightened by our headlights, snort off into the tall grass. Pairs of fiery coals, the reflections from the eyes of nightjars on the wing, dance in the air.

5 February

Two days ago I saw my first wild elephants and was impressed by their muscular power and their liveliness compared to the elephants I had seen in zoos. This morning I will ride my first trained elephant. It seems the perfect vehicle to see wildlife in Kaziranga—an elevated, silent platform borne by an animal that lives here naturally.

As we approach the appointed place we see a large tusker with his *mahout*, or driver, waiting for us in the early light. I am in no hurry to climb aboard. I have never touched an elephant before and I want to run my fingers over his rough skin and feel the sparse stiff black hairs that grow from his head. I inspect his toenails set in his circular feet. As the ele-

phant inspects me with his trunk, I run my hands over one of his long, heavy tusks to the sharp point. His ears, suffused with pink, fan back and forth constantly, flapping noisily. After a thorough inspection to see if I might have something to eat, the elephant, called Rai Bahadur, loses interest in me and begins to graze. He plucks great bunches of grass with his trunk and stuffs them into his cavernous pink mouth.

Even when he is calmly grazing, I can sense the animal's enormous power. This power must at all times be controlled and directed by the *mahout*; if it is not, even a "domestic" elephant can be very dangerous. Belinda, who was brought up with elephants and once had one of her own, warns me never to go near an elephant unless its *mahout* is there. Even working elephants frequently kill people. Nearly all trained elephants are originally caught in the wild.

The elephant's glory, however, is not its strength, but its trunk, the most wonderful instrument in the animal kingdom. It can perform not only the most delicate tasks, like picking up a dropped pen or lens cap, but it can also lift heavy logs. The trunk is used to suck up water for a shower or to be squirted down the throat for a drink. It is a sensitive sense organ, for it really is the elephant's nose. It is also used to gather all its food—from grass pulled out of the ground and leaves stripped from twigs to bark peeled from branches.

We climb on top of the elephant via a tall platform and seat ourselves on an elaborate kind of saddle called a *howdah*. In front of us, astride the elephant's neck, sits Narain Sirkar, the *mahout*. A slim man with a pencil-line mustache, he constantly prods his animal along using the pressure of his big toes behind the elephant's voluminous ears. When this fails to keep Rai Bahadur moving, Narain yells and swears at him. If this is also ignored a blow on the head or a stab with the sharp point of the steel *ankush* gets the elephant going at a brisk pace. Following rhino and buffalo trails we disappear into the sea of grass.

In the distance we hear wild elephants roaring and trumpeting. Judging by their noise it must be a large herd. Winding through the maze of trails we finally come out onto a wide tract of recently burnt country. The old grass has been burnt to the ground and the new growth is only half a meter high. The herd is an indeterminate gray mass among the silk cotton trees in the distance. Belinda persuades Narain to go right into the herd and to let Rai Bahadur mingle with the wild elephants.

The roaring and trumpeting has subsided and by the time we reach the herd all is at peace. The only sounds are those of grass being pulled and the occasional soft rumble. We remain equally quiet for fear of stampeding them. Rai Bahadur joins in the grazing. Soon we are surrounded by about 125 wild elephants. They have accepted the presence of the newcomer and are as yet unaware of the people who have infiltrated with him.

An adult female with a tiny calf comes up, trunk extended, to make friends with our elephant. An adolescent tusker walks over to investigate. Some of the elephants are so close that Belinda, by stretching out her hand, lightly touches one. The animal shrugs but takes no further notice.

Narain keeps a wary eye on four large bulls on the periphery of the herd. The largest of them, an enormous beast, is perhaps the biggest tusker we have ever seen, and he is in musth. Dark liquid streams from glands in his cheeks. Roaring and stomping, the big bull rampages beside the herd and stops only to thrash the vegetation in seeming frustration and rage. The other bulls keep a safe distance. Another tusker in musth stands about 300 meters away, staring at the herd. Suddenly he marches towards the dominant male. For the last fifty meters he rushes in. The big fellow answers the challenge. They stop face to face, heads lowered, foreheads almost touching. For some minutes they stare at each other. Then

without warning the larger bull draws slightly back and charges. With a resounding, hollow "thonk" they ram into each other, head to head. The challenger does not wait for the onslaught of the huge tusks and retreats in a swirl of dust. For more than half a kilometer the dominant bull gives chase.

By the time the winner of the duel rejoins his herd, a large female gets our scent. All hell breaks loose. We are in the middle of a terrifying tumult of sound and movement as mothers and protective aunts gather the infants together. A matriarch, standing taller than the other females, leads the mob. In a short time we are faced by a solid phalanx of massive bodies, a row of snake-like trunks waving in our direction. The adult males do not take part in the rush, but add to the pandemonium with their noise—seeming to try to intimidate us with sheer volume of sound. We are most definitely intimidated. Adolescent males make mock charges from the periphery of the herd. Rai Bahadur remains unconcerned.

Slowly, belligerently, the wall of elephant bodies advances. Screams and roars give way to ominous deep rumbles. The big bull in musth shoulders his way through the females and comes at us like an express train. Very skillfully Narain makes Rai Bahadur slink away as unobtrusively as possible and at just the right pace. The tusker loses interest. He has been distracted by the females that surround him.

A female elephant would have had nothing to fear from the bull. But Rai Bahadur is a male and would have been a sure target. Domestic elephants, even one as majestic as Rai Bahadur, do not have the toughness and agility of their wild counterparts.

Our next destination is Manas Sanctuary and Tiger Reserve. It will be a long journey, to the other side of the Brahmaputra River.

An elephant calf plays under its mother's watchful eye. Young elephants are raised in extended families. The only adults in these groups are females. Adult males are mostly solitary. All females, not just the calf's mother, are solicitous toward and protective of the young.

[CHAPTER 6]

GOLDEN MONKEYS AND GIANT HORNBILLS

Manas Sanctuary and Tiger Reserve—
8 to 20 February 1974

We arrive at the forest rest house on the Indian bank of the Manas River in late afternoon. We look longingly at the forested green hills on the other side, hoping to be able to stay in a small guesthouse there that belongs to the king of Bhutan. We have permission to do so but the river is broad, swift, and just too deep to wade across. There is no sign of a boat of any kind. Belinda is soon deep in conversation with Forest Department staff from both sides of the river.

Belinda works her magic. Several boats are conjured up and two of them are lashed together to accommodate the Land Rover. Two boatmen pole the craft upstream with unhurried skill for about a kilometer and then cross to the other side. We are in Bhutan, in subtropical rain forest. The guesthouse, a small, brightly painted building, is tucked among the trees. A pathway leads to a teahouse overlooking the river, which is much narrower here among the hills. A spreading fig tree covered with clusters of yellow and orange fruits stands on the opposite bank. Giant hornbills, making strange honking sounds, are feeding on them. Downstream a little, on our side of the river, tall trees rise out of flowering shrubs and on the low branches sit the animals that have brought us here— golden langurs. Their black faces are framed with tufts of pale golden fur. The monkeys look at us steadily, calmly, through amber eyes. It is getting dark and down on the plains elephants trumpet.

The next twelve days are a delirium of delight. We walk the hills, spend hours and hours with the langurs, and go out over the wide river flats in India while riding elephants. I find it impossible to separate in my mind what we saw and did on a particular day, but I can vividly remember each incident, the colors, the scents, the sounds, the details, of the animals. In the narrative that follows I have compressed these observations as if they happened on a single day.

★　★　★

As the Manas River rushes out of Bhutan it turns sharply westward and suddenly its waters, no longer squeezed between the hills, lose much of their force. It is dissipated over a wide bed of rounded shingles and finally spent in a maze of sandbanks, gravel beds, and grassed islands. Farther to the west, lush, tall grassland sequined with clear, still ponds stretches between river and hills.

The rising sun catches the white plumes of the seeding grasses surrounding a pool and turns them gold, vivid against the dark, dark green of the still-shaded hills. Perched on the tall grass stems, swamp partridges screech their strident calls. Cautiously a hog deer stag, small but stocky, edges out of the grass. For five minutes or more he scans the open space, tests the air with a sensitive, moist nose before he jerkily approaches the water. He drinks quickly, pushing his muzzle between yellow buttercups.

Without warning a raptor on long wings sails low over the pool. The pied harrier, a male in stark black and white plumage, causes panic. Partridges stop calling, then vanish in the tall grass. Already nervous, the hog deer high-steps back into the tall grass.

With long, lazy strokes the harrier flies westward with the breeze, then rising against the air currents he works back eastward—across more sandbanks—toward the green hills. He is hungry. He is intent on what appear to be sparrow-sized pebbles lying on the sand beneath him, but his eyes are keen enough to see them as a flock of resting, small Indian pratincoles. Standing fluffed out, each on one leg, faces into the breeze, eyes half-closed, the birds appear easy prey. But at any given moment at least a dozen have one wary eye cocked at the sky. With shrill cries they take off en masse in a tight flock and swing down river. Under the indifferent eyes of a ring-tailed fishing eagle and a score of vultures roosting in a silk cotton tree, the swallow-like plovers are once more transformed into a haphazard collection of stones as they land.

Just as the harrier begins to make his turn back to the more open reaches of the river, he spots the movement in a small, boulder-filled pool. He flicks around, losing height so he can make a low-level surprise attack from the rear. The ibisbill, a plover with a long, down-curved beak like that of an ibis, continues to forage. Its head is underwater, its beak probing between and underneath the stones. Soft gray with a black head

Rare golden langurs regarded us calmly from the trees.

and breastband, it blends perfectly with the rounded rocks. Only its red beak and legs stand out. It finds a caddis fly larva and prizes the insect out. As it lifts its head to swallow its catch the harrier strikes. Black talons on yellow feet are buried deep into the plover's body, piercing its lungs and heart. The harrier barely slows in his flight as he makes his catch. By the time he lands on a grassy bank, mantling his black and white wings over his quarry in victory, the ibisbill is dead. Mergansers and Brahminy ducks look up briefly, but soon resume their preening, enjoying the early sun.

Across the river a small piece of mixed forest grows at the base of the rising slopes. Tall deciduous trees from the plains stand over evergreen rain forest shrubs spilled from the hills. The trees are bare for only a short period. Already the silk cottons have spread their flowers and other species are pushing out tender, new shoots. The new growth has seduced a troop of golden langurs away from their hills. Now that the sun is still low the monkeys sit bunched in groups of four or five, sunning themselves high in the bare trees as they groom each other's fur. One lies along a branch on her stomach, legs

dangling, eyes closed while her partner, helped at times by her adolescent young, runs deft fingers through her blond pelt. After a few minutes the two adults change places. The single full-grown male of the troop has two females attending him, but disdains to groom in return. Appetite gradually replaces indulgence and the troop slowly scatters, making their way to the outer branches. Plucking leafbuds with both hands, they stuff their mouths to capacity before chewing.

Before the sun has fully penetrated to the forest floor the langurs leave their tree tops for lower, shadier places. Fearlessly they leap from branch to branch, tree to tree. If they judge the distance too great for an unaided leap, they climb to a thin, outer branch, setting up a rocking motion, and just when it seems the branch must snap, they use the upswing to catapult themselves to the next tree. Each of the adult monkeys uses the same route, the same rocking branches. Mothers leave their larger infants to make their own way—no matter how pitifully the infants scream. The youngsters either stay behind or find their own route. Not being able to leap such great distances, they have to rush twice as far and twice as fast to keep up.

At the lower, greener levels of the forest the langurs' golden blond fur glows. Dashing through the leaves or just sitting, chewing, they appear like pale ghosts in the lingering early morning gloom. Golden brown eyes set in black faces regard the world with neither fear nor belligerence. To each other they show only exuberance and affection.

The forest birds' initial burst of song, when the first gray light seeped through the foliage, ended some time ago. Now that the sun has risen higher and flecks the mossy logs and the leaflitter of the forest floor, they give a second chorus. It is only a little less passionate.

Tucked away in the foliage are a lively array of leaf green colored birds, their greenness making them inconspicuous.

The nectar-feeders among them dip their beaks into bright flowers. Pigeons pull soft berries from heavily laden branches while parakeets tear at harder fruits with their sharp, hooked beaks. A green woodpecker hammers a tree in search of wood-boring insects. A still greener magpie gleans the leaves for spiders and caterpillars. A solitary green-breasted pitta delves into damp moss for snails, pausing frequently among the ferns to whistle his strong triple note. But none of these birds is a plain uniform green, though from a distance they appear so. At throat, face, crest, rump, or chest they have garish touches of brilliant color—blue, iridescent purple, scarlet, maroon, orange....

The green, mostly arboreal birds are matched by a complement of equally deceptively colored ground birds—earth-colored but also trimmed with brightness. Prominent among them are the strong throated thrushes, still in full song. A kaleej pheasant, dark blue with a livid red eyepatch, drums his wings to attract a mate. The male jungle fowl, garish only in direct sunlight, is orange and iridescent green and blue. He scratches his living from among the leaves. Shamas, long-tailed thrushes, flit through the lower shrubs, flashing white signals every time they flick their tails.

But in Manas there is a third group of birds—flamboyant, extravagantly colored species that make these forests exciting beyond anything I thought possible. The birds are of such blatant brilliance and boldness of pattern, and

A great Indian hornbill feeding on wild figs.

they so arrogantly discard the protection of camouflage, that their colors would seem a constant provocation to predators. Yet they are no less numerous than the more soberly plumaged birds.

Both the largest and the smallest birds of the forest are brightly feathered. The male of the diminutive Mrs. Gould's sunbird flashes iridescent purple, scarlet, crimson, and yellow as it flits from flower to flower. Scarlet minivets flutter in gre-garious, twittering parties through the trees. Hunched on a low branch, immobile, sits a red-headed trogon displaying his gorgeous crimson. Almost ventriloquially he calls a leisurely, mewing "cue, cue, cue." High in the treetops fairy blue birds, silky ultramarine and velvet black, test some fruit for ripeness. Not far away a golden yellow oriole sings. On the forest floor a group of twenty white-crested laughing thrushes, cackling raucously, skip and posture with half-drooped brown wings. A verditer flycatcher, a tiny speck of blue, looks on unperturbed. Of most of these birds, only the males are so audaciously colored; the females are more subdued—brown, yellow, buff-colored. They are the ones that sit on the eggs and raise the young. The males can afford their eye-catching glamour—they are expendable.

Overhead, with the hissing, whooshing noise of an approaching storm a pair of great pied hornbills flies toward their favorite feeding tree; huge birds with outlandish casque-topped beaks. Alternately beating their hissing wings and gliding, nearly all their flying energy seems to be directed to keep their bills from dragging them earthward. The pair, as big as vultures, lands awkwardly on splayed feet. Nasal honks, amplified by outsize beaks, greet the newcomers. About a dozen pairs of the hornbills are already in residence among the golfball-sized figs. The fruits are not pendant from the outer twigs, but sprout in clusters from the thick trunk and main branches. They vary from hard, unripe green figs to ripe, squashy, red ones.

Running the gauntlet of the stabs of the settled pairs, the new arrivals find an unoccupied corner of the tree. They settle closely beside each other, shoulders touching. For a while they preen, delicately running their heavy beaks through their feathers. Then the male, with his ruby-red eyes set in an unfeathered, black face, reaches forward. Testing several figs for ripeness he plucks a bright orange fruit. With a delicacy unexpected from such an ungainly instrument, he runs the fig to and fro in his beak, softening it without mashing it to a pulp. Again with unexpected grace, he offers the fruit to his partner. She is identical to her mate except that her eyes are pearly white and ringed in red. She takes the fruit, runs it though her beak in appreciation, then tosses it backward into her gullet. Now it is her turn to feed him. Back and forth they feed each other—not to satisfy their hunger but to reinforce their affection into a strong partnership. Soon the two will seek out a deep hollow in a large tree in which they will nest. The female, after laying her two eggs, will then block up the nest entrance from inside leaving a small slit through which the male will feed her. Once the eggs have hatched and the young have grown sufficiently, she will break out of her prison, but recement the entrance after her. Both parents will then feed the young through the slit and only when the young are big enough to chisel their own way out will they be able to fledge.

By midday it is warm. The langurs drowse. Birds fluff their feathers and preen unhurriedly. The hornbills' long eyelashes droop over their eyes as they teeter on their perches like old men falling unwillingly asleep in their chairs. A troop of Assamese macaques leaves the treetops and descends to drink.

Harsh, insistent alarm calls of birds reach the macaques' ears. Unhesitatingly they abandon their drinking and their play and rush for the trees. Even though she is no threat to them, the tiger striding through the forest draws the abuse of every bird—the hysterical cackling of the jungle fowl, the screech of the parakeets, the grating "che, che, che" of the paradise flycatcher. Her orange, striped coat burning through the green, the tiger moves on, ignoring the agitations. At the forest edge she pauses, briefly, then walks over the mica-gold speckled sand to the water's edge to drink. The monkeys cough and bark at her. For several minutes the tiger drinks and then walks on, leaving a trail of alarm calls.

At dusk, at that period of semidarkness when the white, star-shaped flowers of the jasmine seem to float disembodied in the undergrowth, the sambar and barking deer begin their night's browsing. A Himalayan barred owlet, no larger than a thrush, his white throat glowing like the jasmine, chatters and squawks from a low branch. Rodents leave their burrows and nests in hollow trees and scurry and scratch in the undergrowth—prey for the civets and the leopard cats. First to emerge, from the thicket where he slept all day, is a large Indian civet. His soft, gray fur is neatly patterned with black and white—finely barred along his flanks and boldly striped at his throat and along his bushy tail. For a while he is happy to scavenge fruits dropped by the foraging birds during the day. But soon he trots off to look for mice or lizards or to climb a tree in search of sleeping birds. With agility and liveliness he chases anything he thinks he can overpower. Another kind of civet, the shaggy-haired ponderous binturong, or bear-cat, is slower to emerge. She has been sleeping in a spacious hollow in a half-rotten tree. For some minutes she sits and peers from the entrance of her retreat, tufted ears pricked. Uniformly black dusted with gray, she is difficult to see as she eases into the night, puffing and grunting. Only by chance will she catch a mouse, a lizard, or a bird, for she does not have the speed nor the fierceness of a true hunter. Pride of place as a hunter of small animals must go to a true cat, the leopard cat, with golden eyes and a golden coat spotted with black. Shuffling, snuffling among the ground litter moves a bristly furred hog badger. More badger than hog, it relies on its sensitive, tapering, bare nose to find small animal life among the rocks, the logs, and in the leaf mold. Anything detected is soon ripped from its hiding place with huge, bearlike claws.

Grazers, browsers, opportunists, hunters, they must all be on their mettle to avoid the supreme and indiscriminate hunter—the tiger. All night, from some corner of the forest, comes the bark of a deer, warning of the movements of the big cat.

In just a few days we must leave to make our way to the south, to the opposite end of the country. Once again we will have to navigate the Land Rover through endless throngs of people and dodge in and out of noisy traffic.

To prepare for the journey we sit in the teahouse by the river and try to absorb as much of this enthralling place as we can. After all the rushing about of the last ten days it is necessary to have this quiet afternoon so that we can sort the wonder of it all in our minds. As always birds are around us.

These immediate images of hornbills and woodpeckers swirl about with a hundred others of mountains, rivers, forests, colorful birds, and exotic mammals. Disjointed ideas and thoughts intermingle with them. Why should Manas have this special aura, why should this particular combination of landforms and plant and animal species so excite us? Maybe if I trace the origins of the natural forces that have been at work here over geological time it will become clearer. At night, by the light of a candle while a small owlet calls outside the window, I re-read my notes on the theory of continental drift and subsequent geological events in this area.

Mist shrouds an island in the Brahmaputra River in Assam.

* * *

The theory of continental drift holds that originally all the continents of the world formed two closely connected supercontinents. One of these supercontinents was in the northern hemisphere and was named Laurasia, a contraction of the names of its main components—the Saint Lawrence Basin of North America, Europe, and Asia. The other, in the southern hemisphere, was called Gondwana after a central Indian kingdom and contained South America, Africa, Antarctica, India, and Australia. More than 300 million years ago these two supercontinents fractured into their component parts which, infinitely slowly, drifted to their present positions. Most are still moving.

Among the evidence to support the theory is that if you were to cut the various continents from a globe you could fit them together like the pieces of a jigsaw puzzle, thus re-making the supercontinents. In such a jigsaw, North America fits snugly against Europe leaving a neat space for Greenland. South America's "nose" fits into West Africa's "waist." Antarctica and southeast Africa fit together with India wedged in between. Australia's southern coastline slots into eastern Antarctica. To make the fit almost perfect you would have to cut

along the continental shelves since rising and falling sea levels obscure the true edges of the continents.

Evidence from the study of rocks, fossils, and the distribution patterns of living plants and animals also bears out these affinities. Fossil dinosaurs from India are closely related to those of Madagascar and South America. Almost identical fossil mollusks have been prized from rocks of South America, Antarctica, and India. Certain aspects of Australia's flora are closely allied to those of southern Africa and South America. Marsupials are found in abundance only in the Australasian region and in South America.

As an integral part of Gondwana, India was firmly lodged between East Africa and Antarctica. By the end of the Carboniferous period, about 300 million years ago, the supercontinents had already fractured into the continents as we know them today. But for another 150 million years they stayed closely linked together. Much of the region was under an ice sheet; the evidence of its glaciers was etched deeply into the rocks and is still visible. About 100 million years ago, at the end of the Cretaceous period, the dispersal of Gondwana's various parts began to quicken. "Quicken" may be a term too dramatic to apply to continental drift, for the progress of the continents' supporting tectonic plates was very, very slow. India was thought to have moved fastest during the Oligocene epoch, 38 million years ago, when it crept along at about fourteen centimeters per year. In the following epoch, the Miocene, this slowed to a steady eight centimeters per year.

India broke away from Gondwana towards the end of an ice age—at a time in the earth's geological history when the giant reptiles were dying out and primitive mammals and birds first appeared. Cycads were the dominant plants, but the higher forms, the angiosperms, had already made their appearance. India left Gondwana at what seemed to have been a time of transition in the development of plants and animals.

So the Indian island that drifted northward, the only piece of Gondwana to migrate in its entirety to the northern hemisphere, was host to an assemblage of comparatively primitive plants and animals evolved in a temperate-to-cold climate. As India's climate warmed on the northward journey, plants proliferated and accumulated to give rise to the vast Gondwana coal deposits. Mollusks, spiders, insects, other invertebrates, frogs, and lizards spread throughout the drifting, isolated island. Mammals and birds remained few in number and were still primitive in their development.

India drifted inexorably towards southern Asia, a region that in terms of plant and animal evolution was the very opposite of India. By the time India approached, southern Asia had a young, vigorous, and rapidly speciating fauna and flora.

During the Pliocene epoch, about four million years ago, India and southern Asia collided. A Gondwanan fragment, evolutionary primitive, met the Asian mainland, which had already moved

The Manas River emerges from the rain forest–covered foothills of Bhutan.

into the age of mammals, birds, and higher plants. It had been a long journey for India, lasting some 146 million years.

The collision was a major cataclysm. India's continental shelf, submerged except in the northeast corner, in what is now Assam, rammed the Asian mainland. It warped, buckled downward, slipped beneath the Asian plate, and with its inexorable, continuing pressure began to push up the Himalayan mountain range. The force of the impact cracked the center of the peninsula and huge outflows of lava spread from the fissures. Plants and animals of Gondwanan origin were obliterated from most of central India. On the western coastline the collision caused block-fracturing, subsidence, and the upthrust of the rocks, shaping the mountainous Western Ghats. Since these mountains were unaffected by the lava flows, ancient Gondwana species survive there.

At the time when the Indian plate first collided with Asia there was only a small land connection—not far from Manas. Biogeographers call it the Assam Gateway. It became the first migration route between Indian–Gondwanan species on the one hand and the Indo–Chinese and Malayan forms, collectively known as the Oriental fauna and flora, on the other. The routes to Europe, northern Asia, and Africa were as yet closed by the sea. The Assam Gateway left the way open for an Oriental invasion, mainly of plants. Tropical, wet-climate forests of Oriental origin eventually covered peninsular India and remained its principal vegetation into historic times. Few of the more ancient Gondwanan forms migrated eastward, and most of them survived only as relicts. None of the higher animals and plants, now regarded as classically Indian, are in fact of Gondwanan origin.

By the late Pliocene and early Pleistocene, perhaps between two million and one million years ago, land connections were formed to the centers of species dispersal in

Europe, northern Asia, and Africa. The way was open to invasions from the west and northwest. The migrations took place mainly along the Himalayan foothills and along this route came a procession of mammals, including the Pleistocene giants, who left their remains as fossils in the sub-Himalayan Siwalik Ranges. Mastodons and elephants of eleven different kinds then lived in India. There were giraffes, many different kinds of rhino, hippos, a giant four-horned grazing animal called Sivatherium, several kinds of horse, piglike creatures, buffaloes, bison, deer, and antelopes. Remains of saber-toothed tigers have been found as well as those of a kind of cheetah. More modern animals that no longer live in India such as chimpanzees, orangutans, and baboons also left their remains in the Siwalik hills among those of langurs, macaques, civets, jackals, and others that are still part of India's living fauna.

Mobile species, emissaries from the neighboring zoogeographic regions, invaded India to fill the vacant niches. In peninsular India the plants and animals of East and West met and mingled—the African lion hunts the Oriental deer, the Oriental tiger stalks the African antelope. Intermingling with these forms is a sprinkling of northern Asian species. India became a crossroads of migrations and as a consequence has one of the most exciting and diverse assemblages of plants and animals the world has seen.

In historic times, perhaps less than 5,000 years ago, the western migration route into India began to close. But even as comparatively recently as the Indus River civilization of 2,500 BC there were lush forests along the Indus and Sutlej Rivers—complete with forest-loving rhinos, elephants, and even tigers. We know this from the seals, with beautifully carved figures of these animals, left by the Indus River people. The elephants were depicted carrying some kind of saddle and ropes, suggesting that even then they were domesticated. Since that time the western entrance literally began to dry up. The Sind and Thar deserts in southern Pakistan and western India spread a hot, sandy barrier. Over the last 400 years the process was hastened by human exploitation and mismanagement, which in the end completely obliterated the once lush forests of northwestern India. Elephants, rhinos, and tigers retreated eastward and southward to the forests. The western gateway was shut. The northern route was effectively blocked by the Himalayas.

Only in Assam and its neighboring states of Arunachal Pradesh and Nagaland, at the same place where India first touched Asia, does the gateway to the interchange and flow of plant and animal genes remain ajar. The slow but titanic forces that shaped this corner of the world are still at work. India still pushes against the Asian mainland, and the Himalayas are still, fractionally, rising each year. The northeast is still a crossroads in terms of its fauna and flora and its area of active interchange, but only just. Botanists have been aware for many years of the Assam region's significance as a meeting place of East and West. Joseph Hooker in his seven-volume *The Flora of British India,* published between 1872 and 1897, comments on the Assam forests as follows: "...perhaps the richest and certainly the most varied botanical area on the surface of the globe and one which, in a greater degree than any other, contains representatives of the floras of both the Eastern and Western Hemispheres." Subsequent botanical expeditions to the then–Northeast Frontier Agency, now the Indian state of Arunachal Pradesh, pinpointed the place where the two floras meet—the Abor Hills. The botanist Burkill after an expedition there in 1925 wrote: "Aborland is where the two earth systems meet, a veritable node in phytogeography."

It may seem fanciful, but in Manas I think I can feel something of the vibrance, abundance, and exotic variety you would expect at one of the world's major biological crossroads. But humankind's overexploitation continues and has reached the stage where India's fauna and flora have been reduced to relics. The interchange of species between one corner of the country and another, which was such an important factor in the natural evolution, has stopped altogether. The relics are stagnating.

The Assam Valley and the hills that surround it remained in a more or less pristine condition until about 1900. Only tribespeople lived in the region. Fierce and skillful hunters though the men were, they did not disrupt the natural life forces that flowed so strongly in the valley. Disruption came with the opening of the railways almost to the Chinese border, the establishment of tea gardens, and the immigration of large numbers of workers to harvest the tea. Hard on their heels came cultivators and graziers, lusting after the rich soil and high rainfall. The Assam Valley itself is now virtually denuded of its original vegetation, the animals have retreated to a few pockets. Only the hills remain—though every year fewer and fewer of them still have their original vegetation. Humanity is moving at breakneck speed to shut the Assam Gateway.

What the world stands to lose should this happen, and just how easily it can, we saw here in Manas and in Kaziranga—two of the handful of relics where the pulse of the Assam Gateway's biodiversity still beats strongly.

South Indian Jungles

MARCH AND APRIL 1974

From Assam, we travel diagonally across the subcontinent to the far south—another area of hills, plains, and high rainfall. Here we wend our way through the rain forests of the Ashambu Hills where we look for one of the world's rarest and most endangered monkeys—the lion-tailed macaque. We watch a troop of the glossy black, gray-maned monkeys as they forage for fruits, insects, and small lizards in giant trees that reach into the mist. On sunny days, we are absorbed by the wide variety of life—flowers, snakes, frogs, and lizards, and the occasional elephant. We follow tiger pug marks left in the sand of a creek bank.

On the rolling downs of golden grass of the Kerala High Range, in the shadow of the 2,713-meter-high peak of Anai Mudi, we stalk the elusive mountain goat known as the Nilgiri tahr. These jungles of the mountains of the Western Ghats are as diverse, as enthralling as those of Assam and Bhutan.

Clockwise from upper left: male bonnet macaque yawning; a bull gaur; a bonnet macaque with her baby; Indian chameleon.

Down on the plains we explore the shores of Periyar's artificial lake in a small dinghy. We drift close to bathing and playing elephants. Giant gaur or Indian bison, the world's largest wild bovines, overwhelm with their size and the power they exude. The bulls, glistening black like polished stone, stare at us through pales eyes from among the bamboo. Troops of another kind of macaque—incongruously called bonnet macaques, for they sport unruly hair rather than any kind of hat—swing through the vines. Brilliantly colored birds and butterflies flit through shafts of sunlight and swirl around our heads.

Clockwise from upper left: a Malabar fungoid frog from the rain forest; a balsam flower (*Impatiens sp.*); vine snake; slender lorises: small tree-living primates; Anai Mudi: the highest Indian peak south of the Himalayas.

[C H A P T E R   7]

TIGER HAVEN

By the time we are again in northern India it is early May 1974—the month when the climate is at its most trying. We are on our way to Tiger Haven, Billy Arjan Singh's farm adjoining Dudhwa Sanctuary, right on the border with Nepal. Billy is an old friend of Belinda and her family.

We drive northwest from Lucknow across treeless plains where by midmorning the temperature has risen to 43 degrees Celsius. A searing wind raises billowing clouds of dust that obscure the sun. The few people who are about have scarves and turbans wrapped around their heads, leaving only a slit for their eyes. We should have done the same, for the Land Rover does not give us much protection. Soon our lips are dry and cracked and our eyes, mouths, noses, and ears are gritty with sand.

In the afternoon, as the heat and wind abate, the landscape gradually changes. After crossing the Sarda River and leaving the small town of Palia behind, overgrazed and overcultivated farms give way to natural grassland and marshes. The nearby hills are covered in forest. The small dusty track we turn into follows another, smaller river. On our side there is rich grass, even at this time of year, with occasional large shady trees. The river itself is shaded by jamun and Arjuna trees. The trees and shrubs form an archway over the still-flowing stream. A large mugger crocodile basks on a sandbank. On the other side of the river grows tall forest. The track ends at a clearing where a row of whitewashed buildings stand on the riverbank. We have arrived at Tiger Haven.

The first animals we see, however, are not tigers, but two leopards leaping and playing in the afternoon coolness. Billy comes over to greet us. He is a muscular, powerful man in his midfifties. I had been told that Billy is a taciturn recluse, at times difficult to communicate with. But there is no sign of that as he welcomes us warmly with a smile that transforms his stern, even forbidding, features. The leopards, Juliet and Harriet, had been given to Billy as tiny cubs by the Prime Minister, Indira Gandhi, to raise and to try to introduce into the wild—something Billy has had a measure of success with. Juliet and Harriet stroll over and inspect us and the Land Rover. They briefly allow us to scratch them behind their ears before they're off again, running and tumbling.

There is nothing reticent about Billy as we talk under the stars on a velvet cool evening about tigers, leopards, their introduction into the wild, the problems facing Dudhwa and other reserves in India. He talks with wit about how Dudhwa eventually became a protected area.

I had been under the impression that when Billy bought Tiger Haven's land it adjoined an existing wildlife sanctuary. But this was not the case. He bought the land in the 1950s. The surrounding forests and wetlands, while nominally "reserved," were then ruthlessly exploited. Timber was cut, thousands of cattle grazed there, dead wood was removed, rivers and ponds were fished to exhaustion, and until a few years ago tigers were hunted in the forests. The endangered swamp deer, one of the last herds of which survives in Dudhwa, was saved from being hunted into oblivion solely through Billy's intervention.

Billy exerted all his influence and lobbied the Uttar Pradesh state government; his efforts resulted in 490 square kilometers of forest, marsh, and grasslands being made into Dudhwa Wildlife Sanctuary in 1968.

At first this made no difference. No protection staff was appointed, and grazing, fishing, timber-felling, and all the other activities continued as before. Only tiger hunting stopped—or so we thought. For years Billy looked after Dudhwa on his own, patrolling the sanctuary in his Jeep or on his elephant, evicting graziers and confronting timber-cutters. The Forest Department, the police, and the local courts were not interested in stopping something that had gone on for as long as they could remember. Billy often took the law into his own hands and removed the exploiters himself.

The conservationist Billy Arjan Singh with his leopard Harriet.

He is a powerful and intimidating man. Dudhwa is to a great degree his creation.

★ ★ ★

Billy works very hard to show us tigers within camera range. He has people out in the forest monitoring the cats' movements by following their pug marks. We go out on elephants every morning to look for them. Billy builds *machans*—platforms with minimum cover placed low in trees—and blinds made of grass, in strategic places.

Tiger Haven—8 May 1974

Just after sunrise Billy leaves us in a *machan* about three meters up a large tree. On one side of us is the forest, full of the songs of birds. On the other side is a small marsh overgrown with short, bright green waterplants. Tall grass, dried to a straw yellow, surrounds the pond.

After about an hour rhesus monkeys cough and bark in alarm in the forest. A few moments pass as we hardly dare to move in case we raise the suspicions of the tiger that may be approaching. As the monkey alarm becomes a frenzy we hear the footsteps, crackling on the dry leaves, of *two* animals approaching. We briefly glimpse the striped bodies through the undergrowth before they vanish from sight into the tall grass. For what seems an hour we stare at the place we expect the tigers to emerge. It is probably only seconds later that a tigress, very large to our eyes, strides out of the wall of grass to the edge of the marsh. Looking briefly right and left, but not up toward us, she wades briskly across the shallow pond and disappears into the tall grass on the other side. We take a few pictures, praying that the camera clicks will not upset the tiger and that we can hold our large lenses steady. The second tiger soon appears, a smaller one and most likely a well-grown cub of the tigress', and follows the same route as its mother. For hours, as it becomes progressively hotter, we wait, hoping the tigers will return to sit in the cool water and to drink.

In anticipation of this I climb down from the *machan* and tiptoe along a swept path (so my footsteps will be soundless) to the blind, made of straw, that Billy has built on the pond's edge. Almost immediately the monkeys bark again. And again I hear footsteps on the dry leaflitter; a single animal this time, walking directly toward me. While the blind shields me from the pond, it is open at the back from where the footsteps come closer and closer. Luckily some thick bushes screen me from view.

The sound of footsteps, when they seem just a few meters away, changes to a rustling in the grass even closer. Within touching distance it seems. I have one eye glued to a hole in the blind's side.

A tiger's massive head slowly emerges from the grass no more than three meters from me. I clearly see his eyes, his neck ruff, the muscles bulging on his shoulders, his brilliantly colored and glossy coat. I perspire profusely, as much from excitement as from the heat. I feel as if I am in a fire—the burning sun, the grass dried to yellow straw all around, the tiger's flamelike pattern, and the smoldering in his eyes as he stares unblinkingly at the camera. I do not know how long we look at each other. Perhaps a minute or more. Long enough for the realization to sink in that I should take a photograph. As slowly as I can, in my adrenalin-filled state, I move my head to see through the camera. It is not slowly enough. The tiger utters a growling "whoof" and wheels around, back into the grass. I hear no further sounds. Is he still beside the blind or has he walked silently off across the marsh? Finally I hear his footsteps as he ambles back into the forest. Belinda gets a few pictures as he walks by her *machan*.

10 May

There is no need to hide from Tiger Haven's resident big cats, the leopards Harriet and Juliet. The two run free and during the cooler times of the day ambush visitors, run at them, jump on them, or knock them over. They are particularly attracted to flapping things and most days the leopards confiscate our towels on our way to swim in the river. Often we are too engrossed in watching Juliet and Harriet play in the water to go swimming ourselves. The two race after each other through

A tigress scent-marks her territory.

the shallows then wrestle and play tug-of-war with a stick in the deeper water.

While watching the leopards play and colorful birds come to drink and bathe, I ask Belinda how she first became involved with the jungles and about the two incidents she so far has mentioned only in passing, which influenced both her and Billy in their work with wildlife.

It goes farther back than I can remember. My parents were what you might call social hunters when I was very small. Mostly they went to jungles in Bihar, not that far from Calcutta, truly beautiful forests. They would take out hunting permits and put up amazing tented camps. Cooks and bearers and everything imaginable would be brought from Calcutta. All their friends came to stay. I always went with them right from the beginning. The first time I went, I was six weeks old.

These camps were great social occasions and really an excuse to get away from the city. Everybody would be eating and drinking, playing charades, and singing. That's how I remember them anyway. All the same my parents were very good in the jungle. They would go out hunting, mainly for the pot—wild pig, chital (spotted deer), sambar, jungle fowl, partridge—whatever they had permits for. The hunting wasn't a serious macho thing where you'd always be on the lookout for the biggest and best trophies. They hunted because they enjoyed that way of life.

We sometimes went out spotlighting in a Jeep at night. They didn't shoot at night, ever, we just looked at the animals. It was then that we often heard tigers and saw their fresh pug marks. Once or twice we **thought** *we saw the eerie reflections from the eyes of a tiger. It was very thrilling. But we really never saw one. Despite that I became obsessed, even as a very small child, about tigers. They became mystical animals to me; a hidden presence that dominated everything, yet you never saw it. I found them frightening, mysterious, intriguing, and inspiring all at the same time. To make up for not seeing tigers in the jungle, I used to spend hours and hours in the zoo watching them and I would imagine how they would be if they were in the jungle.*

On those **shikars** *(hunting trips), I was accompanied by a nanny, but the nanny couldn't cope and I would end up going off into the jungle with one of the trackers. Even when I was seven or eight, I could speak Hindi fluently so I would go down to the villages, barefoot and tanned, and play with the children there or go to the stream to explore. My parents weren't very strict with me. This horrified their friends who thought I was "running wild." I really liked the village people and the jungle tribals; I had a great affinity with them. And I still do.*

I was given my first gun when I was about nine. It was a .410 shotgun I used for shooting hares and partridges and other small things.

I loved target practice and clay pigeon shooting. I enjoyed the precision and accuracy of it. I never ever enjoyed destroying a life. That used to upset me a lot, to see the hares kicking their legs and giving their last gasp. Even so I did quite a lot of shooting with my wilder friends even at a very young age. I was always the only girl.

I was fourteen and a half when I firmly made up my mind what I wanted to do with my life, and that was to work with wildlife. I wasn't quite sure how. I didn't want to spend years away from India, studying. I already knew a lot about the wildlife, the problems, the people, and so on, and I knew the language. It didn't take me very long to work out that instead of being a scientist, or a vet—careers that involve years and years of study—I could be a wildlife photographer. But when I decided on what I thought was a brilliant idea, my parents hit the roof. "That's not a career," they said. They were most upset and very much against it—which made me all the more determined.

I had gone to school in England when I was nine, a boarding school and a convent. I hated it at the beginning. When I arrived I had no clue as to how a normal English child should behave. I was used to servants that I could order about. I'd had a pet tiger, an elephant, a house full of deer, a mongoose, and a red panda. I thought that was normal. I had a miserable, really dreadful, first year. It took me that long to realize that I couldn't talk about my life and my interests; my would-be friends couldn't relate to it at all and said I was making things up and bragging. But I wasn't. That was my life. Finally I realized that in order to survive I had to become a proper little English girl. I learned to say and do all the right things.

I did well at school, but I didn't want to stay there. At the age of sixteen I left. I had a return ticket to India so I just checked out and went back to Calcutta. My parents were furious. I insisted that I wanted to be a wildlife photographer and that I didn't need a university degree for that. After much arguing we made a deal. I would go back to England and do a secretarial course and a year at a finishing school. After that they would give me a ticket to Hong Kong, where I would make my fortune and buy the necessary camera equipment. My parents had booked me into one of those debutante-type establishments where you did deportment, makeup, cooking, and flower arranging as well as a secretarial course. I took one look at that and said, "No thanks," and instead did a three-month course in speed-writing. So I was back in India in a few months instead of two years. I got my ticket to Hong Kong and in ten months I had enough money to buy all the equipment I thought I needed, and I came back to India.

Before going to Hong Kong I came here to Tiger Haven with my mother. We had brought with us a young leopard we had raised. He'd

Billy's leopards, Juliet and Harriet, playing.

grown too large and boisterous for the city and had started stalking and ambushing our visitors. So we brought him to Tiger Haven, hoping that Billy would eventually be able to reintroduce him to the wild. Billy wasn't too sure to begin with but soon became very fond of the leopard. He named him Prince, as he thinks of the leopard as the prince of cats. Prince grew up along this river and under Billy's watchful eye gradually learned to hunt. Prince is still out here somewhere, Billy sees him occasionally.

Shortly after returning from Hong Kong I was broke again. I had forgotten that you have to buy film and that it takes a while to get enough pictures together to have something to sell. So I led some wildlife tours around India. It was a brilliant way of getting about and taking

A tigress rests in leaflitter with her cubs.

The Forest Department people were nervous and didn't know what to do. They knew nothing about any poaching going on in the sanctuary. I said, "We must go back to Tiger Haven and get Billy and this photographer, we need a record of this." After a bit of persuasion they agreed. I woke Billy, who was sleeping under a mosquito net out in the open. He muttered something about not going out with that so-and-so photographer and that he'd deal with it in the morning. So then I woke Zuber, who shouted abusively at me for waking him. He eventually calmed down and, complaining all the while, agreed to come. While all this was going on I had to pacify the warden so that he wouldn't disappear.

pictures without having to pay for the travel. After that I got a couple of breaks. I did a story on the wildlife trade in Calcutta for the **London Observer** in 1972. That paid very well.

That same year, I brought the French wildlife photographer Christian Zuber to Tiger Haven. I thought that as he was a well-known, experienced photographer, I might learn something. But I never did, he was a very aggressive, difficult person who did not allow me to take any photographs of my own. Billy did not like him at all. One night the sanctuary's warden drove up to say he was going on a night patrol and would anyone like to come with him. Billy made excuses because I don't think he wanted to be in the same Jeep as Zuber. Zuber said he was too tired. I said, "Yes please, I'd love to come." It was very late, close to midnight I think.

As we rounded a bend in a forest track we saw what looked like a large, pale animal lying right across the road. We couldn't make out what it was. When we were about ten meters away this animal suddenly sprang up, roaring very loudly. It was a tiger with one of its front paws caught in a steel trap. What we'd seen was it lying stretched out with its white belly toward us. She pulled and pulled at the trap roaring and screaming in agony. Ironically that was the very first wild tiger I saw clearly.

We got into the Jeep and went back to the tigress. At our approach she jumped up again, roaring and pulling at the trap. As Zuber was taking pictures a male tiger suddenly walked out of the bushes very, very close to us. My second wild tiger. He was huge and just stood there looking at us and then at the tigress. After a while this second tiger melted into the undergrowth again.

Nobody knew what to do. After long discussions the warden put two forest guards, who were with us, up trees to keep an eye on the tigress. I said, "We need a tranquilizer gun to get the tigress out of the trap. She's in great pain." The only tranquilizer gun that any of us knew about was in Lucknow, which was about 200 kilometers away. I took Zuber's hire car and drove through the night to Lucknow. I went to see the chief wildlife warden for the state and told him what had happened. At first he didn't believe me. Well, poor guy, here was this girl he didn't know rushing into his office saying, "Tranquilizer gun, tranquilizer gun!" In the end I got the gun and the drugs to go with it and rushed back to Tiger Haven.

It was late afternoon by then. Early in the morning Billy, Zuber, and the warden had gone back to the spot but found nothing there. Absolutely nothing. The road had been swept clean, and there was no evidence of a tiger or a trap. Just a few spots of blood were found on some blades of grass. The forest guards who were supposed to watch from their trees had also vanished. If it hadn't been for Zuber's pictures it would have been as though nothing had ever happened.

The photographs were sensational. They received worldwide coverage. It became a big cry for saving the tiger and helped a lot in getting Project Tiger off the ground last year. The pictures became a kind of symbol for Project Tiger.

Later that year, when I was still nineteen, I met my first zoologist. I was on my way to Assam, taking a small group of tourists to Kaziranga and Manas. I went to the office that issued the permits and there was this young English boy, in khaki shorts. His name was Andrew Laurie and he said he was going to Kaziranga too, to work on his doctorate on the Indian rhino.

Our paths crossed again in Kaziranga. In the end I sent my tourists back to Calcutta on their own and stayed on to work with Andrew on his study. That opened up a whole new thought process for me. Until now I loved wildlife, I loved going to reserves and I loved looking and watching—but I hadn't understood the importance of collecting information, to find out for yourself how animals actually lived. With Andrew I became much tougher, much more hands-on in my outlook. We used to collect dung samples, and specimens of the grasses the rhinos eat. We walked everywhere in the park, even at night.

Andrew went to study rhinos in Nepal after that. I joined him for a while and ended up working at Tiger Tops in Chitwan National Park as a naturalist. I was really happy there and got to know the jungle well. Perhaps I enjoyed it because we saw tigers so often. Then I received a telegram from my mother saying, "Need you desperately. Come urgently." I thought something was very wrong and dashed back to Calcutta. Instead, there was this Australian photographer from National Geographic who needed help. After my experiences with Christian Zuber, I was not keen to do that again. But everything worked out fine and now I can take all the wildlife photographs I want and I love it.

★ ★ ★

Billy made tigers magically appear. But we had heard that Kanha National Park was even more remarkable for seeing tigers. It had to be our next place to visit, in this summer season when tigers must stay near water holes. Unfortunately I

had to attend to urgent family matters and returned to Australia for a few months. Belinda, accompanied by John Wakefield and her friend of many years, Anu Sharma, drove down to Kanha. Belinda wrote me letters saying that in Kanha she had found all that we had been hoping for, dreaming about, in the way of getting near tigers. She told me about the stump-tailed female, who had the tip of her tail missing, her two cubs, and the large male tiger she called Arjuna. This is what she wrote to me when, on her last day, she found all four tigers together.

Kanha National Park—23 May 1974

We rounded the corner and there they were—the large male tiger, the tigress, and her two cubs, all lying together on the sand. A breathtaking sight.

We approached them cautiously on our elephants, fearing that we might disturb the scene. One cub, the male, crouched on the bank looking nervously at the big tiger. The male heard us and looked up, snarling warily, but the tigress and her other cub slept on beside him. Once our presence had been accepted we went closer. The tiger lay with his head on his paws, eyes closed, while the little cub slept with one paw over her mother.

When the sun grew hot, the tigers, one by one, roused themselves and padded to the nearby water hole. The male cub drank briefly and rushed off before the big tiger arrived. The tiger strolled up to the tigress and affectionately made a gentle swipe at her with his paw. Then he bounded into the water, sat on his haunches, and with a perplexed expression pawed the water surface. We think that he must have been bothered by his reflection. Then he too relaxed in the deep water, alongside the tigress and her female cub.

After a while we noticed the female cub looking around mischievously. Slowly she swam to the far end of the pool and then sneaked up behind Arjuna. She pounced on him. Instantaneously he leapt around and bared his teeth at her—water flying everywhere. The cub looked startled and hurt while the tigress watched unperturbed. A little later the cub bounded out of the pool and was soon followed by the tigress. Arjuna was obviously enjoying the water and slept on for another hour and a half.

[CHAPTER 8]

FACE TO FACE
WITH THE TIGER

India was transformed while I was in Australia. When I left, in May, the landscape was brown and dehydrated. Dust devils whirled and danced over fallow fields and through leafless forests. Major rivers meandered through narrow channels across their wide beds. Lesser streams ceased to flow and were reduced to strings of small water holes or were dry altogether. The people were listless and left their houses only when they had to. Every day the sun scorched the land mercilessly. A hot sun without moisture is a killer sun—a killer of plants, animals, and people. The monsoon broke in late June and now the land is fresh and green.

Belinda and I meet in Calcutta on 1 August and drive to Kanha. It is a slow journey. Roads have been damaged and bridges washed away by flood rain. Rain is frequent, and where in May the Land Rover's cab became so hot that we could not drive in the middle of the day, now it leaks. We are wet and sometimes cold. But I love the change. The country's overwhelming impression is green, green, green—a vivid, fresh, benevolent green. Instead of day in, day out of depressingly hot sun, the monsoon is a time of changeable weather—lightly overcast one moment, drenching rain the next, followed by bright sunshine. The sun still has a sting to it,

Sal forest in Kanha National Park.

with the added discomfort of high humidity. When we are not wet from the rain, we are dripping with perspiration.

Kanha National Park and Tiger Reserve—
5 August 1974

It is late, about an hour before sunset, when we sign our names in a number of old and frayed ledgers at Kanha's northern entrance gate. Huge, dark clouds are building up in the south. Optimistically we take the Land Rover's canvas top down and while Belinda drives slowly, I drink in the landscape. We are in real, true forest—surrounded by closely spaced trunks of ancient trees with an undergrowth of bamboo and shrubs. The main tree species is sal, *Shorea robusta*. In the distance we see chital lift their heads from their browsing to watch us go by. In the trees above, every so often, a troop of long-tailed gray langur monkeys whoops and leaps through the canopy. A chestnut-colored barking deer watches us gravely from the cover of a small shrub. Brilliantly colored birds flit through the foliage.

We are expected at the forest rest house, right in the heart of Kanha. Belinda is greeted like an old friend; the park staff remember her well from her visit in May. There are no other visitors; we have the grand old rest house to ourselves. The large,

Gray or Hanuman langur monkeys on a branch. The langur on the left shows by its posture that it wishes to be groomed.

sprawling, brick building with a tiled roof has high ceilings and wide verandahs. It is in the midst of a grove of exceptionally tall and spreading sal trees that have rough-barked, dark trunks and deep green foliage. Scattered on the gentle slope below are the more modest dwellings of the park staff, including a row of houses where the elephants' *mahouts* live. Smoke curls from their courtyards as food is being prepared. Several elephants walk briskly to this small village, their grass cutters—the *mahouts'* assistants—riding them. A little way away stands a cluster of grass huts where a community of Baigas, the forests' original hunter-gatherers, live.

A stream flows below the rest house and beyond are spacious, velvet green meadows ringed by forest. A herd of chital grazes there. Birdsong and the rutting calls of chital mingle with the rumble of quiet human voices, the clinking of chains, and the occasional trumpet of an elephant down at the village. Darkness descends rapidly as the clouds roll in. The sharp white light of the lightning illuminates the forest and meadows in blinding flashes. Wind tears at the trees' branches. Rain lashes the rest house. We eat our dinner by candlelight while rain thunders on the roof tiles.

Never before in India have I felt so at one with a place, so at ease with it, and so seized by its mystique. I am over-whelmed by feelings of great well-being but also anticipation. Forest, I begin to think, must be my preferred habitat.

Kanha National Park—6 August 1974

Dawn is cool and fresh, the trees drip with dew or perhaps last night's rain. The sky is clear. The elephants, which have been out grazing all night, are brought in by their grass cutters. The *mahouts* will soon go out to search for tigers. We would have gone with them, but we want to take a long drive over the park's network of roads so that I can get the feel of the place.

The road skirts the meadow, following its border with the forest. Belinda points to a herd of some fifty chital grazing among chindi—small, shrublike palms. Switching off the car's engine, we roll slowly toward the herd and come to a silent stop a short distance from them. For some moments the deer stare at us. They try to get our scent. Sensing no serious danger, they resume feeding. One of the does, grazing near a patch of chindi, suddenly jerks her head up. She looks fixedly at a clump of the palms. She stamps one front foot several times. Instantly all the others are alert; noses twitching, ears straining for suspicious sounds. Fawns trot to their mothers' sides. The doe stamps her foot once more and gives her high-pitched, bell-like alarm call, an explosive "pow," and wheels around. As one the herd turns and moves off. Fawns leap high over the wet grass, does skip gracefully, and the stags, heads held high, trot stiff-leggedly, their shoulders and haunches rippling with muscles. It is a low-level alarm—a strategic re-treat rather than a frantic rush from a dangerous predator.

The cause of the alarm soon tiptoes from among the chindi. Lifting its feet high so as not to get wet, a jungle cat steps out into the sunlight. It is much too small to be a threat to the deer. The cat looks at us through yellow-green eyes. It has uniformly grizzled yellow-brown fur, with just a few black bars on its legs and tail. With its back toward us, it sits down briefly to scratch its chin then walks off among the dwarf palms.

The track leaves the meadows and winds back into the forest—an almost pure stand of sal. The Sulcum River's sandy banks are crowded with tall, dense stands of bamboo with polished-looking, yellow, straight stems. In the clear space among several clumps, Belinda spots the faint movement of a patch of red fur. Quickly she maneuvers the car into place so we can have a clear view. Three red dogs, the wild dogs of In-dia, raise their heads to look at us, white teeth gleaming, their faces bloodied. They have brought down a chital yearling. We are just in time to watch them tear the last pieces of flesh from the carcass and bolt them down. Only a few scraps of fur and some splinters of bone remain of the chital when the dogs canter down to the river to drink. Silently they trot on again, warm red-brown forms with bushy black-tipped tails, and vanish into the forest.

We ford the Sulcum's clear waters, shaded by Arjuna and banyan trees. On the opposite bank a dark brown sambar doe and her fawn browse on a shrub while shaded by the gigantic leaves of a small teak tree. The track rises up a spur that leads to a high ridge. Soon we leave the pure stands of sal and en-ter a mixed forest. The trees here are more slender, more ele-gant than the solid and robust sal. There is more bamboo here mixed with bauhinia, lagerstroemia, and fig trees. White gar-denia and purple indigo flowers splash the undergrowth. Gi-gantic, thick woody vines snake up among the trees and smother their crowns with foliage and large bunches of creamy white flowers. The vine is another species of bauhinia. The fresh scents of flowers and vigorously growing leaves mix with the odors of decay in the ground litter. Orange and white fungi sprout from a rotting log. Red jungle fowl scratch among the moldering leaves of the forest floor. Langurs feed on the flowers of the bauhinia vine, high in the canopy. They tear off a handful of flowers, eat a few, drop the rest, and then grab another bunch. Chital are attracted to this extravagant way of eating and gobble up the flowers as they fall.

We pass several small hills made up of enormous black rocks piled one on top of the other. The rocks themselves are not really dark, but are covered with a black lichen. These *chattans* are islands of rock and mixed forest in the sea of sal. At one *chattan,* with enormous bauhinia vines snaking and looping among the rocks, we disturb a troop of langur mon-keys★ in their feeding. With breathtaking recklessness they hurtle out of the trees in great leaps that shake the branches and scatter the leaves. The male booms his territorial call as he bounds through the canopy. Those in taller trees slide down the trunks and then gallop away over the rocks, their long tails curled like question marks over their backs. Rough, tough an-imals with long tails—not prehensile, branch-grabbing tails like those of South American spider monkeys, but balancing organs to steady them in their daring leaps.

The meadows are the habitat of one of India's rarest ani-mals, the hard-ground swamp deer, or barasingha, a different subspecies to the ones we saw in Kaziranga and Dudhwa. At this time of year they are in the tall grass meadows of another part of the park. These deer, the males with huge antlers, were once counted in their thousands throughout central India. Kanha's herd is the only one that remains. Four years ago their numbers reached their lowest point—just sixty-six. In this year's census 138 swamp deer were counted.

Chital alarm calls, urgent calls from many throats this time, come from the forest on the other side of the meadows. Belinda grabs my arm and says, "Tiger!" We drive quickly to-ward the commotion. A huge herd of chital, more than 500 I would guess, comes pouring out of the forest; a river of pale brown, white-spotted bodies flows out over the green mead-ows. Even the stags are running at full stretch. The stampede is not entirely in fright. Many deer, especially the younger ones, make great exuberant leaps and run around their elders. Young stags begin to spar, locking antlers and pushing back and forth. We sit and wait, hoping a pursuing tiger will appear. None does, but one roars among the trees, a moaning, long, drawn-out roar.

We return to the rest house just as the wind bends the

★ The word *langur* is derived from the Sanskrit *languria*, which means "hav-ing a long tail."

A herd of chital runs along the edge of sal forest.

crowns of the trees and the first big cold drops of rain fall. It is only a brief thunderstorm and not much rain comes down. Before long the sun is out again.

In the evening Mahavir, one of the *mahouts,* comes to see us. He and his colleagues have found a sambar stag freshly killed by a tiger. We will go looking for the tiger tomorrow, he says. Be ready at first light.

Kanha National Park—7 August 1974

As we walk onto the rest house verandah, Mahavir guides Pawan Mala, his elephant, to where the Land Rover is parked. By climbing onto the top of our vehicle, we can step straight onto the elephant. She will not have to kneel down, which is a strenuous and difficult maneuver for her. Pawan Mala is an elderly elephant approaching her sixtieth year, and not nearly as comfortable to ride as Kaziranga's Rai Bahadur. But she has other virtues. She is exceptionally good at finding tigers and will stand perfectly still to allow the taking of steady photographs. She is large and well-rounded, even for

an elephant, and somewhat lazy. She needs constant prodding from Mahavir, verbally and with stabs of his *ankush,* a short iron rod with a sharp point and hook at the end. Mahavir, a bald, round-faced man in middle age, his teeth stained red from constantly chewing betel nut, keeps a lively conversation going with Belinda. It is about village gossip, park management, family problems, and adventures with tigers. It is all in Hindi and I soon tune out and watch the chital, sambar, langurs, a drongo sitting in a sapling, a covey of bush quail scratching among the fallen leaves as they look at the elephant plodding by. They all perceive her and her human cargo as part of the forest and not to be feared. Had we been on foot, they would flee before we could even see them. Tigers too have become accustomed to the elephants.

Mahavir spots the kill, a sambar stag lying under some bushes. He points silently with his *ankush*. The tiger has eaten the deer's entire hindquarters. With such a large meal inside him, he cannot be far away. He has probably gone to the nearest water. Tracks on the sandy streambed confirm the tiger to be a male. The prints are broader and larger than those of a female.

A jungle fowl cackles at the creek ahead. Has he seen the tiger? Silently Mahavir, pressing his toes behind the elephant's ears, urges her along. Her large feet make faint whispering sounds on the sand. The first of the sun's rays, instantly warm, pierce the forest canopy as we follow the fresh pug marks. Rounding a twist in the meandering creek, Pawan Mala stops dead in her tracks. The tiger lies half submerged in a shallow pool. Bamboo branches frame his alert form. The sun makes stripes of light and shade through the bamboo that so closely resemble the tiger's pattern, he is difficult to see.

A tiger snarls at us from the undergrowth.

Soon the tiger relaxes and sprawls in the water. Several frogs climb onto his rump. A tiny blue kingfisher perches over the far end of the pool. Scarlet dragonflies skim and whirl over the water. One lands on the tiger's ear. He twitches it away.

Mahavir eases the elephant closer and closer. Pawan Mala picks up a small stick with the tip of her trunk and flicks it toward the tiger; a trick, we fear, she has been taught by her *mahout*. The tiger sits up and snarls, exposing huge white canines. Resentment and defiance seem to smolder in his green eyes. He is comfortable and cool after his meal and does not like to be disturbed. But perhaps he does not like our close presence either, for he soon gets up and melts away into the forest, up the slope of a *chattan* covered in bamboo. Within seconds he has disappeared from view, though he is probably only twenty or thirty meters away. We try to follow but Pawan Mala has difficulty negotiating the loose rocks of the steep incline. She plods slowly on. Suddenly we are aware of the tiger above us. Lips curled back, eyes blazing, he seems ready to spring. He looks us straight in the eyes from just a few meters away.

With a coughing roar that makes me shrink down low on Pawan Mala and my heart race, the tiger rushes us. The elephant, chewing a succulent piece of bamboo she has uprooted, stands her ground. At the last moment the tiger swerves to one side then bounds up the hill. Mahavir is keen to follow, but we call it off. We have intruded enough.

In the afternoon Belinda and I sit on the verandah while a steady soft rain falls from a windless sky. We talk about how much we have seen in just two days. So much and of such a special nature that it has made a profound difference to me. There is some unfathomable dimension to these forests, meadows, and rocks that affects me. I sensed that even before we saw the tiger. But then we did see the tiger and these feelings deepened. Even though I had looked a tiger in the eye, close-up, and standing on the ground and level with him at Tiger Haven, I still felt a certain detachment there. Perhaps because I was confined behind the straw blind.

This afternoon's encounter had a completely different quality. I no longer felt an outsider, looking on dispassionately. I felt as if I had slipped into the tiger's realm, as if I had reached some understanding of its world. The adventures of the last few days also heightened my senses about the other animals—tiger prey and nontiger prey—from gaur to frogs, and from wild dogs to dragonflies.

Belinda tells me she experienced a similar transformation when she was here in May. She was not close to just one tiger then but six, and for days on end. There is no doubt that it was in Kanha that both of us came under the tiger's spell.

Perhaps these affinities were planted in our minds during our childhood—mine in cold damp Holland, Belinda's in Calcutta and the jungles of eastern India—by Rudyard Kipling's *Jungle Book* stories. It was here in Kanha and the surrounding district that Kipling set his stories. Seoni and the Wainganga River are not far from here. In these forests, or ones identical to them, wily Bageera the leopard and Baloo the wise old bear taught Mowgli, the boy raised by wolves, the law of the jungle. It is where Hathi the elephant and Kaa the python lived and where Mowgli defeated Sher Khan the tiger. Strangely enough Kipling himself was never in this part of India, yet so vivid is his writing that he captured the spirit of these jungles.

Those are vague notions in our heads. But we determine that we will come back to try to penetrate the tiger's world further.

Now we must wait for the rains to stop and the streams to go down, and then make our way to the marshes of Keoladeo on the densely populated plains of northern India, where the monsoon has stirred the energies and passions of countless birds.

[CHAPTER 9]
A GIFT FROM THE MONSOON

Keoladeo Sanctuary—27 August 1974

Monsoon. We are breathless from the concentrated energy of tens of thousands of birds nesting closely together, with the luminous brilliance of color. Aquatic grasses sparkle vivid green under an unclouded sky, birds mill around in swirls of pink, yellow, blue-gray, white, and black. The green babul trees, *Acacia nilotica*, are freckled with yellow flowers, which when they fall float like yellow puffs on the black-brown water. Fields of immaculate water lilies appear at dawn, bumblebees and wasps blunder from flower to flower seemingly dazzled by the white. As the sun becomes hot the lilies fold their petals and withdraw from the assault of the heat. Smaller, yellow lilies retreat further and bend their closed flowers under the water.

The birds also calm down in the heat. They pant with open beaks, spreading their wings to shade their eggs or newly hatched young. Ten minutes in the relentless sun would addle the eggs and kill the hatchlings. Movement resumes with evening cool, in a frantic rush as though the swamps are about to dry and nesting must be completed at a desperate pace. Painted storks fly to their chosen

sites, bringing green sticks for nest building; egrets dance on their nest platforms; white ibises flap and posture as they mate; jacanas chase each other through the sedges; spoonbills raise their crests in anger to defend their nest sites; cormorants etched black against the sky fly in V-formations to a distant fishing ground; pairs of openbill storks clapper their beaks at each other; sarus cranes dance and trumpet; a dead tree, collapsed into the swamp, is gaudy with emerald parakeets; bright squirrels and weaver birds scurry around the water's edge. As the sun slips from the still cloudless sky a pack of jackals wails, howls, laughs from a thicket beside the swamp.

★ ★ ★

How can a small patch of marsh, eight-and-a-half square kilometers out of the sanctuary's total of twenty-nine square kilometers, support such density of life—countless plants, insects, fishes, and birds plus a daily influx of cattle and goats? The answer is simple. It is a gift from the monsoon, reinforced by a man-made system of dikes and channels.

The monsoon is a yearly phenomenon that is looked forward to with a mixture of eagerness and

A male and a female painted stork preen each other, a gesture that reinforces their pair bond.

anxiety, for it often comes in violent excess. Meteorologists, city dwellers, villagers, and forest tribes all speak of the monsoon as some animate, tangible object that swarms up from the south and envelops the whole country in a wet embrace. Weather reports refer to it as "punctual," "stalled," "advancing," "weakened," "vigorous," "fully established." Its progress through India makes daily headlines.

There are four distinct seasons in northern India. Winter, which lasts from December to February, is pleasant with warm days and cool nights. Summer, from March to June, is the season of heat and dust. The southwest monsoon, which begins in late June and lasts to September, is the only period of significant rain. Postmonsoon, in October and November, is cooler, lush, and with clear skies. In the far south of India there is a second monsoon, the northeast, which brings rain from October to December. There is no comparison between the Indian seasons and those of temperate or even equatorial zones. Winter changes abruptly to harsh summer

Unlike most cats, the fishing cat revels in water. It does not hesitate to plunge into streams and pools after fish. Somewhat larger than a domestic cat, it is a fierce hunter on land as well, where it has been known to kill and eat dogs.

in March, with very little of spring's softening intervention. In June the rains arrive suddenly, immediately cooling and soothing the cracked, blistered earth.

The monsoon is the life-giver on whose bounty the country must exist for the entire year. Rains from winter depressions and premonsoon showers amount to no more than 10 percent of the total—they are minor refreshments. Of Keoladeo's total annual rainfall of 640 millimeters, 575 millimeters fall during the monsoon.

A conspiracy of intense heat, trade winds, and mountain ranges molds the monsoon. During the summer, temperatures as high as 50 degrees Celsius build up over the deserts and the Gangetic Plain. Keoladeo lies at their junction. The heat eventually results in low-pressure areas that suck in the moisture-saturated trade winds from the Arabian Sea. The Himalayas, stretched across the top of the subcontinent, stop winds and rain from being dissipated in the remoteness of central Asia. Mountain ranges, some as high as 2,000 meters, along the west coast, to a lesser degree along the east coast, and in Assam and its adjoining states, regulate where the monsoon clouds will drop their moisture. In the Western Ghats and in parts of Assam more than 2,500 millimeters of rain falls in a year while Cherapunjee, in the hills of Meghalaya, was once the wettest place in the world with an average rainfall of 10,500 millimeters. In 1861 the area received 22,600 milliliters, 9,100 of which fell in July alone—more than 300 milliliters for every day of the month.

★ ★ ★

Siberian cranes gave their unison calls close to our blind, a sound that embodies all the romance and wonder of Keoladeo's marshes.

I have to return to Australia again for a few months and Belinda attends to other matters. By the time we set out on our assignment once more it is winter, dry and cool. We hasten back to Bharatpur and the marshes of Keoladeo.

Winter shows Keoladeo's other face—a brown, cool, open face. Only a few of the monsoon birds remain. Since October there has been an influx of migrant species from geese to wagtails, culminating in the arrival of the Siberian cranes in early November.

Keoladeo Sanctuary— 30 January 1975

Long before sunrise we are up and dressed, ready to try to photograph Keoladeo's rarest birds, the Siberian cranes. At this hour the temperature is barely above freezing and we are wrapped in thick parkas. Along the main road a pair of fishing cats stands momentarily dazzled in our headlights. Woolly in their winter coats they look like oversized tabbies; supercats, capable of killing small calves, goats, and even dogs.

At the turnoff onto the *bundh* (dike) we switch the car lights off and drive slowly on for a kilometer or so. The blind stands in the marsh about 100 meters from the *bundh*. I hoist the backpack with camera gear, trousers, socks, and boots onto my back, pick up the tripod and in my shorts wade out into the icy thigh-deep water. Weeds and grasses grab at my legs. After a dozen staggering paces my legs are numb and I do not feel anything. Five minutes later, which seems more like five hours, I reach the blind's dry platform. Fighting cramps I wrap up in everything I have brought and still shiver. A dusky horned owl laughs his "wruck, wruck, wruck."

Siberian cranes are the shyest birds at Keoladeo. The blind faces their feeding area and I must be in place before daylight when the birds come in from their roosts. Soon the sky reddens behind me but the swamps are still wrapped in a low, blue mist. The birds who are already at these feeding grounds ignore me—wood sandpipers, egrets, and pond herons fish and chase insects behind the blind. If I poked a finger out I could touch some of them. Out in front greylag geese and pintail ducks upend in their search for the tubers and stems of water plants. Surprisingly two kinds of small bush birds are also out on the marsh. Yellow wagtails and blue-throats walk on the half-submerged weeds looking for insects. Larks sing in the sky. A white-breasted kingfisher has chosen the main pole of the blind as its lookout perch. Time and again it dives, then resettles on the pole, its prize in its beak. Before swallowing the catch it bashes it thoroughly—showering me with fish scales and beetle wing cases.

The sky is cloudless and as the sun lifts over the horizon the mist is dispelled, and blue changes gradually to purest gold. The grasses are no longer green but straw yellow; no water lilies or babul trees flower.

A sweet, musical "ku-wang, ku-wang, ku-wang" comes from above and a party of seven Siberian cranes flies overhead. Where will they land? The swamp is wide and my field of operation is narrow. They circle once then spiral down to settle near the *bundh* in front of me but about 200 meters away—too far. Others come in twos and threes and then one group of nine. A pair with a chick of the previous year lands slightly to my right—almost within range.

By seven o'clock a line of fourteen cranes is spread out in front of the blind. Pure white with red facial discs and legs, the birds are magnificent. As they fly in they show their black primaries but these are tucked under white secondaries and invisible once they settle. Smaller than the gray sarus cranes, they nevertheless tower imperiously over the many egrets and storks in the swamp.

The cranes preen and soon begin to feed. The tubers of sedges are virtually their only food at Keoladeo and they must expend much energy to get them. With great heavings of their necks and chest muscles they clear away the water plants and then dig deep into the soft mud with their beaks. Their reward? A marble-sized bulb. Pairs with chicks often have to surrender their prizes to the incessantly peeping, insistently begging youngsters. Slowly, while feeding, a small group moves to within camera range and I get a series of good photographs.

I have my sandwiches spread out and am sipping hot tea from a thermos when the kingfisher makes its spectacular catch—a frog that fully stretched is as long as the bird and close to half its weight. The frog is held in a viselike grip just behind his front legs, but he fights back pushing with his muscular hindlegs at the bird's eyes and face. The kingfisher needs all its strength to whack the frog against the blind's pole.

The life-and-death struggle so absorbs the kingfisher that I am able to part gently the grasses that cover the blind and push my head through. The bird keeps bashing the frog, overbalancing and nearly falling off at every mighty swipe. I reach down and pick up a camera. Holding it only about half a meter from the bird I begin to take pictures. After about ten minutes the frog hangs limply from the bird's beak. Its tiny frame heaving, the kingfisher just sits for a while. Its battle is not yet over, it still has to swallow the frog. Soon it swallows the head and body and only the frog's giant, webbed feet protrude, one on each side of the bird's beak, like some elaborate mustache. One, two, three more convulsions and they too disappear. The kingfisher bathes, preens—but catches no more food.

At 3:30 a herdsman puts the cranes to flight and they move to another swamp. I am free to leave my cramped quarters and struggle back to the *bundh*.

★ ★ ★

Our National Geographic assignment is coming to an end and we are getting pressed for time. We drive west, into the arid zone, on the last leg of our adventures.

This whitebreasted kingfisher has exhausted itself killing the frog.

Into the Arid Zone

SAURASHTRA PENINSULA—MARCH 1975

To reach the drier areas of western India we drive right across Rajasthan and the north of the state of Gujarat. We arrive in the Saurashtra Peninsula, which juts out into the Arabian Sea, during a severe drought. It is a time of hardship for people and their livestock as well as the wildlife. We pass lines of women striding across bare dusty plains carrying water from distant wells in pots on their heads. A man who has unhitched his magnificent bullocks from their wagon to let them drink at a roadside pond confides that soon he may have to move from his farm to seek grazing for his animals. These kindly, nonaggressive people have a great respect for wild animals as well as their domestic ones. This may be one of the reasons why certain mammals, long exterminated from the rest of their once-considerable geographic ranges, survive here.

Above: village women in the Little Rann of Kutch. Right: *shikaris,* traditional hunters—now guardians—of the lions of the Gir Forest. Left: a rest stop for a bullock-drawn cart.

The Asiatic wild ass was once a common animal across Iran, Pakistan, and western India. Only about 400 now remain and all of them live in Saurashtra's Little Rann of Kutch. At this time of year the Rann's salt flats are bone-dry and herds of wild asses race our Land Rover

across its expanse. When we fall behind, they wait for us to catch up.

The Asiatic lion once moved from Greece, right across the Middle East, to central India. It too is now confined to Saurashtra: the last 200 Asiatic lions live in the Gir Forest. With the Gir's *shikaris*—hunters turned protectors—we follow wild lions on foot. Some of the lions inspect us closely. A three-quarter-grown cub invites us to play. We decline.

Blackbuck were once the most numerous large mammals on the plains of northern India. In the 1920s and 1930s people in cars sometimes had to wait twenty minutes or more for a vast herd of the antelopes to cross the road. As recently as 1942 there were 15,000 blackbuck in Velavadar Sanctuary, which is also in Saurashtra. Now there are only 3,000 in the last great wild herd.

Even during the heat of the day, the blackbuck do not seek the shade of the few scattered acacia trees. They remain in the open, among the whirling, twisting dust devils where the dominant males prance and skirmish to keep their harems of females together. They take little notice of us as we weave in and out among them.

Velavadar is the last stop on our assignment. With great reluctance we head back across the deserts of Rajasthan to New Delhi. It will be difficult to adjust to life in the city again and on the way we talk for many hours about how we might resume our life of observing and living among Indian wild animals and plants.

Above: Asiatic lions. Below: wild asses in the Little Rann of Kutch. Left: blackbuck in the dry and bare Velavadar Sanctuary.

An Act of Audacity

A painted stork on the monsoon-filled marshes.

For Belinda the year traveling around India, in 1974 and 1975, was a time of consolidation. More than ever she became aware of the astonishing diversity of habitat and wildlife in her country. She had also been able to realize a long-held dream—to photograph wild animals full time. She blossomed as a photographer and in time became one of the best.

For me those were days of excitement, discovery, and constant wonder. All the mammals large and small that had so stirred my imagination I had seen for myself, close and in their natural habitat. The birds in their variety and spectacle were a never-ending source of surprise that often left me speechless. They still are and do. The forests, the grasslands, the deserts, and the wetlands combined to build a picture of one of the world's great natural regions. The splendor of it was something I had not expected.

Through Belinda's guidance I slowly relaxed in India. I no longer panicked at the dense crowds, I did not gnash my teeth any more at

the interminable hassles the country insists on putting in everyone's way. With a few notable exceptions, I came to appreciate the people as warm and helpful.

Both of us longed to look more deeply at the wildlife, to stop traveling helter-skelter, and to examine a few special places in detail—Kanha, Kaziranga, Keoladeo, and others we might discover.

During our travels we had become acutely aware of the building pressures on a number of reserves and individual species such as wild asses, Siberian cranes, great Indian one-horned rhinoceroses, and Asiatic lions. The tiger, on the other hand, was beginning to flourish under Project Tiger. When we got to New Delhi at the end of our National Geographic assignment we decided to find a place to live there and to try our hand at making films to record as much as we could. It had not been done before. Over the ensuing months I sold my house in Australia and we settled in New Delhi.

Our filmmaking began with what in retrospect was an act of great audacity. We made our pitch to a number of production companies. Our strengths were that we knew the wildlife and that we could work effectively in India. Our weaknesses were that we had little or no experience in filmmaking and that we had no equipment whatsoever. We must have been persuasive for we secured a contract to make four half-hour films for the Time-Life series, *Wild Wild World of Animals*. Time-Life gave us an advance with which we bought a sixteen-millimeter cine camera, sound equipment, and enough film for two of the stories. We bought the camera in Paris and shipped it to New Delhi, untried. Without exposing a test roll—there was no time—I set off to shoot our first film. Belinda in the meantime had contracted hepatitis and was staying with her family in Calcutta. We shot the whole of our first film, on Indian snakes, and sent the unprocessed rolls to New York. When well into our second film we received a telegram to say the snake footage was outstanding. If it had not been, our involvement with Indian wildlife would have been cut short.

Our second film was about monkeys in Sariska Sanctuary in the state of Rajasthan.

[PART III]

FARTHER INTO
THE JUNGLE

In 1900 [Kanha] contained as much game as any tract I saw in the best part of Africa in 1908. I have seen 1500 head consisting of 11 species in an evening stroll. It is nothing like that now, but it is probably true to say that it contains more numbers and more species than any other tract of its size in Asia.

Dunbar Brander after a visit
to Kanha in 1928

Herds of Lightsome Monkeys

And in every bush and thicket
Herds of lightsome monkeys play.
—*The Ramayana,* circa 1000 BC

SARISKA WILDLIFE SANCTUARY—
DECEMBER 1975 TO APRIL 1976

The Ramayana is the most popular of India's two great religious epics. Its heroes and heroines embody all the virtues of Hinduism: devotion to duty and to family; steadfastness in adversity; and self-denial. Rama, heir to his father's kingdom, is the principal character. With his wife Sita and brother Lakshman, he is banished unjustly from his country to wander in the wilderness for many years. Sita is abducted to Lanka

Above: a gray or Hanuman langur.
Previous pages: a great Indian one-horned rhino with jungle mynas in attendance.

(Sri Lanka) by the demon Ravana and much of the story revolves around winning her back. Noblest of all Rama's supporters in finding and fighting for Sita is Hanuman. He is powerful—able to pluck trees out of the ground, build causeways by pushing hills into the sea, and uproot whole mountains. He can generate cyclones and whirlwinds, fly without wings, and assume any form at will. But he is no mere brute: a Sanskrit scholar and classical musician, he is cultured. In his service to Rama, he shows himself to be a unique exemplar of obedience and selfless service. But Hanuman is only half human: he has a man's physique but the face and tail of a langur. He is one of the most widely worshipped deities in Hinduism today. His spirit is believed to be alive in the long-tailed, black-faced gray or Hanuman langur monkey.

Hanuman langurs live throughout the length and breadth of India, from the Himalayan foothills to Cape Comorin, from Gujarat to Assam. And nearly everywhere they are sacred. In rural India, Hanuman is particularly popular and village people take great care to feed his living incarnations.

There is another very common monkey in northern India but it lacks the langur's elegance. The rhesus macaque is red-faced and short-tailed. It is brown, squat, and muscular, with stubby hands. It is typical of the opportunist rhesus that some of the langur's sacredness should have rubbed off on it and that it too is fed and cared for at

Above: rhesus macaques besiege visitors and pilgrims.
Left: rhesus macaques groom one another.

Clockwise from left: female gray or Hanuman langur with her infant; gray or Hanuman langurs; rhesus macaques with infant; rhesus macaques surround a village bus.

Hindu temples. Both species thrive under this benevolence and are common in cities and villages as well as in the forests.

Sariska Wildlife Sanctuary, which is only a few hours' drive from New Delhi, has become one of our favorite reserves. In the Sanctuary's heart it is still possible to see some of the truly wild inhabitants of eastern Rajasthan. A few tigers, hunting deer and antelope, survive in the deep valleys and rocky hill ranges. On the reserve's borders are forest shrines dedicated to Hindu saints. The shrines are not buildings but ancient, rugged fig trees whose roots are watered by warm springs. Pilgrims come here and feed the resident monkeys. At these shrines and in the surrounding forests we make our film: we watch pilgrims at Talvraksh as they are besieged by pugnacious rhesus macaques at the tea shop. Later we sit with the monkeys as they peacefully groom each other among giant Arjuna trees.

At Bhartrihari we become part of a troop of the exuberant, elegant, long-limbed and not at all aggressive Hanuman langurs. These winter days spent in warm sunshine while young langurs do headstands and pull at our shoelaces or when a group of females hand a newborn from one to the other in loving gestures, are among our most exquisite times in the jungles.

By the end of April, Sariska becomes intensely hot and dry. But in Assam it remains cool, and thunderstorms, harbingers of the monsoon, wash over Kaziranga almost daily. It is time to begin our film there on the great Indian one-horned rhinoceros.

[CHAPTER 10]

FIRE AND FLOOD IN KAZIRANGA

Kaziranga National Park—
2 May 1976

Silently we are carried along, about four meters above the ground. When our elephant, once again Rai Bahadur, disappears in the grass below us we can look out over the top. How fortunate we are to be here on these wide, green, and comparatively cool plains under clear blue skies. We have escaped the heat, the dust, and brown lands baking under a white-hot sky of northern and central India. We can breathe deeply here and we feel as if a great weight is lifted from our shoulders.

Rai Bahadur walks on and on in a steady rolling gait; a soporific movement in the warm sun. As Belinda chats quietly with Narain, the *mahout*, about our plan of action, I doze intermittently. There is a dreamlike quality about the afternoon. In the brilliant light under the wide sky the animals appear to move in slow motion. Wild pigs regard us gravely then slowly melt away into the tall grass. Water buffaloes lazily raise their heads as we approach and indomitably stand their ground. Thirty or so elegant swamp deer, the stags crowned with embryo velvet antlers, their orange-brown summer coats glowing among the greens, glide in an undulating line of bodies across our path. Another species of deer, smaller, stockier, and lacking all grace in its movements, skulks among the tall grass. In winter these hog deer were a uniform brown in color; now their fur is paler with a reddish tinge. Some, especially if they are in the sun, appear faintly spotted, a reminder of their close relationship to the chital—one of the most graceful of deer. Hog deer are the most numerous of the larger mammals in Kaziranga, and they are the main prey of the tiger and other predators.

A rhino and her three-quarter-grown calf emerge from the tall grass and make their way to the lush, short growth at the water's edge. I jolt awake for this is what we have been looking for.

Moving upwind Narain guides Rai Bahadur toward the rhinos. When within fifty meters of them, without uttering a command, he makes Rai Bahadur kneel down and I scramble to the ground. Belinda hands down camera, tripod, lens, film magazine, and battery. Equipment assembled, I begin filming. Beside me, one of his tusks lightly brushing my shoulder, stands Rai Bahadur like a lumbering guardian angel. His constantly flapping ears fan the back of my head.

Grazing all the while the rhinos work their way in our direction. After gathering lush grass into their mouths with their prehensile upper lip they pull the bundles up, roots and all, with a jerk of the head. In a single bite the muddy roots are then discarded.

This is the best way to see rhinos. Being on their level, the animals' bulk is more impressive, more ominous. I can sense their power. Heavy folds of thick skin around the neck and legs give them an armor-plated look. This impression is reinforced by the rivetlike knobs that stud the rhinos' skin. Mother and daughter are so close now that I can see every wrinkle on their lips, the crust of dried mud on their backs, the fringe of reddish hairs on the tips of their ears. Cattle egrets drift in on the breeze and land on the rhinos' backs, then jump to the ground. Darting in and out between their feet the elegant white birds snap up grasshoppers, frogs, and other small animal life.

The rhinos seem truly magical beasts akin to the unicorn and the griffin. I am so enraptured that I do not realize how close they are. But Narain, ever watchful, guides Rai Bahadur in front of me at the critical moment then gently claps his hands. Tossing their heads, the two bulky animals snort and gallop off; so large, so stolid, and so easily intimidated. Rai Bahadur kneels down again. Standing on his bent back foot and gripping his tail I heave myself aboard. Rai Bahadur then strides out to a nearby mud wallow trying to get us there before it is too dark to film.

We can just see two rhino horns and two pairs of ears sticking out of the wallow. I descend once more and with camera and tripod tiptoe to a good vantage point. As Narain urges Rai Bahadur forward I start the camera rolling. I can hardly believe my ears and eyes. With a dreadful slurping, sloshing sound the rhinos rise out of the mud. Clods of dark gray sludge dribble down their bodies; they look like monsters suddenly conjured up out of a primeval swamp. Both are males and annoyed at the intrusion. It takes all my willpower to stand fast. Rai Bahadur intercedes and I breathe again.

One of the rhinos has a deep gash in his side. In spite of the soothing, cooling mud the wound oozes blood. Nearly every rhino has scars, fresh wounds, or both. A few days ago we saw one with a gaping hole, the size of a football, in its side. Adult rhinos have no natural enemies and nearly all injuries are from fights with their own kind. Their main weapons are their very sharp teeth, not their horns. Birds, mainly jungle mynas and crows, keep the wounds clean by constantly pecking at flies and maggots, and the animals' actual flesh.

The two big males turn and gallop off when faced by the huge tusker. Big and round as they are, the rhinos are agile and light on their feet; they run and trot, twist and jump in a springy gait—all actions that the elephant cannot perform. It has only one gait—a walk, slow or fast.

★ ★ ★

On our way back to Arimora we pass Mihi Bheel. The sun, a golden globe, hovers above the horizon. Half-submerged in the lake, a buffalo tosses his head, shattering the calm water.

Trying for a last meal of the day, a ring-tailed fishing eagle, the wind screaming through his wing feathers, hurtles out of the sky at a group of spot-billed ducks. But the ducks see him coming, dive, and are safe.

In the east, lightning dances through ink-black clouds. To the west the sky remains clear for the last moments before the sun sets. A near–gale force wind springs up. The storm ruptures the large, globular seedpods on the silk cotton trees growing in a grove on the lake's edge. Seeds spill from the pods; each small, black seed is wrapped in a voluminous piece of light, pure white fluff. The fluff is the silk cotton. The cotton acts like a parachute, enabling the seeds to travel far from the parent tree. So numerous are the pods that it looks as if a snowstorm rages among the trees—"snow" with enormous flakes that look extrawhite against the black sky. Soon the ground around the lake is lightly covered with white. Moments later the sun sets and the magic is extinguished.

9 May

Mist hangs ragged over the Mikir Hills. Low, scudding clouds race overhead. It drizzles. The light is subdued and flat. The larger animals, rhino and buffalo, are dark and glistening with rain and appear even larger and more forbidding. A female rhino and her small baby, only a month or so old, are asleep. The tiny pinkish youngster, looking like a windup toy, lies huddled against its mother, between her massive head and an outstretched front leg.

But the weather is changeable in these premonsoon days and the clouds, except for those clinging to the hills, are swept away. It is humid and hot in the sun. A tiger lies in the

A water buffalo bathes in Mihi Bheel.

is almost dark though there are still two hours until sunset. These last fires of the season burn off the old grass and seedling trees that have sprung up during the wet season, simultaneously stimulating new growth in the grass and killing the small trees. Without these fires, trees would soon proliferate and turn grassland to woodland, making them unsuitable for rhinos, buffaloes, and swamp deer.

18 May

Standing in the back of the Jeep, peering over the top of the grass, Belinda sees the elephants, at least 150 of them, drinking and bathing at the edge of the lake. We leave the car on the track and walk through the tall grass to the lake. Most of the elephants are adult females with their offspring of various ages. Small babies are numerous, blowing bubbles in the water through diminutive trunks and pestering other youngsters. Adolescent males play vigorously. Around the outskirts of the herd roam and rage the big males in musth.

Suddenly all sound and movement stops. Inquisitive trunks snake in the direction of something in the grass that is hidden from our view. The noise resumes, redoubles, trebles in volume. Babies are gathered. Subadult males rampage, rushing into the grass bellowing. Enraged yet frightened, they swing their front legs back and forth in frustration. Hog deer rush off into the grass. A swamp deer barks in frantic alarm.

A tiger, cool and deliberate, glides like a shadow out of the grass. He sits down with his back to the elephants, his color a flame among the green. Young tuskers charge at the tiger, trumpeting, then come to a ground-pawing halt only a few meters from him. The tiger rubs his ear against some grass stalks, ignoring the turmoil he causes. The swamp deer rushes into the lake and stands facing the tiger while thrashing the water with her forefoot. In a few lazy strides the tiger moves back into the grass, never once dignifying the elephants' presence with so much as a glance.

★ ★ ★

The first half of July has brought continuous, heavy rain. In the hills whole villages have been swept away by landslides. Even the sluggish Brahmaputra, usually flowing between sandy banks more than two kilometers apart, cannot cope with the volume of water and overflows its banks. Towns and villages are inundated in slowly rising water. By the end of the

Soft-ground swamp deer in their summer pelts.

water at the edge of a small lake to escape the oppressive heat. Moments later we watch a male rhino leave his patch of grazing and make for the same pool. Twenty meters from the tiger he lies down in the mud and rolls over to give himself a thorough coating. The two ignore each other.

We arrive at Mona Bheel just as a herd of about fifty elephants approaches the water. One by one the giants emerge from the tall grass to drink at the lake's edge. A female in estrus has three tuskers of various sizes and a large *makhna*★ vying for her attention. The biggest tusker takes possession of the female. With his trunk lying along the ridge of her back and his tusks digging into her flanks, they walk in tandem round and round. She stops and he mounts, his front legs straight out along her back.

In the distance columns of black smoke rise into the sky, flames leap and dance thirty meters above the grass, and even from where we are, several kilometers away, we hear the roaring and crackling of the fire. Thick smoke obscures the sun. It

★ In the Indian elephant, females are mostly tuskless, and even some adult males are naturally without tusks. The tuskless males are called *makhnas*. *Makhnas* often make up for their lack of tusks with greater body weight. The largest, most powerful Indian elephants are often *makhnas*.

month, nearly all of Kaziranga is submerged. Water buffalo and rhino, who enjoy a certain amount of water, are the last to move to higher ground. Most of the deer and the elephants migrated to the Mikir Hills weeks ago.

There is a strip of unprotected land between Kaziranga's now inundated grassland and the forests of the hills. A major highway runs through it, bordered by tea plantations and rice fields. Day and night the national park staff patrol this area, guarding against poachers and rescuing animals from the floods. A baby rhino, apparently swept away from its mother, is picked up and adopted by the forest guards. Three tiger cubs were not so lucky and their floating bodies are pulled out of the floodwater. Scores of hog deer and a few swamp deer have drowned. Rain continues unabated.

28 July

When the morning's first gray light seeps slowly into the darkness we slip into the eight-meter-long dugout canoe. Two forest guards, skilled boatmen, paddle us across the Diphlu River. Large trees that stood perched on the levee bank five meters above the stream two months ago are now in two meters of water. We must duck to avoid the lower branches, covered in orchids with sprays of pink or yellow flowers, as our canoe glides along. Insects, flushed from the grass, race up the tree trunks. The hills are hidden and a slow drizzle continues intermittently. It is cool. We make our way along clear channels through the grass and soon realize that these are the roads we drove along earlier in the year. Only the very tips of the tallest elephant grass, the topmost half-meter or so, project above the water. These tips are the last refuge for the grassland's myriad insects. Each blade-tip is heavily laden with grasshoppers, bugs, beetles, caterpillars, and ants; ants clutch eggs and larvae snatched at the last minute from drowning nests. Spiders too cling tenaciously to the grass-tips, which sway with the crawling, clinging multitudes. Many of the tiny animals think our boat a more substantial haven and try to clamber aboard. Spiders come running across the water surface on velvet feet.

Paddling with sure, rhythmic strokes, the guards take us to the Gandamari guard outpost. The floor of the small hut—made of bamboo, reed, and thatch—is only a few centimeters above the water though the whole structure stands on stilts four meters high. We tie our boat to the verandah. Somehow

the guards light a fire and make tea, just as the wind drops and the rain stops. It is dead calm. Birdcalls suddenly burst forth. Songs of reed warblers, bulbuls, and orioles float across the vast, still expanse of the lake. Orange-colored bitterns and red-wattled lapwings calling "did he do it, did he do it" skim over the water. A small flock of cotton teal, the world's smallest duck, flies fast circles over our heads, quacking excitedly. Scores of river terns, immaculate black and white birds with orange beaks, wheel and dive after tiny fishes.

31 July

In the extreme western corner of Kaziranga is Kanchanjuri, a small piece of ground that is more a lower slope of the Mikir Hills than part of the Brahmaputra floodplain. It is a few meters higher in elevation than the rest of the national park and is covered not in grass but in rain forest. The floodwaters have not reached here.

All night it rained, but this morning, though still cloudy, the rain stops. The Kanchanjuri forest drips. We are showered as gusts of wind shake at the upper branches. The earlier scents

During the monsoon, Kaziranga's guards patrol in dugout canoes.

of fresh new growth have given way to earthy, decaying smells. The constant moisture rots the fallen leaves, branches, and whole trees that have crashed down in the hurricanes that lashed the park. But as well as decay there is massive regeneration; the forest bubbles with new life. Plants are adorned with fresh new leaves of every imaginable shade of green. Trees, shrubs, herbs, and grasses pulsate with insects from tiny aphids to giant grasshoppers and lazily basking birdwing butterflies. Rhino beetles—one-horned, two-horned, three-horned, and some larger than a matchbox—struggle out of the soil and rotting vegetation, spread their wings, and lumber noisily off into the forest. On bushes and shrubs sit katydids so closely resembling the foliage that the insects have veins and spots on their wings that are exactly like those of a leaf.

Most orchids, like this vanda, flower during the monsoon.

Others resembling twigs and withered leaves scurry about the forest floor. Spiders in silver webs snare small, brown butterflies. Scarlet dragonflies on golden wings scoop flies and mosquitoes out of the air. Beetles of the purest gold walk among raindrops on a grass stalk. Caterpillars of every imaginable color and shape devour the new leaves almost as fast as they grow.

Above us a troop of monkeys rushes through the branches, seeming to bathe in the water drops. These are capped langurs, named after their helmets of backswept dark hair. Their tails are enormously long, even for a langur, and fluffy at the tip. The monkeys are mostly dark gray in color, but with a beautiful orange-brown chest and pale golden tufts of long fur on their cheeks. In the soft mud are fresh footprints of a tiger, always so impressively large, and of a rhino made since the rain stopped less than an hour ago. We walk down to where the forest meets the grassland. Crashing and splashing, throwing up clods of dirt, a herd of water buffalo stampedes. The trees at the edge of the forest stand in shallow water. An otter dodging between tree trunks chases a fish and catches it.

From a tall, bushy tree come the wildest and also the loudest cries we have ever heard, "wahoo wahoo," "hoop hoop hoop." These must be the hoolocks, or white-browed gibbons, India's only ape, which we know are occasionally seen in this part of Kaziranga. The duet, with echoes from other pairs high up in the Mikir Hills, goes on and on at such volume it seems the animals' throats must burst. We move carefully, for hoolocks, unlike most of the animals in the park, are shy. As we draw near the chorus subsides. We hear only deep, guttural gurgles. Scanning a giant tree through binoculars I suddenly see him—hanging from his long arms, his mouth shaped in an indignant O as he looks down at us. He is black all over except for his pure white eyebrows. In a fork of the giant tree, just below him, sits the female, brown but with a black face. She has a small, serious-faced baby clasped to her chest. We sit quietly and for some minutes we and the apes look at each other. Suddenly, hurling themselves from branch to branch, using only their powerful long arms, they move into the next tree and resume their wild chorus.

We wade out into the floodwaters, making for a tree about a 100 meters away so we can climb it and get a view. Soon the water is waist-deep. On a log floating by sits a monitor lizard, his giant claws stolidly clutching the wood; he flicks his forked tongue at us. A cobra streaks away, making for a shrub that it climbs swiftly and expertly, then raises itself on its coils and hisses with its hood spread. Frogs leap out of our way, hotly pursued by fast-swimming watersnakes. Heart-rending cries coming from dense clumps of grass tell of a snake's successful chase. The water is chest-high when we reach the tree.

As we settle down in one of the higher branches, fighting with large black ants who have chosen the same tree as a refuge, the sun comes out. Instantly it is burning hot and stickily humid.

The heat has also affected the Assamese macaques—thickset brown monkeys—who have gathered in a tree not far from ours. The adolescent macaques tumble and play on the outer branches. Part of the game is to leap into the water with as much splashing as possible, then rush up the tree again, followed by another leap. It is so hot we follow the monkeys' example and plunge into the water, though with considerably more caution. They watch us, squeal, jump up and down, and pull faces at us—just like the small boys who gather around wherever we stop in an Indian village or town.

★ ★ ★

Kaziranga National Park is one of the most critically important and most brilliant links in the chain of the world's wildlife reserves. Part of the floodplain of a great river, it is a tapestry of tall elephant grass and lush, sweet pasture knee-high to a rhinoceros. It is veined by strips of dense forest that fringe sluggish streams and dotted throughout are ponds and lakes. This kind of country is called the *terai*. Once, hundreds of years ago, the *terai* covered a great arc of land right along the base of the Himalayas from Burma to the Indus River in Pakistan. All the well-known mammals of Asia, the tiger, elephant, one-horned rhinoceros, gaur, many kinds of deer and monkeys, as well as birds and other animals, were then found in the *terai*.

Now only a handful of the tiniest fragments of the natural *terai* remain and Kaziranga's 430 square kilometers are undoubtedly the most important and have the most varied wildlife. But it is only a tiny relict of a once seemingly limitless area. Besides being representative of the *terai*, Kaziranga has much other special wildlife such as the hoolock gibbon, the Gangetic dolphin, the capped langur, the green-billed malkoha, the kaleej pheasant....

Though for the most part a well-guarded national park, Kaziranga is not an entirely safe haven. Most years about two-thirds of it is inundated by monsoon floods. Many animals, including some rhinos, are swept away on the current and die. Species from elephants and tigers to pheasants and pythons must seek refuge on higher ground. But little of this lies inside the park. To reach the safety of the slopes of the Mikir Hills the animals must cross rice fields and tea plantations and face the ire of their owners. Even the hills are not secure as they are rapidly being stripped of their rain forests.

The day-to-day work to keep Kaziranga operating and to protect the animals from poachers rests on the capable shoulders of R. N. Sonowal. He is a youngish man, a typical Assamese with almond-shaped eyes, bronze complexion, and a shock of shiny black hair. Reticent and modest, he was difficult to get to know. But during our earlier visits, sitting in his office, drinking tea, exchanging jokes, we gradually broke through his reserve and were rewarded with many insights into the trials of managing such a park.

The most serious problem is the running battle with poachers. Poachers, and in the early part of the century, trophy hunters, almost wiped out the great Indian one-horned rhinoceros, *Rhinoceros unicornis*, Kaziranga's most highly esteemed animal, the animal that has become its symbol.

As early as 1908 the Indian rhino was an endangered species. Only a dozen remained in Kaziranga and a further dozen or two lived in isolated pockets in other parts of Assam, North Bengal, and Nepal. This was the time when the rhinos reached their lowest numbers.

The Indian rhino is possibly the most coveted animal in history. Every part of its anatomy is desired, as a magical cure for a long list of diseases, as an unfailing charm, and in India as an aphrodisiac. To many people in Asia the rhino is a walking apothecary that could cure them of all diseases and keep them so vital that they would stay young and potent forever. To the Chinese the Indian rhino is much better medicine than rhinos from Africa and other parts of Asia.

Powdered rhino horn fetches about two dollars per gram. As the average horn weighs about one-and-a-half kilograms the value is roughly 3,000 dollars at the point of use. The poachers, of course, get much less—about 600 dollars for a good-sized horn. For people who can expect to earn about twenty-five dollars a month, if they work hard, that

A female hoolock gibbon. Pairs of these gibbons, the only species of ape in India, demarcate their territories with wild choruses that reverberate through the forested hills.

represents the savings of a lifetime. The temptations are great, but so are the dangers.

The sad thing is that the aphrodisiac and medicinal properties are completely spurious. The rhinos are relentlessly hunted for nothing. The horn is merely "an epidermal outgrowth of agglutinated hair"—a bunch of compressed hair. Exhaustive laboratory tests, carried out in Switzerland, failed to find any exciting chemicals in the horn.

A rain forest grasshopper. Insects proliferate at the onset of the monsoon.

It is not just the horn that is sought after. Nearly every part of the rhino is believed to be imbued with some special quality: its blood, urine, meat, skin, and even the fetus.

So the slaughter continues and it is Sonowal's job to stop it in Kaziranga. He has been very successful. In 1968, when he was first posted here, a total of about 380 rhinos lived in Kaziranga. In 1975 the number was over 800, which is approaching the optimum population for the park. The measures Sonowal takes are drastic. The park is patrolled by 113 regular forest guards reinforced by fifty-five of the paramilitary Assam Home Guards. All are armed with .303 rifles or twelve-bore shotguns. They can shoot on sight any unauthorized armed person they see in the park. Most patrols are on foot and radiate out from twenty guard outposts located in strategic places. Some patrols are mounted on elephants.

The shooting between poachers and guards began in 1968 when a forest guard was killed. There have been subsequent exchanges of fire and a number of poachers have been shot dead. But it is more usual that the poachers surrender when challenged or melt away in the high grass. Before 1968 about one rhino a month was poached but since then the number has been kept down to two or three a year. None were poached in 1972 but 1975 was a bad year when six were taken. The poachers' returns are just too high and they keep trying.

The poachers are tough people, usually Miri aboriginal people, plains people, who know their way about the grasslands. When they decide to try to get a rhino, a hunter is sent ahead to select an animal with a large horn and to study its movements and those of the guards. Then, usually on a moonlit night, a party of four or five or even a dozen men, depending on how much of the animal they intend to bring back, go in for the kill. They may shoot the rhino from close range with an ancient muzzle loader, often as much of a hazard to the poacher as to the rhino. But guns are noisy and alert the guards. More often the animals are trapped in pits dug along well-used trails.

★   ★   ★

On the evening of our last full day in Kaziranga, in the monsoon of 1976, there is the tiniest sliver of moon. The Milky Way blazes from a clear northern sky. In the south, lightning illuminates billowing clouds from within, like gigantic Chinese lanterns. Countless fireflies wink in unison as they spiral in waves around the trees. During the night a furious storm breaks but the next morning the early sun bathes Kaziranga in purest light. Everything glows and shines. For the first time during our many visits we are able to see the snow-covered peaks of the Eastern Himalayas, over 150 kilometers to the north. But already thunder rumbles in the clouds burgeoning over the hills.

This morning we leave Kaziranga by air for the roads are closed. We fly from Jorhat and pass low over the national park; it appears and disappears among the monsoon clouds. How pitifully small it looks—a tiny enclave between a single curve of the Brahmaputra River and the Mikir Hills, and how vulnerable to the human pressures that have already denuded most of the Assam Valley.

★   ★   ★

We spend the rest of the year making films in Australia and Papua New Guinea. We return to India in January 1977 to begin work on our film on Kanha's tigers.

[CHAPTER 11]
TIGERS OF KANHA

Kanha National Park and Tiger Reserve— 30 January 1977

In the early hours of the morning, well before sunrise, the forest just below our bungalow shakes, literally vibrates, with the full-throated roars of two tigers. The roars roll back and forth like thunder, punctuated with snarls, coughs, and hisses. The tigers, both males judging by the volume and depth of their voices, are fighting. The protracted battle is more than a dispute over freshly killed prey or territorial boundaries. Those are usually brief. It sounds more like a challenge for territorial possession fought out between well-matched animals. On and on it goes as we stand entranced on the verandah.

At the first glimmer of daylight we climb aboard Pawan Mala. She strides out while Mahavir, her *mahout*, and Belinda work out where we might find the combatants. The forest drips with dew; icy drops fall on our heads. We skirt along the edge of a wide meadow. In these moments before the sun rises the open space is thinly veiled in mist. The light has a blue tinge adding to the impression of coldness. The distant hills, visible above the fog, are deep purple. Tall sal trees stand as dark, brooding islands in the lakes of pale grass.

The last time we were here was during the monsoon when the air, while it was not raining, was crystal clear and the meadows and forests were intensely green. Now the leaves on the sal and bamboos are yellow, ready to fall.

We leave the meadow and enter the forest. Luckily there is little undergrowth and visibility is good. A sambar doe with a yearling at heel high-steps through the leaflitter, every muscle taut with apprehension. She sniffs the air and her ears scan for suspicious sounds. From a little farther on we hear the sudden bark of another sambar. She stamps her front foot hard on the ground and barks again. She must have caught a tiger's

scent. Mahavir slows Pawan Mala. For a few minutes we beat back and forth. The tiger, when we find him, is lying on his side among sal saplings. He looks dreadful and does not even raise his head as we approach. We stop about ten meters away. Beside him lies a dead sambar, a fully grown stag, perhaps weighing as much as 300 kilograms. Part of the deer's rump has been eaten.

A slow trickle of blood drips from the tiger's nostrils. His muzzle from between his eyes to his nose is a raw wound, the skin completely gone, exposing part of the nasal bone. Despite his disfigurement Belinda recognizes him by the marks on the sides of his face as the same male who consorted with the stump-tailed tigress and her two cubs nearly three years ago.

In most cases we name the tiger after the tree under which it rests when we first see it. Belinda initially saw this male under a huge Arjuna tree. Arjuna is also the name of a mythological warrior of great prowess and courage. It seems that Arjuna the tiger has lost the night's battle, though he gained the prey.

Another tiger roars deeper in the forest. Arjuna immediately sits upright. This obviously causes him pain, and he moves stiffly without his usual fluidity.

Mahavir makes Pawan Mala amble off into the direction of

The tiger Arjuna was badly wounded in his fight with the younger, larger Snarl.

the sounds of the second tiger. We find him almost immediately, only about half a kilometer away on the edge of a patch of bamboo. We draw in our breath as we take in his huge size and bright orange color. He lies sprawled on a carpet of brown and yellow fallen leaves. But he raises himself up onto his forequarters, resting on his "elbows." Head lifted imperiously, he stares us directly in the eye. He growls deep in his throat and curls his lips back in a snarl. In his winter coat he looks magnificent, his neck ruff almost lionlike in its shagginess. Humps of muscle stand out on his shoulders and ripple down his front legs as he shifts his position slightly. His cushioned paws look deceptively soft and fluffy but conceal retractable sharp hooks, weapons he used to rip Arjuna's face. His tail lashes from side to side in what appears to be barely contained fury, which is also reflected in his pale green, fiery eyes. We have not seen him before and name him Snarl after his aggressive disposition.

Some minutes pass in a tense mutual appraisal then Snarl suddenly relaxes as if he no longer considers us a threat. His tail comes to rest and his eyes lose their intensity. Slowly, luxuriously, he yawns—making us gasp in surprise once again; his canine teeth are enormously long. This is a male of larger than average size and at the height of his powers. Arjuna by contrast is getting old, his canines chipped and broken. Snarl has no major wounds, just a few puncture marks and scratches on his shoulders and front legs.

For three more days Arjuna is at his sambar kill. On the fourth day we see his pug marks going down a sandy dry streambed heading out of his old territory. Snarl has taken over.

It is a cold winter. Several days in a row the grass is white with frost, though the days are warm and still. Swamp deer stags strut and rut on the meadows. Steam rises from their mouths as they bugle in the cold air of sunrise. When not fighting or sparring with each other, they thrash the grass and the chindi palms. Having gathered large bunches of vegetation in their antlers, they walk about on stiff legs with their heads held high as if the hanging gardens are a kind of status symbol.

February becomes drier and warmer. No longer is there any dew. The rivers cease to flow. Sal and other trees shed their leaves, which accumulate, dry and brittle, on the ground. It becomes difficult for a tiger to make a silent stalk. By early March it is spring, briefly. Soon the migratory birds, the flycatchers that haunt the bamboo, the harriers that shadow the meadows, the ducks that gather on the marshes, and others will move north to the Himalayas and beyond. Resident birds are in full song and some begin nesting. Peacocks spread and raise their trains, strut and dance to attract the females. Other birds await the approach of the monsoon, about three months away, before nesting.

Among all this exuberance there is bad news. Arjuna has been found dead by forest guards about ten kilometers from his old territory. His face was hideously swollen from his infected wound. We still see Snarl regularly.

Since early spring we have occasionally seen a tigress along the dry creek known as Desi Nulla and on the meadows and outcrops of granite around it. We have had glimpses of her three cubs and suspect she hides them in a cavern somewhere among the boulders. The first time we saw her it was still cool and she lay sunning herself across a black rockshelf beneath a tree with silken white bark that flakes off in tissue-thin layers. We have named the tigress Kulu after the tree she rested under.

18 May

Yesterday was hot and we did not go tracking on Pawan Mala till late afternoon. Not far from one of the last small pools in Desi Nulla, surrounded by boulders and shaded by a spreading bauhinia tree, we found a freshly killed swamp deer doe.

Snarl—named for his aggressive disposition—yawns, showing his huge canine teeth. A tiger's canines, both upper and lower, are long and dagger-like, shaped for a stabbing bite that can sever the spinal cord of a deer, killing it instantly.

Kulu and her cubs cool off in a small rock pool. At the height of the dry season, when the days are searingly hot, tigers and others concentrate at the few remaining water holes.

Only a little had been eaten. For an hour we searched high and low for Kulu, for this is in her territory, but we could not find her.

At sunrise we are back at the pool, more a muddy puddle covered in green slime. The coolness of night still lingers. Kulu lies on the high bank among rocks. To our astonishment all three cubs, well-grown now, are with her, lying on boulders not far from their mother. To our further delight the cubs do not run away this time. All have rounded stomachs. The remains of the swamp deer, just the forequarters, head and neck, lie in the grass on the opposite bank. Jungle crows fly in and settle in a tall silk cotton tree just above the deer's remains, cawing raucously. Higher in the tree sit a score of vultures, their long, almost bare necks hunched into their shoulders. More glide in. A troop of langurs feeds in a sal tree right above Kulu.

We take up a strategic position in the shade in the streambed not far from the pool. Pawan Mala is soon busy feeding on bamboo and grass. All four tigers ignore us, but Kulu stays alert to the activities of the scavengers. Even when lying down, seemingly asleep, she growls when she hears a vulture flying in or crows going to her kill.

As the sun rises higher the tigers, panting and their feet dragging, move deeper into the shade. The cubs come together, play halfheartedly, and lick and nuzzle each other before stretching out again. A little later, one after another they go up to Kulu and rub against her. The smallest cub, a female, rubs her head and the full length of her body under Kulu's chin and flops down, lying across her mother's paws.

The crows and vultures seem to think this family affection distracts the tigress' attention. The vultures, one after another, hop down to the lowest of the silk cotton's branches. A few adventurous crows land on the carcass, raising buzzing clouds of flies from the putrid meat. Kulu growls, hisses, and spits. But she is too full of food and too content to take further action. She stretches out and dozes. A single vulture glides silently down and lands on the swamp deer's shoulder. For minutes it stares at the tigress but there is no reaction. The scavenger begins to eat. Three more vultures join it. A jackal materializes out of the grass and makes off with a discarded leg bone. Soon there are a dozen noisy vultures on the carcass. Kulu gives no warning that she is aware of what is going on. She leaps up, jumps over one of the cubs, streaks fifteen meters across the creek, and, roaring, charges the birds. The crows take instant evasive action but vultures are large, clumsy birds that need room and time to spread their wide wings and take off. Kulu is among them in an instant and swats first one then another with swipes of her front paws, breaking their backs. The birds die slowly in the sun. The crows and the other vultures leave and do not return.

Kulu picks up the deer carcass and drags it to the pool where she dumps it in the water. She pants with the exertion and stretches out full-length beside it. The cubs come down the bank and join her—four tigers crammed into a tiny pool. We leave them but will return in the late afternoon.

The tigers are back in the shade. Where Pawan Mala stood this morning lie the remains of a langur—which is a great surprise. How could Kulu have killed one of these sharp-eyed, cautious monkeys? Did it come to drink?

At dusk the cubs become lively and play in the manner of all cats. They "attack" each other from ambush, stalk and pounce on their mother's tail, jump, and chase. Running and tumbling they slide down the bank, down to the pool. They drink some of the stagnant, malodorous water.

Kulu is suddenly alert. She stiffens and stares across the meadows. In the far distance we faintly hear the "aroom" of a tiger. With a quick glance and a soft throaty noise at the cubs, meaning "do not follow me," she sets off at a quick pace. Disconsolately the cubs climb the bank, lie down on the rocks, and stare after Kulu as she disappears into the darkness.

22 May

Two days ago Kulu brought most of a chital stag to the cubs at the small water hole. She did not wait long to stride off again along the creek. Yesterday she did not come to the cubs, morning or evening. They looked rather forlorn and had not eaten much.

This afternoon we decide not to go to the cubs but to investigate the pug marks of a male tiger that had been seen this morning about three kilometers away deep in the forest.

We pick up the pug marks of a male *and* a female tiger walking side by side up a dry creek. Those of the male are especially large. We follow them until they leave the nulla. On and on the elephants tread in the hot afternoon; through bamboo thickets, down steep-sided valleys, across small clearings, through tall forest, and along dark, cool gullies shaded by fig trees.

We hear a tiger's coughing roar, short, not the usual drawn-out "aroom." It came from a ravine where there is a small pool. The *mahouts* urge the elephants on but it seems an eternity before we get to the place. There are fresh pug marks around the pool. The sand around it is still wet from the water that dripped from the tigers' fur. The elephants drink their fill and cool themselves by spraying their undersides with water from their trunks. Up ahead chital "pong" furiously. We must be close but unless the tigers stop we will not catch up with them. The sun is close to setting.

We hurry up a gentle forested slope. Then we see them, two tigers lying only a few meters apart in the open space between two huge sal trees. The tigress is Kulu, a long way from her cubs, and with her is Snarl, looking as magnificent as ever.

Kulu walks over to Snarl, who makes throaty noises at her overtures. She lies down again, a few paces away, with her four paws gathered under her. Her head is down and stretched forward, almost touching the ground and her tail is slightly raised. As darkness falls rapidly Snarl gets up and straddles Kulu. They mate. He roars and savagely bites her neck and ears, puncturing her shoulders with his canines. After a few moments Kulu turns her head and roars, full-throated and spitting, in Snarl's face above her. He answers with an equally ferocious roar and leaps backwards, moves away, and lies down. Kulu stretches languidly and rolls on her back.

Slowly, not wishing to tire the elephants unduly, we go back to our bungalow. It is dark by now. To our knowledge few if any people have seen wild tigers mating, certainly not at such close quarters.

One of Kulu's cubs, killed and partially eaten by Snarl. These cubs were almost certainly not Snarl's. Such infanticide may be the practice of males who have come into a new territory and are eliminating the genes of their male predecessors.

18 June

A month has passed since we found Kulu and her cubs feasting on the swamp deer. Premonsoon showers have freshened the meadows and water holes but the creeks are not yet running. It is still hot but now it is also humid, very uncomfortable weather. We have found both Kulu and her cubs and Snarl from time to time. They too find it hard to cope with the heat and spend as much time as they can at the few pools, where they lie in the water. When not in the water they hide in ambush for the deer, pigs, monkeys, and gaur that must come to drink.

This morning we are tracking in the area where Kulu and Snarl mated, for yesterday we saw the pug marks of the tigress and her young heading in this direction. All six tracking elephants are out this morning, moving on a broad front through the forest.

Rada's *mahout*, up ahead on the hill, shouts to come and see what he has found. It is unspeakably horrible—one of the cubs, dead, its hindquarters eaten. It looks fresh and two elephants go off to look for the cub's killer. We dismount and look closely at the young tiger. It is a male. He is not really that small, about ten months old. Ticks and mites crawl out of his fur and leave him while blowflies hover around and settle on his forequarters and nostrils. His windpipe has been crushed and there are deep puncture marks through his rib cage. He did not die from a casual swipe from a powerful and intemperate tiger but was deliberately killed, as prey would be. Only two days ago we filmed him sitting on a rock watching langurs in the tree above him, stretching, yawning, and dozing on his back, paws in the air.

Dev Bahadur comes back and his *mahout* says he saw a large male tiger that looked like Snarl walking off into the hills. He caught up with him, but the tiger would not stop. While we are all huddled around the dead cub we hear long, drawn-out roars on the hill above us, "arooom, arooom." Heart-rending sounds to our ears. We can just make out that it is Kulu, her remaining cubs close beside her. They walk in the opposite direction to where her territory is.

The *mahouts* and two Baiga trackers do a *puja*, a ceremony and prayers, for the cub, then pick up his remains and take them to the park headquarters. When we arrive there some of the tiger's whiskers are gone. The others are quickly removed and burnt by the range officer. Tiger whiskers are believed to be very dangerous by the Baiga. They think that if they are given to someone in food the person's intestines will be punctured and he or she will surely die.

★ ★ ★

A corner of our hilltop bungalow's verandah catches a cooling breeze. We sit in this marginally more comfortable place to think about this morning's events.

Why should one male tiger (Snarl) kill a cub and another (Arjuna) consort with a female and play with her cubs? When Arjuna and Stumptail were together, she was not in season and the two did not mate.

There are other records of tigers killing cubs, including several in Kanha. It has been theorized that infanticide by males, which has also been recorded for lions and langur monkeys, is perpetrated by those who have just taken over a new territory or troop. The new male kills the young so that the females will become receptive again and he can mate with them. In other words he destroys the genes of his predecessor so he can perpetuate his own. Arjuna, an older male who had been established in his territory for some years, may have been confident that Stumptail's cubs were his offspring and therefore did not kill them.

This male strategy does not suit the females, however. The female's genes are perpetuated in all her offspring no matter who has fathered them. Kulu's cub was close to a year old when he was killed and she had made a great investment in raising him. She, therefore, would have gone to great lengths to protect him. Is that why she mated with Snarl, to appease him? Her cubs were still too young for her to have another litter. Such speculation is all very theoretical and full of unanswered questions. It could simply be that Arjuna was more tolerant and that Snarl has a nasty streak in him. Too little is still known about tigers in the wild.

★ ★ ★

Over these months, while making "Tigers of Kanha" for the television series *Wild Wild World of Animals*, we feel we have penetrated the tiger's mysterious world just a little. But we want to know more and more about them. Above all we want to spend time with them, to observe them, in their seductive and exhilarating jungles.

Before we can return to the tigers' world we have a unique opportunity to fulfill another long-held dream—to make a film about Keoladeo's marshes.

Death and Renewal on the Marshes

When we visit it in the winter of 1979–1980, Keoladeo's future is in jeopardy. People have it by the throat and it is slowly dying. The threats to what to us is one of the wonders of the world (what other place supports 364 species of birds in so small an area?) impels us to make a one-hour film on Keoladeo. We want to follow the lives of the birds and other animals through the cycle of the seasons.

For a year we live at Keoladeo. The winter is not an auspicious time for filming, for it is a season of exceptional drought, the worst in forty years. The monsoon has failed. Animals are dying. It is a sign of Murphy's Law at work, we think, that we begin a film on wetlands when these are drying up in front of our eyes.

In other ways it is a dream come true. By being on the spot all the year round, we can follow the birds' life histories, how they are affected by the weather, how they interact with other species, how everything fits together.

Most days Belinda and I go to some corner of the park to look for events to film. These are the times I perhaps enjoy most for there are always new and unexpected things to be discovered: an owl's nest; a python's lair; the hatching of a sarus crane egg, the explosion of insect life after rain. I say perhaps because on other days we film from a blind set up at a bird's nest, at a special feeding place for pelicans and storks, or in the midst of the nesting colony of waterbirds. There is something very exciting and wonderful to be just a few meters from birds going about their business of courtship, nest-building, and caring for their young.

Above: Keoladeo's marshes in winter.
Left: a pair of sarus cranes give their unison call.

euphoria with its energy and spectacle, as it did six years ago. No one expressed that feeling better than an anonymous Buddhist monk writing 2,000 years ago:

> When the drum of the clouds
>   thunders in heaven
> and all the ways of the birds are
>   thick with rain,
> the monk sits in…ecstasy
> and finds no joy greater than this.

Before completing our film on Keoladeo we spend a week at Ranthambhore, half a day's drive to the southwest, to record the songs of woodland birds. Sound recording for

the film is a problem in Keoladeo because of the incessant noise of traffic, industry, and domestic animals. Besides, there are tigers in Ranthambhore.

Clockwise from upper left: a sarus crane with its chick and egg; a spotted eagle feeds on a fish stranded by lowering water holes; a stone curlew nests despite the drought; nesting median egrets; a blacknecked stork harasses a flock of rosy pelicans in Keoladeo's last fishing hole.

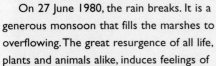

On 27 June 1980, the rain breaks. It is a generous monsoon that fills the marshes to overflowing. The great resurgence of all life, plants and animals alike, induces feelings of

[CHAPTER 12]

AN INTERLUDE WITH A TIGRESS

Ranthambhore Wildlife Sanctuary and Tiger Reserve—27 November 1980

For an hour or more we have been driving straight toward a range of rocky hills. It is only at the last moment that we realize that we enter Ranthambhore Sanctuary via a narrow cleft cut in these same hills by a small river. We feel something enticing and beguiling the moment we drive through enormous wooden doorways set in a centuries-old stone gate.

After passing through a ravine we enter gently rolling hills covered in forest and knee-high grass. Nilgai antelope graze the pristine slopes. In the forest stand elegant, ancient buildings, long since abandoned and now crumbling in the suffocating embrace of banyan tree roots. Langur monkeys lounge nonchalantly on the roof of an ancient pavilion.

Rounding a bend, we are confronted by an escarpment of rock several hundred meters high and topped by medieval battlements. The fortifications enclose a city, now uninhabited, whose architecture, in the shape of domes, spires, and square block towers, goes back more than 1,000 years. A Bonelli's eagle, its white underside streaked with bold brushstrokes of black, sails along the cliff.

We drive through cool, dark forest. A leopard slinks across the road just in front of us and insinuates itself into a dense patch of thorn bushes growing beneath tall trees. Even though there is no dappled sun and shade, the leopard's pattern makes it virtually disappear among the dry foliage. But

A tigress lying in ambush.

we can clearly see the glitter in its eyes as it watches us from about ten meters away.

On our left the forest thins out and we see the water of a lake flickering through the trees. A little farther on the road seems to end at the steep ramp that zigzags up to Ranthambhore Fort on top of the cliff. It is broad enough for elephants, used in battles and ceremonies centuries ago, to have walked up and down. At the end of what would once have been a city square, however, the road continues after passing through another gigantic stone gateway. The old square is deserted and overgrown with trees. From the hollow in one of them a diminutive collared scops owl looks down through slitted eyes. A forest guard is there to meet us. He says he will show us to our accommodation and that Mr. Fateh Singh Rathore, the reserve's field director, will join us this evening. We drive on a few hundred meters and find ourselves in one of the world's truly magical places.

The forest rest house is an airily built pavilion, painted a red-pink color, and has domed roofs, a courtyard, and a wide verandah. Beside the window of our room grows a gular tree, a species of fig. So close that we could shake hands with them, a group of Hanuman langurs is eating its fruit. The verandah overlooks a sizable lake and beyond are low hills covered in golden grass and dhauk trees. Directly below the verandah, kingfishers are perched on grass stems overhanging the water and bronzewinged jacanas walk over the water lily leaves. To one side, in an area of shallower water, ducks and geese dive and dabble while painted storks scissor the water with their beaks trying to catch fish. Seven sambar stags with impressive antlers have waded out and are up to their chests in water while they feed on aquatic plants. A few meters from them, on a small island, large mugger crocodiles bask in the midafternoon sun.

On the other side of the rest house, the courtyard faces Ranthambhore Fort, but the view has been usurped by a banyan tree of enormous proportions and reputed to be the second largest in India (the largest is in Calcutta). Although it is a single living plant, it is more a miniature forest than a tree. There are numerous trunks, between them covering perhaps a quarter-hectare, each of which began life as a proproot trailing down from a horizontal branch. Over time some of these roots, after reaching the soil, thickened, were covered in bark, and became trunks. It is a tree you can walk about in. A few of the trunks are of monumental size, while others are thin and elegant. Connecting them all are thick, horizontal branches, some so low that they bend down to the earth. The canopy reaches from the top of the tree to the ground, giving it the appearance of a gigantic green dome whose roofing tiles are leathery, interlocking leaves.

The only entrance into the tree is an archway of stems facing the rest house's courtyard. Scores of langur monkeys rest inside the dome. Sprawled over the branches, they rest and groom each other. The young swing from aerial roots. High in the vaulted canopy, tree pies, gray hornbills, green pigeons, parakeets, and barbets feed on the banyan's marble-sized red fruit.

The afternoon inside the tiger reserve is a kaleidoscope of geese and ducks among water lilies, sambar pulling up lotus stems, brown fish owls sitting over water holes, chital and peafowl on grassy meadows, bush quail scratching around small memorial plaques where a widow committed *suttee* (burned herself alive in her husband's funeral pyre), nilgai strolling through the ruins of a village, fifty or more vultures wrapping a sambar carcass in flailing wings and pulling out its entrails with bloodied beaks, and green bee-eaters pirouetting in flight as they catch dragonflies above the treetops.

When the sun is about to set, we stop the Jeep under a tree on a rise overlooking a small lake. Most of the lakebed is dry—only a little water remains in one corner—and a herd of sambar grazes on the succulent grasses that have sprung up. Around the edges of the lakebed grows tall, dry grass. It is a perfect combination of prey and cover for a tiger. We decide to stay and see what happens. Gray partridges scratch in the dust almost beneath our Jeep. Painted sandgrouse pick grass seeds off dry stems. Above us green pigeons converse in bubbling, flutelike voices. White-necked storks and black-winged stilts sift the last muddy water for food. Nothing could be more peaceful.

We examine the tall grass around the lake minutely through our binoculars. Belinda grabs my arm and signals for me to be absolutely quiet. She has detected a slight movement in the tall grass directly below us.

There is another movement. As our eyes become ac-

Below Ranthambhore Fort is pink-colored Jogi Mahal, one of the most exquisite rest houses in India's jungles.

Sambar apprehensive about the presence of a tiger.

sambar. In what seems an eternity of suspense that makes our palms sweat, the deer move closer—thirty meters, twenty, two more meters, another step, and another. The tigress' black tail tip moves slightly from side to side. She turns her ears back, then forwards again. She tenses her leg muscles and places her feet for an explosive power takeoff.

There must be a shift in the wind. The leading doe jerks her head up, stamps her foot. All the other sambar are instantly alert. As the doe opens her mouth to bark her alarm, the tigress springs out of the grass. The sambar wheel around and, with an equally powerful takeoff, sprint off across the dry lakebed. For a few moments the tigress gains on the deer. She makes a leap at one and tries to knock its feet from under it with a swipe of her paws. She is so close that she grazes the sambar's leg, but she does not knock it over. The tigress has lost the initiative and she stops. Panting, she watches the sambar gallop up over the bank and into the dhauk forest. "Aroom," she moans several times. She walks over to the remaining puddle of water, vacated by the birds, and lies down to drink—lapping with her pink tongue. Soon she too walks off into the forest.

It is dark by the time we arrive back at the rest house. An oil lamp burns at the window of our room. A fire has been lit under the banyan tree and three chairs arranged around it.

Ever since we drove into the reserve at midday I had experienced the mental equivalent of my eyes becoming rounder and wider with astonishment at each new revelation—entrance gate, fort,

customed to the patterns of grass blades, light, and shade, a patch of them resolves itself into the striped form of a tiger. It is no more than thirty meters from us. There is no doubt that the tiger is aware of our presence, but it has decided to ignore us. All its attention is concentrated on the unsuspecting sambar. They are still out of the tiger's range. After a few more minutes the tigress slowly and carefully begins to move. With her belly almost touching the ground, she turns and comes out of the grass. She is still hidden from the sambar. Taking a few steps, placing each foot with exquisite care so that not a twig snaps nor a stone rolls, then freezing for a few moments and never taking her eyes off the sambar, she moves around the lake edge. She reenters the grass and disappears from our view, but we can follow her progress by the slight movements of a few grass blades. The sambar are now moving directly toward her. One of the does seems to be nervous and keeps raising her head and sniffing the air. But the wind is not in her favor.

The tigress moves forward until her face is screened from the sambar by just a few grass blades. We can see her perfectly, but the deer cannot; their eyesight is not good enough. As long as the tigress remains motionless, she is invisible to the

Fateh Singh Rathore, field director of Ranthambhore Tiger Reserve.

leopard, lake, rest house, banyan tree, thousand-year-old buildings inhabited only by wild animals, a tigress hunting. What I find most compelling about Ranthambhore is that it has been reclaimed by nature, completely and unequivocally, where everywhere else humanity is stealing from nature. Above all, in the process of reclamation, something mysteriously romantic, wild, unpredictable, and totally splendid has been created.

Then to top it all off there is Fateh Singh Rathore, Ranthambhore's colorful, passionate, and incorruptible field director. He is the man who is overseeing the last handover of Ranthambhore to the natural forces. Fateh materializes out of the darkness and joins us at the fire beneath the banyan. He is an extroverted man with a sweeping mustache and a strong voice. He wears an immaculate, wide-brimmed felt hat, a cravat at his throat, and a greatcoat to keep out the cold. He offers us whisky and soon we are deep in conversa-tion about tigers and how Ranthambhore came to be the exotic place it is. Toward midnight the fire has died down. There is a lull in the conversation. Crocodiles and fish splash in the lake. From behind us, between the banyan and the fort's rock escarpment, comes the sound that electrifies the forest and makes our hair stand on end. A tiger roars in his full-throated voice that echoes off the rocks once, twice, then it is silent again.

★ ★ ★

The experience of that afternoon has sharpened and rekindled our fascination with tigers. With Fateh's encouragement our thoughts turn to making a film on tigers, a film that we hope will reveal something of the animals' secretive life. We would do it partly in Kanha and partly in Ranthambhore.

Sambar run from a tiger's charge.

TIGERS! TIGERS! KANHA AND RANTHAMBHORE

... there is a stirring of the blood in attacking an animal before whom every other beast of the forest quails, and unarmed man is helpless as the mouse under the paw of a cat—a creature at the same time matchless in beauty of form and color, and in terrible power of offensive armature— which draws men to its continued pursuit.

Capt. James Forsyth,
on tiger hunting in the Kanha area,
in *The Highlands of Central India*, 1871

I wanted to do everything I could to restore Ranthambhore; to stop grazing and tree felling, to remove villages and so on. I wanted to give Ranthambhore back to nature and let nature do with it what she could. Ranthambhore means everything to me. After I die I want my body to be put in the land there so that the tigers can walk over me.

Fateh Singh Rathore,
Field Director, Project Tiger, Ranthambhore
March 1987

[CHAPTER 13]

HOW TO FILM TIGERS?

After completing the film "Birds of the Indian Monsoon" in Keoladeo, we spent some time in both Kanha and Ranthambhore. We saw many tigers, some of them at very close range. The tiger, more than ever, got into our blood.

Late one afternoon, sitting in Fateh Singh's Jeep on a hill overlooking one of Ranthambhore's lakes, I turned to Belinda and said, "I think we should…" Before I could finish the sentence, she said, "Yes, I agree, the time is right." That is how we decided to make our tiger film. We had become proficient at filmmaking over the last six years. Tiger numbers were on the increase all over India. In Corbett National Park, in Kaziranga, in southern Indian reserves, but especially in Kanha and Ranthambhore, it was now possible to see tigers for long uninterrupted periods, in daylight and up close. As far as we could gather from our reading, this was the first time in history when this was so, probably because no one had tried to get close to wild tigers before. There certainly

Belinda photographs Saja.

were more tigers in the past, but they were always seen as dangerous adversaries and hunted down.

Because we had served our apprenticeship, as it were, in filmmaking, and we did not know how long the good relations between people and tigers would last, it was time for us to seize this chance. There might never be another.

Yet to convince a production company to fund the tiger film took another act of audacity. To *see* a tiger is one thing, but to *film* it in long, steady, and close sequences that build up into a coherent story, is quite another. Apart from our twenty-five-minute film in Kanha, it had not been attempted before. But the techniques we used then, to film handheld from the back of an elephant, would not be good enough for a full one-hour film.

We traveled to Washington, D.C. and spoke to the executive producers of the National Geographic Society's television division. We talked to them with passion about tigers and the Indian jungle. We showed them "Birds of the Indian Monsoon." We showed them Belinda's still pictures of tigers. The producers quizzed us closely about just how we proposed to make the film, how long we would take, and how much it would cost. We were able to work out a plan in which just Belinda and I would work in the field, instead of the usual crew of four or five people, and so resources could be stretched over two years. This was the minimum time required, we thought, to penetrate the secrecy of such an elusive, and as yet little-known, animal.

The two executive producers went into another room to discuss our proposal and make their decision while we stood at a window high up in the National Geographic Society's building and looked down at the city traffic. After only a short time the executive producers returned. Yes, they agreed to our proposal. We would make a National Geographic television special on tigers in India. We shook hands and took the next plane back to New Delhi.

Over the months that we waited for the Madhya Pradesh Government to give us permits to film in Kanha, we thought hard about just how we were going to film the tiger. We could try to stalk it on foot. We dismissed that idea immediately, not because it is dangerous, for if you know what you are doing it is reasonably safe, but because for us to try to approach the jungle's stealthiest animal by stealth would be futile.

Another possibility would be to film from a *machan* at water holes, at fresh kills, or at other places favored by the tiger. On further reflection and after a few trials, we rejected this idea too, for we would only be able to get limited footage of a tiger walking by or drinking at a water hole. We would not be able to follow them.

To do that we needed something that could be transported by the elephants. Why not a full-sized elephant made of fiberglass, on wheels so that it could be pulled along by the real elephants? One of us could sit inside the body of this artificial animal and film through a hole in its side. When the tiger moved, our Trojan elephant could be pulled along and follow it. We even took measurements and made inquiries with the Van Ingen brothers, famed taxidermists in Mysore, asking if they could make such a beast. They said they could. We decided against this rather fanciful idea also, mainly because the places favored by tigers were too steep and rocky for us to maneuver a wheeled elephant.

We could not film handheld from the back of an elephant because the animal never stands completely still, nor could we expect it to. Elephants like to feed, to swish at flies with their tails, to flap their ears to cool themselves, to shift their weight from one leg to another.

In the end the solution was quite simple. We built a massive tripod that could be raised to a height of four meters, to stand beside the elephant. We would then put the camera on the tripod and film while leaning out from the *howdah*. This proved workable but always remained a difficult operation. Such a tripod is very heavy.

In Ranthambhore, where the habitat is more open, we always filmed from a stripped-down Jeep.

Finally, after the central government had applied consid-

erable pressure on our behalf, the Madhya Pradesh forest department issued us our permits.

On 18 April 1982 we arrived in Kanha to begin filming. Right on the boundary of the park, Bob Wright, Belinda's father, had just opened Kipling Camp, his jungle lodge.

Our last day's filming was on 27 April 1984, just over two years later, in Ranthambhore.

To avoid repetition and for the sake of brevity, we have compressed the events of these two years into one in the narrative that follows.

Filming with the elephant tripod.

[CHAPTER 14]

THE STORY OF BANSERI AND SAJA

Kanha National Park and Tiger Reserve— April and May

We have come to live in Kanha; we are no longer visitors. Our attitudes and perceptions as a result are slightly different. We find that we look a little more sharply but also more affectionately at the forests, the meadows, and the animal life. The elephant people, the *mahouts,* and the forest people, the Baiga tribals, are our close neighbors. They are the ones who truly know the jungle and the ways of the animals. Of the Forest Department's officials, the park's managers, we see as little as possible although our relationship with them is reasonably cordial.

Our home is the upper cabin, a square concrete building with a wide verandah. It is on top of a ridge surrounded by tall sal trees with an understory of indigos, wild gardenias, and a few bamboos. At the base of the ridge is the magnificent old forest rest house we stayed in during our first visit in the monsoon of 1974. It is now a museum and interpretive center.

Kanha National Park's core area is 940 square kilometers. It would be futile for us to try to see every part of it, to find all eighty or so tigers that live there or even a large number of them. We would like to get to know a small number of tigers well, to see them often and to observe their daily

Tiger pug marks in the mud. Forest staff use tracings of pug marks to estimate the number of tigers in an area; this is a technique that may yield inaccurate figures (see pages 134 and 135).

lives as closely as we can. For that we need elephants and these are only at Kisli, at the western entrance to the park, and at the central Kanha village near the upper cabin. The two places are about eight kilometers apart. The loveliest bamboo jungles

are near Kisli, and Kanha has wider meadows and the wonderful rock outcrops overgrown with mixed forest known as *chattans.* Otherwise the two places are very similar. All the animal life can be seen around them. Occasionally we go farther afield to look for a particular herd of gaur or to the area where the barasingha, the swamp deer, drop their fawns. But Kanha to Kisli is our beat.

Each place has six elephants. In Kisli we work mostly with the magnificent tusker Shivaji and his charismatic *mahout,* Sabir. The other elephant we will use there is Pawan Kali, whose *mahout,* Lucknoo, has the sharpest eyes for spotting animals and an uncanny ability to find tigers.

Pawan Mala, the venerable old elephant we worked with to make "Tigers of Kanha" in 1976, has died of old age. Mahavir has a new, young female elephant called Tara. They are both at Kanha. Mahavir's friend Gunpath is the *mahout* of our favorite elephant, Bundh Devi, a large, good-natured, and tractable animal. She is unperturbable, has a comfortable gait, and fears nothing—not tigers, not difficult terrain, not strange objects like giant tripods.

To a large extent the character of the elephant reflects that of its *mahout.* If a *mahout* is excitable or fearful and dithery, so is the elephant. But if the *mahout* is calm and decisive the elephant will be the same. Mahavir tends to be lazy but when the occasion demands knows exactly what to do and does it with energy. So does Tara. Gunpath is a gentle, kind man who hates a fuss yet has a determined streak in him. Bundh Devi has a similar disposition. Lucknoo likes to move quickly and gets quite excited when he finds a tiger. Pawan Kali is a fast-moving, slightly nervous elephant. Sabir wants total control. He has a flair for the dramatic and enjoys a show of power, intimidation even. In his case the influence from elephant to *mahout* is greater than usual. How can it not be, with Shivaji such a dramatic and powerful animal?

Mohan Lal Durbai is a Baiga boy whose voice has just broken. He is sturdy and well-muscled for his age and has large, callused feet. He has never worn shoes and has never been to school. For most of his life Mohan has lived in Kanha's Baiga village. When he was nine or ten he began work as a day laborer for the Forest Department, mostly building and maintaining the roads. Mohan has a wonderfully open face with a ready smile and is full of exuberance and a kind of innocent bravado. He is not intimidated by tigers or by the forest department bosses. Mohan loves the forest and knows about the plants and animals

At the Upper Cabin, our home while we were working in Kanha. From left to right: Mungal Baiga; the zoologist Paul Newton; the authors; and Mohan Baiga.

like no one else we met. He is a forest spirit like Mowgli in Kipling's *Jungle Book*. I can well imagine Mohan running through the forest living with the animals, talking to them, having fun with them. In fact, the original Mowgli was very likely modeled on a Baiga boy.

Mohan and another Baiga boy called Kua become our assistants. The two are beguiling company.

25 April

The six elephants have gone ahead to track tigers along the Sulcum River. We will join them at a pond on the other side of the meadows. The sun is just above the horizon. It is still refreshingly cool and we tingle with the excitement of our first sortie after the tiger. A large male and a female with cubs have been seen regularly along the river. On this first day we have not yet brought our giant tripod. Before we try to use it we want to get the feel of the jungle again and to familiarize ourselves with the elephants and the tracking techniques. It has

been more than a year since we seriously looked for tigers.

At Shrawantal Belinda climbs onto Tara who is under the control of Mahavir. I join Gunpath on Bundh Devi. Mahavir is round, smooth, and voluble where Gunpath is thin, wizened, and laconic. But none of us talks as the elephants spread out and the search begins. We enter dark, cool sal forest. The air is scented with the slightly lemony aroma of the trees' new leaves and the sweet perfume of flowering gardenias. A troop of langurs feeds on the white froth of flowers covering a bauhinia vine sprawled over a rock outcrop. The colors of birds are bright brushstrokes on the forest's green and brown canvas.

The language of alarm of those hunted by the tiger, pug marks in sand or mud, scrapes in the soil, the smell of scent marking on a bush or tree trunk, the movements of scavengers—all these signs of tigers come rushing back. We slip easily into the tiger's realm again. Soon we will be so attuned to it that we will be able to divine their presence from the subtlest signs—a slight movement in the grass, a footfall on dry leaves, a hint of orange among the foliage, a spot of blood from freshly killed prey.

The elephants push through the bamboos that line the river's sandy bed and move onto one of the few remaining water holes. The river ceased to flow months ago. A tigress with two cubs come to drink here but also to lie in ambush for thirsty sambar, chital, and wild pigs. The sand is crisscrossed with old pug marks. Several large footprints of a male tiger are preserved in the dry mud at the edge of a small pool. The skull and some other bones of a chital, a recent tiger kill, lie under some bamboos.

Mahavir spots fresh pug marks, this morning's, going from the main water hole up a dry nulla. Out in the riverbed the sun is already hot and the tiger is probably looking for a cool, shady spot or perhaps has gone back to its kill. We cannot hear any crows or see any vultures—scavengers who rarely fail to spot a kill—so there probably is none. Belinda and Mahavir, who have gone ahead on the younger, more energetic Tara, find the tigress lying beneath a *Cassia fistula*, an Indian laburnum tree, which the Baiga call *rela*. We call the tigress Rela. In a month or so the tree will be covered in large bunches of canary yellow flowers. Gunpath says they see this tigress regularly.

Rela is restless. Perhaps she wants to get back to her cubs. All six elephants have gathered around her. She snarls at some that go too close to her, and swishes her tail. Soon she gets up and walks back to the river, over to one of the pools, and lies down in the water. Her colors blaze among the dark rocks. After drinking for a few minutes she rises again and walks off into a bamboo thicket.

KANHA NATIONAL PARK (WESTERN)

FOREST ROADS
CLOSED ROADS
VALLEY MEADOWS
FOREST CHAUKI (Guard Outpost)

Not to scale.

26 April

Mahavir and Gunpath are older men only a few years away from retirement. While always willing to help, they are set in their ways, as are their elephants. So to try out our big tripod we go to Kisli to work with Sabir and Shivaji. Sabir is in his late twenties and is passionate about elephants and their training. Shivaji is the best-trained elephant. Sabir can make him do almost anything with minimal commands.

We are out in Kisli's jungles before sunrise. I am on Shivaji surrounded by boxes of camera equipment and the heavy pan and tilt head that has to be placed on top of the tripod. Belinda is on Pawan Kali with Lucknoo, carrying the tripod. The plan is that when we find a tiger, Belinda and Lucknoo will put the tripod in place while I ready the camera. Once the tripod is in position, Sabir will maneuver Shivaji close beside it and I will put the camera with the pan and tilt head on top, hoping that the tiger will not walk off in the meantime.

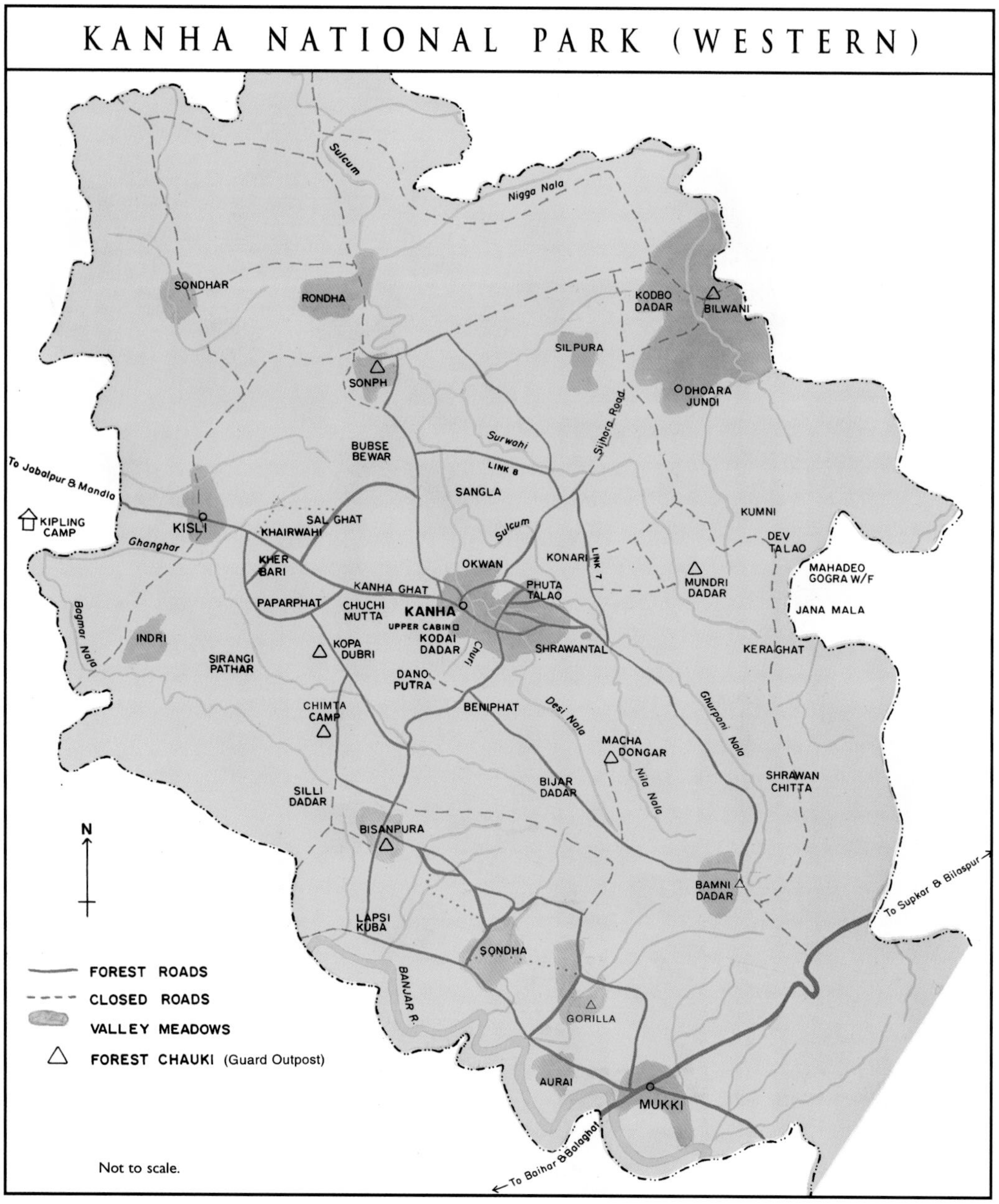

Even before the sun is up we hear chital alarm calls several hundred meters away. That by itself is not a definitive sign, as the deer will give their high pitched "pongs" of alarm at almost anything, even a suspicious-looking log. But we also hear the double bark of a male langur. The elephants seem to recognize the sounds too for they hurry on without urging. After a few minutes we are under the tree where the langur is still barking. The chital have gone. The monkey stares at a particularly dense patch of jamun saplings, their fresh new weeping foliage a perfect screen for a tiger to hide behind. We approach the place from opposite directions. When about ten meters away, Shivaji stops stock-still and blows down his trunk, hitting the end of it on the ground at the same time. This makes a hollow snorting sound that means "there is something strange and unusual ahead." Shivaji raises his trunk high and tests the air, then points it at the center of the clump of trees. Slowly, without uttering a word, guiding the elephant only with his feet, Sabir directs Shivaji toward the group of trees. Lucknoo has trouble controlling Pawan Kali, because in a similar situation a few months ago a tiger rushed out from cover and bit her on the tail, severing the tip. She now snorts, shakes her head, and, walking backwards, trumpets loudly. Shivaji walks on. He pushes through the leaves to the center of the grove where there is an open space. A tiger lies beside his kill, a huge sambar stag. The big cat lifts his head and looks quizzically at us for a moment, then lowers it again and closes his eyes. Lucknoo finally persuades Pawan Kali to join us.

The large male tiger Langra.

The kill must have been made during the night. The tiger's lethargy may well be the result of his enormous meal. His stomach is hugely distended, having taken in most of the deer's hindquarters—about forty kilograms of meat. The tiger is a large male. When he finally sits up we can appreciate the power of his forequarters but also the open look on his face, conveying a sense of innocence almost. There is no sign of hostility towards us. The *mahouts,* who see him now and again, call him Langra, which means lame one. They have called him that not because he limps, for he does not, but because his left hind foot is slightly misshapen, something that shows in his pug marks.

Langra settles down to clean himself. Moving slowly and carefully, for there is not much room in the small clearing, Belinda puts the tripod in place. Pawan Kali is not too sure about this strange contraption and in her skittishness threatens to topple it. Once she tries surreptitiously to kick it with one of her hind feet. Eventually the tripod stands in the right place. Sabir now puts Shivaji in exactly the right place with great economy of movement. I lean out from the *howdah* and place the camera on top of the tripod. Leaning out farther, somewhat precariously, I film Langra as he grooms his fur. He yawns at us, showing his long, perfectly white canine teeth.

To begin with Shivaji unintentionally hits the tripod with his flapping ears and swinging tail, but Sabir soon controls

that. After a few minutes, Shivaji becomes fidgety and wiggles about, which could tip me off the *howdah*. So when I am actually filming, and Sabir has soon worked out when that is, the *mahout* lies forward on the elephant's head and covers his eyes with his hands. When Sabir does that Shivaji stands completely still. At those times the tripod is rock steady; the method works.

When we have been with the tiger for more than two hours, practicing our operations, we hear sambar alarm calls not far away. Langra is instantly alert. When another tiger roars he is on his feet immediately and strides off, abandoning his kill, something a tiger does only with great reluctance. For a while we follow him, Shivaji walking alongside the tiger for about a kilometer. But the roars of the other tiger keep receding and we go back to pick up our tripod and return to Kisli.

2 May

We have had no further luck with tigers in Kisli so over the last few days we have concentrated our search in the Kanha area. We have seen Rela a few times, and a male tiger. We tried our elephant tripod with Tara and Bundh Devi, at first with disastrous results, the tripod falling over several times. Once it fell close to Rela, who ignored it totally. There has been no sign of Rela's cubs.

The other Kanha tigress that supposedly has cubs has her territory at Churi only a kilometer or so behind the upper cabin. Churi is a sandy creek, now dry except for a single small water hole. It drains a bowl of gently sloping hills covered in sal and bamboo interspersed with small areas of open grassland. Adjoining the creek on the northern side is an outcrop of huge boulders that rise about forty meters to a plateau. The resident tigress is thought to have given birth to her cubs in a cavern high up on the edge of the plateau. She has not been seen in that area for a while, so we reason the time has come for her to visit this part of her territory. We take just the two elephants—Tara and Bundh Devi.

Our guess is right. We find her not through alarm calls, pug marks, or other clever deductions; when we reach the water hole, there she is, lying in it. As we approach she gets up and lies in the shade of a clump of bamboos; it is a thin shade as only a few leaves remain on the branches. We name her Banseri.

Banseri basks in the early morning sun.

We try putting the tripod up and filming her. But Bundh Devi is not equal to the task yet. While we mill about Banseri does the most wonderful things—she walks through bamboo, gets into the pool again, drinks, drapes herself over a beautiful rock, lies in a cavern, yawns, scratches, washes her face. Finally I think I have everything set up just right. As I start the camera rolling Banseri gets up and walks directly at Bundh Devi. Gunpath cannot stop her from backing away. I have just enough time to switch the camera off but have to leave it standing on the tripod. Banseri walks up to it, sniffs it thoroughly, and lightly bites one of the legs. I hold my breath for if she knocks the tripod over the camera will be smashed. But she does not, she merely scent-marks it with a spray of urine. The tripod is now part of her territory.

At that we give up on filming for the day and concentrate on enjoying Banseri. To be *always* preoccupied with filming and cameras, with trying for the best angle, becomes tiresome.

We move closer to Banseri as once more she lies regally and languidly on a shelf of rock. It is only now that we realize what an extraordinarily beautiful tigress she is. When she walked about we noticed how perfectly proportioned she is—not massive, but compact and elegant. She walked with her tail held horizontally with only the tip curled upwards. Now we see that her head is finely featured with longer than usual, somewhat pointed ears. Her long, white whiskers rise out of black dots on her upper lips. But she is not delicate. Her muzzle is broad, her teeth are strong and white. She has powerful shoulders and large paws. She is more athletic and less bulky than a male such as Langra. Her eyes are steady, round, and greenish in color. The pattern around her eyes looks like makeup and emphasizes their clarity. All tigers have these lines of "makeup," but in Banseri they are so bright and well drawn that they give her face a look of extra alertness. The stripes along her body are narrow and relatively closely spaced. On her shoulders and flanks there are lines of brown spots between the stripes. Her chest has larger than usual areas of white. Her shiny, short summer coat makes her look sleek. She probably weighs between 130 and 140 kilograms—the average for an Indian tigress.

She has an amazing temperament. Slowly we move closer, till we are about five meters from her. She lies on an elevated rock and looks down at us alertly but without malice or threat. I can see every hair, every nuance of color and pattern. To have this wild animal, her superb head lifted, look calmly straight at you, is an affecting experience. More than anything else it makes me feel part of these jungles—something that looking through the camera alone could never do.

The mutual inspection over, Banseri rolls onto her back and, paws in the air, goes to sleep. We notice her teats are swollen. She must have cubs nearby.

6 May

We take a break from bobbing about on elephants to look at some of the other wildlife. Driving along the edge of the forest, where it meets the meadows, Mohan spots a tiger coming out of some tall grass. We stop in a gap in the trees with a good view of the open space. Very slowly and deliberately the tiger walks toward us, head down, shoulders hunched. A herd of chital face the tiger and with tails raised give a few desultory "pongs" of alarm. A langur in the trees above us utters a half-hearted bark. As long as they can see the predator moving out in the open they are not greatly agitated. The chital move toward the tiger, to within ten or twelve meters. The tiger, a male with massive forequarters, raises his head and gives a low moaning roar. He stops and roars again, full-throated this time, "arooom." It is a loud, menacing sound that emphasizes his power.

There is no doubt that the tiger can see us and our vehicle for we have made no attempt to hide. Still he comes toward us. When he reaches the forest undergrowth he thrusts his face into the leaves of a small bush. He pushes another bush down with his shaggy head, then gives a grimace—lips drawn back, tongue out, and teeth showing. He has smelled the scent of another tiger. Immediately he backs up to several trees and bushes and squirts them with his scent. We can smell it clearly. It is not as pungent and catlike a scent as we had expected.

The tiger continues to walk toward us. It is already hot and he is panting. Saliva drips from his chin. When he is about five and a half meters from the car—I measure it with an imaginary tape measure—the tiger stops, looks at us for a few moments, then lies down in the leaflitter. All four of us are gripped with excitement, especially Mohan. There is a kind of joy on his face as well and he keeps saying, "I knew it. I knew it."

The tiger is under a tall tree with large, soft leaves. Its dark gray bark is cracked and fissured both horizontally and vertically, giving it the look of crocodile skin. The tree is *Terminalia tomentosa*, or saja. We name the tiger Saja. Mohan says that the saja tree is the dwelling-place of the great god of the Gond people and when they swear an oath they do it on a saja branch to make it binding.

Saja the tiger is an old male.

His teeth have yellowed and the tip of his upper right canine has broken off. There are nicks out of his small, rounded ears. He is by far the largest tiger we have seen and could weigh more than 250 kilograms. His head is broad with bold, black markings across the top. Scars of old wounds are slashed across his muzzle. Many of his whiskers are broken. His neck ruff, even in his summer coat, is pronounced. It will be majestic in winter. His flanks are thin; he must be hungry.

Saja, Belinda determines, is the same tiger we have seen several times over the last four days. His range covers most of the Kanha meadows as well as those of Banseri at Churi and Rela at the Sulcum River. The tigresses' cubs are most likely his offspring.

Saja yawns several times then flops on his side and dozes off. We ask Mohan what he meant when he said, "I knew it." "Well," he says, "the tiger is very special to the Baiga. Tigers will never harm us even though we spend all our lives in the jungle. Also Baiga get very upset when a tiger is killed. We are not afraid of tigers and they know us. When this tiger came toward you and lay down here, I knew you were just like the Baiga. A tiger will never kill either of you. You have special connections with it."

Seeing first Banseri and then Saja so close and so at ease, all kinds of thoughts come to mind. What exactly is it that makes a tiger a tiger? Why is it the way it is? What forces shaped it to reach predatory perfection and gave it extraordinary colors and patterns, making it the most vivid among mammals? First of all, I suppose it is this way because it is a cat and cats are the most specialized land carnivores. The evolutionary forces that shaped them are all directed toward catching live prey—in the case of the tigers prey sometimes larger than

The tiger Saja, an older but still large and powerful male.

Identifying Tigers

Whenever we see a tiger well, Belinda sketches its facial pattern, in both the right and left profile. These patterns of stripes and squiggles are as sure indications of a tiger's identity as fingerprints are for people. These drawings turn out to be very important. Without them it is at times difficult to tell one tiger from another—to determine, for example, if the tiger near us is the same one we saw two days ago. Even the *mahouts*, who see tigers more often than anyone, often make mistakes about their identity. Tigers can appear very different under different circumstances: thin when hungry, fat when they have just eaten, different colors in the shade or sun, summer or winter. They appear different when angry to when they are relaxed. Only their patterns never change.

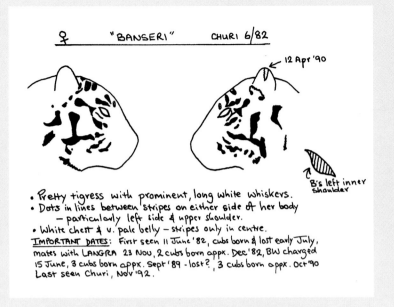

♀   "BANSERI"   CHURI 6/82

12 Apr '90

B's left inner shoulder

• Pretty tigress with prominent, long white whiskers.
• Dots in lines between stripes on either side of her body — particularly left side & upper shoulder.
• White chest & v. pale belly – stripes only in centre.
IMPORTANT DATES: First seen 11 June '82, cubs born & lost early July, mates with LANGRA 23 Nov, 2 cubs born appx. Dec '82, BW charged 15 June, 3 cubs born appx. Sept '89 - lost?, 3 cubs born appx. Oct '90 Last seen Churi, Nov '92.

themselves. Cats cannot supplement their diets with fruit or other vegetable matter as other carnivores such as bears and members of the dog family do. The cats' digestive system can deal only with meat, skin, and bones. Nothing else. They must catch other animals consistently; their specialization enables them to do it ruthlessly and efficiently. These same forces have made the tiger the largest, the most dramatic, and the most mysterious of all the cats—the ultimate cat, the ultimate power in the jungle.

The tiger is a solitary, stalking hunter. With great power in its shoulders, it is fast over a short distance, but it cannot sustain that speed in pursuit of prey as wolves and wild dogs can. A tiger must lie in ambush or stealthily approach its potential prey. The pattern of its fur, so flamboyant in isolation, is entirely suited to this end. Even to human eyes, which are acute among mammals, tigers are difficult to spot in the jungle. Their pattern is almost a perfect match for the grasslands and forest undergrowth where they live. For deer and other hoofed animals, whose vision is not especially sharp, the tiger's pattern makes it virtually invisible, even when fairly close and screened by minimal cover. Only when the tiger is seen moving or is scented can these animals detect their nemesis.

Sight is the tiger's most important sense organ. It can spot prey from a long distance and in almost any light from bright sunshine to all but the darkest night. Cats' eyes are six times more sensitive to low light levels than those of humans. As a

consequence the cats' eyes are large so that they can gather more light. They also have complex muscles in their pupils so that these can open wide when it is dark or close to pinpricks in sunlight.

To gauge their leaps at prey and their high-speed charges through the vegetation, cats need binocular vision. It is almost as good as that of humans; in fact only primates have more accurate binocular vision than cats.

Tigers can hear a wide range of frequencies, both higher and lower than ours. They can pick up the high frequency squeals and squeaks of prey species and the low frequency sounds of their movements through the undergrowth.

Its sense of smell is no help to a hunting tiger. Compared to those of other carnivores such as dogs and bears, a tiger's sense of smell is poorly developed. A good sense of smell requires a long, tapering nose, but cats have short muzzles—they have sacrificed an acute sense of smell for a greater, swifter killing power. The cat's short jaw and well-developed cheek muscles give it an extraordinarily powerful bite. A long nose, and therefore a long jaw, reduces the strength of a dog's bite.

The power of a cat's jaws is reinforced by specialized teeth. The daggerlike canines in both the upper and lower jaws, but especially the upper jaw, are very long and shaped for an effective stabbing bite. When attacking comparatively small prey, such as a chital doe, the tiger will kill it with a bite to the nape of the neck, placing the canines so that they stab be-

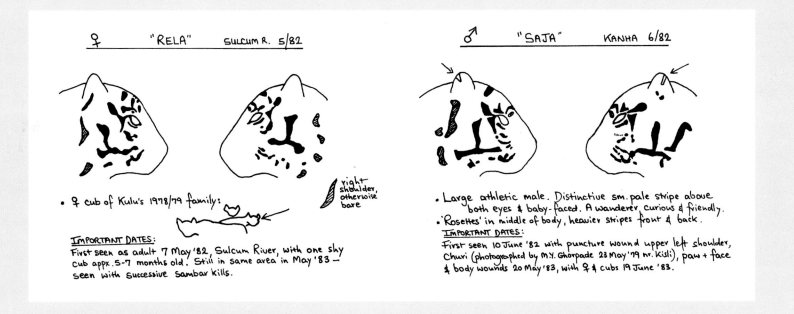

♀   "RELA"   SULCUM R. 5/82

- ♀ cub of Kulu's 1978/79 family:

right shoulder, otherwise bare

IMPORTANT DATES:
First seen as adult 7 May '82, Sulcum River, with one shy cub appx. 5-7 months old. Still in same area in May '83 — seen with successive Sambar kills.

♂   "SAJA"   KANHA 6/82

- Large athletic male. Distinctive sm. pale stripe above both eyes & baby-faced. A wanderer, curious & friendly.
- 'Rosettes' in middle of body, heavier stripes front & back.

IMPORTANT DATES:
First seen 10 June '82 with puncture wound upper left shoulder, Churi (photographed by M.Y. Ghorpade 23 May '79 nr. Kisli), paw + face & body wounds 20 May '83, with ♀ & cubs 19 June '83.

tween two vertebrae and sever the spinal cord. Death is then almost instantaneous—and a quick kill is important to a tiger as thrashing hooves and thrusting antlers or horns can injure it. The tiger's cheek teeth are also specialized. They are long with sharp ridges and act like scissors that cut easily through the toughest skin and the most sinewy meat.

But before a tiger can kill its prey, it must catch it. Here too there are special, feline adaptations. Once a tiger has positioned itself for attack, it needs speed to outrun its prey *and* power to bring it down and kill it. The difficulty is having both speed and power in the same limb. Powerful arms or legs such as you might see in a gorilla are relatively short and heavy with large muscles and are therefore slower. Limbs built for speed, in a deer for instance, are long and lean, so giving a longer stride. While the legs of cats are slightly elongated, these carnivores achieve a lengthening of the stride by having a flexible backbone that can stretch and contract. Cats do not have collarbones and therefore the shoulder blade has freer movement and allows the front limbs to go farther forward—again lengthening the stride and giving more speed. In the tiger the collarbone is reduced to just a small bone that "floats" in the muscle and is not attached to the skeleton. This is the so-called "lucky" bone that was much prized by hunters.

The flexibility of the spine and shoulders is what gives cats their characteristic grace, their sinuous agility and suppleness. In some species it also results in extreme speed. A chee-

tah, for example, can outrun the gazelles on which it preys. The tiger has given away some of this speed for power, which resides mostly in its shoulders and front legs. As a result it is explosively fast over about fifty meters and then has the power to topple, hold, and kill prey that may weigh 100 to 150 kilograms more than itself. It can even lift such heavy animals and drag them into cover.

At the moment of capture two more feline adaptations come into play—one is a mechanical "device," the other a sense organ. In its final leap the tiger strains forward and extends its claws, which had been concealed in sheaths on its toes. The sheaths protect the claws, from being blunted and also reduce the sound of the animal's footfalls during stalking. By extending their claws the tiger's soft, quiet feet are changed into hooks that grab and hold its prey.

As the tiger reaches out to give its fatal bite, it is guided to the most effective spot by its whiskers. These sensory hairs are directed forward at the time of the killing bite. There is a close coordination between the tiger's eyes and the sense of touch from its whiskers.

Despite being the best equipped and most efficient of hunters, life for a tiger is tough. Prey is difficult to bring down. Only about one in twenty attempts at a kill is successful and the prey's hooves, horns, teeth, and quills can inflict incapacitating wounds. Other tigers are always a threat. There is much wear and tear. Canine teeth, the killing instruments, are often chipped or broken. Tigers in the wild are not long-lived. The longest lived tiger in captivity died at twenty-two years of age. In the wild the average life span is much shorter—about twelve to fifteen years.

9 May

Not even the early morning is cool. At 6:00, when we leave the upper cabin on Tara and Bundh Devi, it is already 30 degrees Celsius. The *mahouts* allow the elephants a leisurely pace. We are off to Churi to see if we can find Banseri and her cubs. We have only gone a little way down the hill and entered a small meadow, when Belinda notices spots of blood on the grass and the signs of a large kill having been dragged. At the same time we become aware of vultures flying in low and landing in an area of rocks. The kill is a chital stag, now under a blanket of pushing and shoving vultures. At our approach they stop their quarreling for a moment and look at us—sixty or more long, snakelike, bloodied necks pointing in our direction—then they continue stripping the chital's skeleton.

Banseri is not at the water hole, although there are fresh tracks including those of cubs. We decide to comb the boulder-strewn slope directly below what the *mahouts* assure us is her cave. The vegetation is mostly bamboos, which here on the dry slope have shed all their leaves. One or two bauhinia vines coiled over the rocks add a touch of green. We can hear no alarm calls and there is no sand or mud for footprints.

Belinda sees Banseri first, lying round-bellied and replete between rocks directly below her cave. The tigress lies with

her feet gathered under her. I see a slight movement about fifteen meters behind Banseri. A cub lies sprawled along a horizontal vine and wriggles about trying to get comfortable. Another cub stares down at us from a rock a few meters farther away. They are about the size of Labrador dogs, and half inquisitive, half fearful. But it is hot and the tigers, panting heavily, are not about to move out of their shade. The sun rises higher, shifting the shadows from a gular tree, and Banseri is forced to seek a cooler place. After yawning several times she gets up slowly, walks up the slope, and disappears into the coolness of her cave. The cubs, a male and a female, follow her, also in slow motion. We are pretty sure they will not move till the afternoon.

Late afternoon is even more oppressive. Clouds and humidity make the heat less bearable. Banseri and her cubs lie across a slab of flat rock at the entrance to their cave. Towers of black, gray, and white clouds boil up and intermingle directly above us. Now and again the sun shines through a window of blue sky. The tigers sit up, face into the wind that has sprung up, and sniff the rapidly cooling air. Dead leaves are blown noisily across the hillside. A few heavy drops of rain splatter on crackling dry litter. Thunder rumbles in the distance. The first premonsoon storm has arrived, almost. After these few drops, the rain and wind cease. Thankfully the coolness remains and the tigers no longer pant.

Banseri leaves her cave and walks down toward us. When she is about halfway the cubs race after her, scattering the dry leaves. Banseri stops and flops down in that loose, supple way of tigers. The cubs pounce on her. The young female climbs on top of her mother and bounces up and down on her, while the male lies on his back under Banseri's chin and reaches out

for her whiskers with his paws. Banseri rolls over and briefly hugs the female cub to her chest. The young leap to their feet and, bounding and rolling in a ball of striped bodies, come closer and closer. The *mahouts* make the elephants stand as still as possible. The cubs have seen the elephants from a distance quite often, I imagine, but they have never been this close. As if suddenly aware of their recklessness, they stop and stare at us. They look back at their mother, but she is lying down again and takes no notice. Another quick look at us and the cubs run back and lie close to Banseri. She rolls over onto her back, letting the slight breeze cool her underside. Our hearts beat faster. Will the cubs suckle? As far as we know this has never been observed in the wild. They do not.

When the light begins to fade, Banseri walks off into the forest, the cubs close on her heels. In the subdued light the white spots on the back of her ears stand out brightly. We have often wondered if these have some function. Could it be they are there as beacons for the cubs to follow? It has also been suggested that they signal threat, for when a tiger is about to attack it will swivel its ears so that the white spots point forwards.

On our way back we look in at the waterhole where, to our utter surprise, we see a tiger drinking. Banseri walked off in the opposite direction, so it cannot be her. It is Saja. We are apprehensive about seeing him here. Will he kill the cubs as Snarl did a few years ago or is he more tolerant?

Saja, as usual, ignores the elephants and having drunk his fill crosses a small meadow and walks off into the sal forest, away from Banseri's fortress.

Purely by chance we catch up with Banseri again. She is alone. She moves with great care in a crouching position. She takes a few quick steps, then freezes. She is stalking something hidden from our view. After a few more slinking, cautious steps, she puts her tail straight up and explodes into the grass. There are no alarm calls. When we reach her, Banseri has a chital doe in her jaws. She bit it in the nape of the neck and the deer is already dead. After a few minutes Banseri releases her grip on her kill's neck, grabs it by the throat, and carries it off as though it were as light as a feather.

It has been a memorable day: to see the cubs for the first time; to see Banseri and Saja in the same area; to see Banseri make a kill—and all of it only a short elephant ride from our cabin. It makes good sense, therefore, to concentrate our filming efforts on these four tigers.

28 May

Over the last several days we have had glimpses of Banseri at Churi, which culminated in yesterday's unforgettable meeting when she suckled her cubs—which we have related in the Preface. We have also met Saja several times. He usually comes over toward us for a closer look, whether we are on an elephant or in a vehicle.

From what we know of his movements, Saja should be back on the central meadows today and in this heat we expect him to be at, or in, one of the three water holes remaining in the creeks. We find him in the second, a malodorous puddle just big enough to hold him. Flame of the forest trees and some tall grass shade and hide him. The heaving of Saja's

Banseri kills a chital stag and drags it into cover.

ribcage as he pants sets off waves across the pool. The elephants, like all of us, feel the heat and we do not stay long. Luckily Saja is near a narrow trail where we can just drive our Jeep. To keep him in view, we must sit in the full sun. We shade ourselves and our equipment under large umbrellas, but even so the lenses of our cameras are soon too hot to touch. As so often happens these days, big clouds build up and we can hear a distant rumble of thunder.

By midafternoon Saja drags himself slowly and stiffly out of the pool. He walks to a small shaded area of short grass right in front of the Jeep. It is only now that we realize he is injured. Small trickles of blood ooze down his face, shoulders, and left front paw. He has a deep cut across one toe, a laceration down his upper lip, cuts—such as would be made by another tiger's claws—across his right shoulder. Small holes puncture the skin of his chest, throat, and left shoulder. Again and again he licks a wound on the underside of his foot, which seems to be the most serious. They are all fresh but superficial wounds. Did Saja fight with another tiger or did he try to catch a porcupine?

Injuries attended to, Saja rolls onto his back, about three meters from us, and soon dozes. Every now and again he shakes and jerks his injured paw into the air to keep the flies off. When the clouds come over, the thunder crashes, the wind whips through the trees and grass, and the rain pelts down on his belly, Saja stays as he is, not even twitching an ear—while we try to control our umbrellas, which have been turned inside out by the wind. Soon the sun is out again.

29 May

Belinda has a hunch this morning that tiger tracking will be fruitful. We make an unpromising start. On and on we go without hearing any alarm or seeing a single track. At Churi a troop of langurs is doing acrobatics in and out of Banseri's cave. Near the water hole two red dogs trot off into the grass. According to Mahavir and Gunpath this is not a good sign, for tigers go out of their way to avoid the wild dogs. Tigers do keep their distance from large packs of dogs that may number over twenty, but two dogs? On we go. Nothing. Even Mohan, the keenest tracker, says there is no point in going on. We decide to press on just a little longer. Then there is a chital call from up ahead. Belinda, Mohan, and Gunpath on Bundh Devi go one way while Mahavir and I go another on Tara. We

find Saja almost immediately, lying replete on a bed of leaflitter. Belinda finds Banseri with one of her cubs about 200 meters away. Banseri has a sambar kill several days old. When we go over to her, she is eating it. Banseri cuts off big chunks of meat with her cheek teeth and bolts them down. The second cub joins her. With stomachs distended the two young lie in a patch of dense shade. But does Banseri know Saja is so near? Is he a threat to her cubs?

After about twenty minutes Banseri stops eating and drags her kill closer to the cubs. She rakes dry leaves over it with her paws till it is completely covered. Lying down beside the stinking, fly-covered carcass, she thoroughly cleans herself. She cleans each toe very carefully, licking away any meat that might have adhered to her claws. She draws her paw, licked wet with saliva, across her face and behind her ears.

Heavy footsteps on the dry leaves approach. Saja comes striding along, takes hold of the carcass, and, surrounded by a buzzing cloud of flies, drags it a few meters away and finishes it off. Neither Banseri nor her cubs react in any way. The four tigers obviously know each other well.

In the late afternoon Banseri, closely followed by the cubs, walks over to the shade of a banyan tree. The cubs play perfunctorily but it is still too hot to be really energetic. Saja follows a few minutes later. He groans with the discomfort of overeating as he lies down. He pants incessantly in quick, shallow breaths. One of the cubs goes up to him, rubs itself against his side, lies down with its head on Saja's shoulder, and is soon asleep. The other cub, the female, lies against her mother. Belinda's hunch was right, as it so often is.

Postscript

After we finished filming in Kanha, in July 1983, we had sporadic reports about Banseri and Saja. In 1986, when we were in Australia, we received a letter from Belinda's father saying that Saja had been badly wounded in a fight with a younger male on the Kanha meadows. Four months later forest guards found Saja's emaciated body a long way south of his old territory.

Shortly after returning to live in India, Belinda visited Kanha. There on 12 April 1990 she found Banseri with three small cubs at her old cave at Churi. The last time Belinda saw the tigress was in August 1992 when she watched her kill a chital stag on the meadows just below Churi. That was the last time anyone saw Banseri.

[C H A P T E R   1 5]

THE MONSOON COMES TO KANHA

In June the heat in Kanha does not abate but the humidity slowly increases. The meadows are brown and tinder dry. The chital and barasingha have difficulty in finding nutritious grazing. We see Banseri, Rela, Saja, and the cubs regularly at the Churi and Sulcum water holes where they lie lethargically in the water for hours on end.

We build a well-camouflaged blind about ten meters from one of the last few water holes in the Sulcum River and plan to spend several days there to observe the animals that come to drink.

14 June

On our way to the river at first light, we stop the Jeep where the track emerges from the forest and enters the meadows. We usually pause here to listen to the sounds of the jungle.

In the distance, then closer and closer, we hear a plaintive call "pee-pee-piu, pee-pee-piu." The bird whose song it is lands in a small bush. It is a mostly black bird with a crest and a long tail. Its underside is white. Belinda and I smile in delight at this appearance of the pied-crested cuckoo. This is the first sign that the monsoon is imminent, that the oppression of summer is about to be lifted. The cuckoo is the unfailing harbinger of the rains. The bird migrates from Africa just in advance of the southwest monsoon and is perhaps propelled by its winds. The rains are at most a week away.

The blind is a metal cage covered in light cloth and camouflaged with grass and leaves. There are peepholes and openings for the camera lens on all four sides. For most of the day it is shaded by Arjuna trees. The pool is only a few meters across but is quite deep. In the early twilight a few frogs jump around the muddy edges. A small fish leaps and splashes. With the camera on its tripod, a stool with a large soft cushion, some food, and lots of water I am ready to spend the day in what will undoubtedly become a hot box.

First to arrive are three racket-tailed drongos who land among the flowers of a gardenia tree on the far side of the water hole. They sing for a few minutes giving perfect imitations of the calls of a serpent eagle as part of their repertoire. Other birds closely inspect the blind and hop all over it. A black-naped blue flycatcher peers back at me through one of the peepholes. We are literally eyeball to eyeball. A shama sings from just a meter away, its voice deafening at that close range.

The sun rises above the treeline and it is hot. A pair of white-breasted kingfishers bathes by dashing into the water, briefly submerging, and flying to their favorite perch. There

A threatening monsoon sky over the Kanha meadows. The grass has withered under the summer sun but the trees, with their deep roots, have put on new leaf, anticipating the monsoon.

they fluff and preen themselves with such vigor that their exertions must cancel out the cooling effect of the water. A procession of other birds comes and goes—coucals, doves, several species of cuckoo, an oriole, tree pies. An immaculate blackwinged kite, pure white with gray and black on its wings, looks at the blind through large, ruby-red eyes. But as with the other birds the blind causes it no concern. Shikras, a kind of goshawk, drink with their wings held high above their heads. Some bathe by walking into the water and just sitting down.

A pair of jungle crows and their two fledglings have taken up residence at the pool and bathe frequently by wildly and noisily splashing about.

From the peephole on my right I see a barking deer cautiously approaching through the bamboos. Every few steps it stops, listens, and tests the air for the scent of predators. In its nervousness it constantly licks its face with its long, prehensile tongue.

Downstream, not far away, a tiger roars. The barking deer freezes, one forefoot off the ground. Langurs, sambar, and chital, still hidden from view, give alarm calls. The barking deer brays its call, surprisingly loud for such a small species, and dashes off, scattering the babblers at the edge of the pool. The alarm dies down and there are no further tiger roars. More and more birds, untroubled by the commotion of the mammals, come to drink and to bathe. A checkered keelback snake slithers from a small cavity and slides into the pool. A few minutes later it emerges with a small fish in its jaws. The snake catches two more fish in quick succession. It probably dredges them from the mud at the bottom of the pool. If it is not careful it will become a meal itself for one of the crested serpent eagles that haunt the water hole.

I am so engrossed in filming the snake, that I do not hear the footsteps on the dry leaves till they are quite near. With my heart beating faster I look through the peephole. It is not a tiger approaching the blind, but a sambar doe. Back at the pool three more sambar, a female, her young fawn, and a yearling male, have materialized out of the bamboo and stand under the gardenia tree. For about fifteen minutes the deer stand there, muscles taut, all senses alert. Finally the tension goes out of them. Relaxed, they slowly walk to the water's edge. All four jungle crows land on the largest sambar and pick parasites from the corners of her eyes, her ears, tail, knees, hooves, and back. A fledgling lands on the deer's head with one foot on each ear. It goes through all kinds of gyrations trying to keep its balance as the sambar twitches its ears.

The tiger must have moved on, for langurs and chital approach the water hole. The monkeys, a troop of about twenty-five, come tumbling down the bank. The chital approach the water with great caution and anxiety. At this time of year every water hole is a potential deathtrap for them.

The langurs are not rushed. In twos and threes they sprawl at the water's edge and with their faces in the water right up to their nostrils, they drink. A female with an infant at her breast submerges the young and drinks for such a long time that I begin to think the baby might drown. Once the entire troop has had enough to drink it disperses over the rocks.

Close to midday a group of jungle babblers, starling-sized birds with ragged pale brown plumage, comes out of

Sambar and chital drink at a water hole in the Sulcum River.

the shade and lies in the hot sun. With feathers fluffed, panting with their beaks open, tongues out, and pale eyes staring at the sun in a rigid pose, the birds look demented. Crows, coucals, and mynas also lie on the hot sand as if hypnotized by the sun. Do they sunbathe to make life too hot for feather parasites?

By midafternoon the day slowly cools. Four whitenecked storks, with fluffy necks and large, heavy-lidded, sad-looking eyes probe the pool for fish and frogs, and perhaps a keelback snake. The kingfisher dashes in among the storks' red legs and catches a fish.

When a shaft of light pierces the forest and lights the water hole a herd of about twenty-five chital comes cautiously along the riverbed and moves to the water. They drink, pressed tightly together in a line, legs braced for a quick get-away. With the sun on their spotted, warm brown coats and their delicate elegance, the line of drinking chital is one of the most beautiful sights in all the jungle. As if to enhance the effect, a male paradise flycatcher flutters down onto a branch directly above them.

When I finally leave at dusk, bats flit over the water surface and drink on the wing. Who knows what dramas will occur here during the night. Will the tiger kill a chital or sambar coming to drink?

Throughout the night, at the upper cabin, we hear the pied-crested cuckoo's call. It is a haunting sound that appealed to the romantic nature of the Moghul emperors in the sixteenth and seventeenth centuries. Akbar noted that the call "makes love's unhealed wounds bleed anew." Jehangir referred to the cuckoo's "soul-piercing lament." And when will the rains come?

19 June

We have spent several more days in the blind. Most mornings there were fresh tiger pug marks around the pool but we never actually saw a tiger come to drink, although some days, by the sound of their roars and the alarm they spread, we knew they were close.

More and more pied-crested cuckoos have arrived. There is an influx of rain quail whose whistling calls of "which-which" are heard all over the meadows. Another call for rain. The humidity has increased and high clouds drift in from the southwest.

We are at the Sulcum River to remove our blind. There

are no fresh tiger pug marks. Before taking it down, we walk downstream to see what has happened to the only other remaining water hole we know of. It is muddy but there is no standing water left. When we return to the blind, there are fresh tracks of three tigers—a male, a female, and an adolescent—around the pool and in the sand near the blind. The blind itself has been scent-marked by one of the tigers. We did not hear them or see them, nor have we heard any alarm calls even though we were only a few hundred meters away.

21 and 22 June

Dark clouds advance from the southwest—an almost black blanket that rolls over and envelops the hills. There is no thunder or lightning and no hurricane wind, just a gentle breeze. Rain comes gradually. First a drizzle, then bigger drops, and finally sheets of water fall out of the still air. Chital run out of the forest and stand in the rain. On and on it pours. By late afternoon the ground is saturated. Slow trickles slide down the slopes and percolate into the creeks and rivers. For a while the sand of the Sulcum's bed absorbs the water, but eventually here too a thin trickle runs into the water hole where we had our blind. The big drops of rain beat the water surface into a froth. A lone pond heron stands beside the pool, water streaming from the tip of its beak.

The constant hiss and roar of the rain on the Upper Cabin's roof and on the surrounding trees lets up about an hour after dark. The rain slows to a gentle drizzle and then stops. It is only now that we become aware of the cacophony of frog voices in a newly formed pond at the bottom of the hill. It seems very close. Carrying a flashlight with a strong beam, we walk down to it. The sound is so loud that it seems closer than it really is. The soaring dark trunks of the sal trees are sprinkled with fireflies.

At the pond the sound of hundreds of frogs of many species—each with its own "song"—is so loud that Belinda and I cannot hear each other talk. We can only point and use sign language. In the middle of the pond, which is a depression in the forest floor about four meters across, sit five male bullfrogs. Their urge to spawn has turned them from a nondescript browny green to a bright yellow. Every time they utter their booming calls, blue vocal sacs swell at their throats. Three smaller, species float in the water, twittering and quacking as great balloons pulsate beneath their chins.

These vocal sacs act as resonators. So strong are the waves of sound and so taut the vocal sacs that water droplets bounce off them and waves ripple across the water with every call. Each male frog is intent on out-shouting its neighbors so as to attract a female. A few couples have joined and are spawning.

Rain continues intermittently throughout the night. At dawn the forest still drips, but the rain has stopped. Only the bullfrogs and toads are still calling at the pond, which has become part of a large sheet of shallow water. All the little nullas and gullies that have been dry for more than six months are running to overflowing. Clouds, detached from the general blanket, swirl around the hills. Wisps of mist lie sinuously over the meadows and trail into the forest. It is beautifully cool.

Wherever there is standing water, even right out in the open meadows, bright yellow male bullfrogs are calling. Some clasp even larger gray-green females. In one tree-lined pond, scores of the frogs splash and jostle in a thunderous chorus. A pair of mongooses has killed a yellow bullfrog, dragged it onto a termite mound, and is eating frog legs. A honey-buzzard swoops down and grabs another bullfrog, which screams loudly—silencing, for a few moments, the courting males.

Sunrise is not perceptible in this gray, wet world. Already there is a flush of green on the meadows. The true monsoon rains have banished the dry, cracked earth, the bleached brittle grasses, the extreme heat, the scarcity of water, the tiger's ambush at the few water holes, for another year. By midmorning the rain sets in again.

24 June

Over the last few days the skies have been gray and the rain, while not constant, has been frequent with some heavy downpours. Last night the clouds cleared. In the skies washed clean by the monsoon, the stars sparkled with a clarity we have rarely seen here. The frogs, after their first night of passion and fervent song, have fallen silent. This morning the

After the first heavy rains of the monsoon, countless frogs emerge to breed. Courting male Indian bullfrogs turn bright yellow and make their voices resonate through blue vocal sacs.

birds regain their voices. As the sun rises above the horizon all of Kanha—the forests, the meadows, the *chattans*—sparkles with dew and is scented with the aroma of growing plants and damp earth. The short grass meadows' new growth looks like an even carpet of green velvet. Chital come pouring out of the forest, running and skipping as never before. Their warm colors glow in the early sun.

A pair of jackals with three half-grown pups comes trotting out of a thicket of chindi palms and inspects the herd of chital with an eye to taking one of the small fawns. The male jackal is muscular with dark golden fur and a luxuriantly bushy tail. The female is smaller, grayer, paler. She is solicitous of her pups, licking them and playing with them. Not far away an all-male troop of langurs sits on termite mounds, drying their fur in the sun. One of the larger monkeys slowly climbs off his perch and casually walks toward the jackals. When he is near one of the pups he charges after it. The two run in big circles over the meadow—scattering the chital. When the pup begins to tire and the langur is gaining on it, the male jackal intervenes and chases the langur at full speed. He is much faster than the monkey, catches up with it, and nips it on the thigh. The langur leaps into a small tree. The jackal stands beneath it. As soon as the jackal turns and walks away the langur jumps down and slaps the ground with one hand and grimaces, taunting the jackal. He turns around and runs at the langur, who climbs back up the tree, just high enough to be out of reach. Up and down, back and forth they go. Finally the jackal trots back to his family—followed by the langur for a short distance—and they trot off into the forest.

All the barasingha stags have shed their antlers and both males and females are in their tawny summer coats. Already the stags are growing new antlers, but they are no more than knobbly orange stumps.

The meadows, at this time of year, offer the best grazing. Many animals such as gaur, sambar, even most chital, are seduced into leaving the forest. This morning an unruly mob of

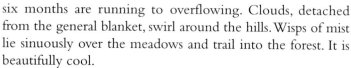

Gaur, or Indian bison, come out of the forest to feed on the fresh new grass on the meadows.

fourteen wild sows and their collective thirty tiny striped piglets come swarming from among the sal trees. My first, rather incongruous, thought is, Will those rough, tough animals soil and tear up the meadows' immaculate carpet?

When the sun is still low but already warm, what look like plumes of smoke waft from termite mounds and from holes in the ground. These are the alates, the reproductive male and female termites, pouring out of their nests on gauze wings for their one and only nuptial flight. Bee-eaters, bulbuls, shrikes, pied-crested cuckoos, and a host of other birds fly after the insects and catch them on the wing. They make little impression on the swarms and soon the taller grass blades are alive with alates shimmering their golden wings among the silver sparkle of the dew. Male and female termites find each other and descend to the soft ground where they shed their wings, mate, and perhaps become founding kings and queens of new colonies.

In the forest the sensation of walking in greenness is even greater than on the meadows. The sun filtering through the new leaves, especially those of the bamboos, spreads a muted green luminescence. Cicadas' shrill voices compete with those of the orioles, drongos, babblers, and other birds. A scarlet minivet, a stain of bright red, bathes in drops of dew clinging to the leaves of a shrub. Red millipedes walk up the stems of the bamboos, now also a vivid green. The leaflitter is dark with a plum-colored bloom and is soft and supple under our feet. A giant orange weevil, more than five centimeters long, lands on the leaf of a small teak tree. In a patch of wet sand a line of tiger footprints leads to the river. They are Saja's.

After just a few monsoon days it is already difficult to remember the rigors of summer—when the bamboos were bare, the meadows were brown and barren looking, the leaflitter crackled, and the light was harsh and burning. From brittle harshness to gentle greenness in three days.

All the life, plant and animal, that had been in retreat from the assault of summer is on the march again in the monsoon's hothouse.

25 June

The elephants will soon retire to a place deep inside the jungle where they will remain, without having to do much work, until the park reopens at the beginning of November. Before they leave for their deserved rest, we go tiger tracking for a few days. We persuaded the park management to let Shivaji come to Kanha for this period.

Top: a giant weevil struggles to gain a foothold on the smooth leaf of a teak tree. Bottom: many kinds of invertebrates erupt out of the ground—like these velvet mites eating a winged reproductive termite.

This morning we meet six of the elephants at the edge of a small meadow surrounded by forest. The plan is that the *mahouts* on their elephants will thoroughly search the meadow and if they find a tiger one of them will come back to fetch us.

Normally we do not walk out into the grass, even when it is only knee-high as it is here, in case we accidentally stumble on a tiger. Should the tiger be on its prey or have small cubs, it would more than likely attack. But the six elephants, walking abreast, combed the small meadow without seeing a tiger. Above us a troop of langurs is feeding in a tall tree with a comprehensive view of the stretch of grass. Chital graze at the far end. Both species are at peace and we have faith in their ability to detect tigers. So I pick up a camera and walk toward a small grove of trees where orchids are flowering in cascades of pink, while Belinda sits on a rock and watches the langurs. I have to cross a small nulla. As I climb up the far bank, when my eyes are about level with the ground, a tiger raises its head above the grass no more than two meters from me—a blaze of orange among the green. For a few seconds we look into each other's eyes. Before I have time to think what to do, the tiger gives a coughing kind of roar into my face, leaps up, and bounds off—in the same direction as the elephants. I am pretty sure it is Banseri. Luckily her cubs are not with her and she runs in the opposite direction from where Belinda is. The elephants must have passed within a few meters of her.

Minutes later Sabir returns excitedly on Shivaji and says they have found a tigress. And, he says, she came running from behind them! We explain to Sabir what happened as we climb onto the elephant's ample back and go into the forest. We catch up with the other elephants and Belinda transfers to Bundh Devi.

We find Banseri, for it is indeed she, lying on the topmost rock of a small *chattan*. She and the rock are swathed in bamboo. The only place from which we can film her is a narrow ledge very close and slightly below her. Belinda somehow manages to put the large tripod in place. Banseri is unconcerned and lies asleep on her side with her paws dangling over the rock's edge. Sabir slowly and quietly guides Shivaji into place. It is difficult for the elephant, for there is only just enough room for three of his feet. But he stands like a rock. I put the camera on the tripod and begin filming. As I look over the camera at Banseri, she suddenly sits up, eyes blazing. With lips curled back she hisses and spits at me and makes a slashing movement with her unsheathed claws. She gathers her legs under herself as if ready to spring. Does she recognize me from our earlier encounter? I quickly look at Sabir but he, while very watchful, remains calm. I continue filming. The moment passes. Banseri flops onto her rock again and goes back to sleep. She does not even lash her tail in annoyance.

28 June

Long periods of heavy rain interspersed with breaks of stinging sunshine continue. The ground is saturated and soft. In the forest, sal seeds have germinated into thick jungles of seedlings. Wild rice and other grasses have almost reached knee-height on the meadows. Chital have gathered in huge herds of up to a thousand individuals.

After initially being captivated by the chital's elegance and beauty, I have taken them rather for granted, and thought of them as the dullards of the jungle, merely the food of tigers and leopards. During these days of the superherds on the rejuvenated meadows, I realize how shortsighted I have been. I now appreciate the spectacle of hundreds of the deer galloping and courting in high spirits, but also the intriguing interactions between individuals.

Yesterday the wide bed of the Sulcum, which still flows in only a trickle, was so densely crammed with chital that we could not see the grass and sand, only the solid press of hundreds of deer swirling about. They took fright at something and leapt the two meter high riverbank in a fountain of graceful arching bodies. On and on they washed over the bank. On top of it there was a crush to avoid some obstruction. The chital bounced off each other in their leaping rush—fawns, does, and heavy-antlered stags.

This afternoon we sit in our Jeep at the edge of the meadow between the Upper Cabin and Churi. A huge herd of chital emerges from the forest and moves slowly toward us as the animals graze. Some of the largest stags walk through the herd, holding their heads high, constantly licking their lips as if in agitation and nervousness. They search for does in estrus. Frequently they stop and give their labored, hoarse rutting calls, "huhh, huhh, huhh." Several stags on the edge of the forest rise on their hind legs and rub their faces in the leaves of trees, marking them with the scent from glands on their face.

Duos of stags, well matched with similar-sized antlers, go through ritualized combat trying to settle their dominance without engaging in an actual fight. The two walk parallel to each other, heads held low, antlers lying along their backs, ears down, eyes rolling so that much of their whites are showing, nostrils flared. They look slightly sinister with the hair on their necks and backs standing on end. After a few stiff-legged steps they stop and paw the ground, sending up arcs of grass and soil. A few more steps and they violently thrash a bush with upward thrusts of their antlers. Usually the less dominant stag will turn away and walk off. But two adversaries in the center of the herd slowly, threateningly, face each other and raise their heads, signaling their intention for a direct attack. They charge head to head. Their antlers clash in a loud report. With muscles on their hindquarters straining, they push back and forth. They disengage, then charge in again using their antlers like rapiers. Each tries to injure the other with the sharp points and at the same time to parry the thrusts of his opponent. One of the two finally runs off, out of the herd.

Banseri snarled at me after I met her at close range while out on foot.

the subdued light the reddishness of their fur stands out. Keeping a wary eye on the dogs the chital return to their grazing but they stay bunched together and keep their tails raised.

The dogs stop playing. All of them stand up and after a few moments' inspection of the herd canter toward it. As one the chital run, their hooves drumming across the meadow. They do not yet move at a full gallop, more an easy lope, keeping a constant distance between themselves and the dogs. They still give no alarm calls.

The dogs spread out behind the herd and change into a fast run. Now the chital go at a gallop. We keep up along one of the roads. A chital doe with a gaping wound on her shoulder, no doubt the result of an earlier attack, lags behind. She steps among some bushes and stands perfectly still, hoping the dogs will run by in their pursuit of the herd. Her stratagem does not work. The dogs make straight for her. She runs again but her wound has impaired her speed.

The fight is not for the possession of a harem of does, as it would be for most species of deer, but for dominance within the mixed herd. The dominant males are the ones that mate most frequently, though not exclusively. The males are so preoccupied with their rut and strut that they are less vigilant than the females. Tigers and leopards catch significantly more stags than does.

Without giving any kind of alarm, no foot stamping, no calls, the superherd suddenly bunches together into a gigantic spotted ball. With their tails raised, showing their white undersides, all the chital, even the most amorous males, look intently toward the forest.

A pack of eleven wild dogs comes trotting out of the undergrowth, their pink tongues lolling from between strong white teeth. For a while they watch the chital, who stare back at them. Many of the dogs are playful subadults. They soon roll about like overgrown pups while the adults lie down to rest. Their flanks are thin, so they have not eaten recently. In

The dogs overtake her. One grabs her by the nose, others tear at her flanks, one of the subadults has her by the throat. She is down and eviscerated within seconds. Ten minutes later only a few bones remain. There is nothing left for the jackal

The red dogs, or dhole, are relentless hunters of the forest. Even the tiger gives them a wide berth.

The Sulcum River dries almost completely during summer (opposite page), but quickly flows again after monsoon rains (right).

that comes trotting up. All of it has happened in silence.

For most of the year the wild dogs remain deep in the forest. When the chital mass on the meadows at the breaking of the monsoon the dogs emerge in the open to pursue their most numerous prey.

★ ★ ★

There are many recorded instances where a pack of wild dogs has driven a tiger off its kill and some reports of wild dogs killing tigers. Zoologists think that direct attacks on tigers by red dogs are very rare and are usually disputes over a kill that have got out of hand. Red dogs are not active hunters of tigers. However, there is one eyewitness account of a pack of about thirty dogs attacking a tiger. In the fight the tiger killed twelve of the dogs before he himself was killed and eaten.

A chital, or spotted deer, stag in velvet. He cannot use his antlers in combat while they are in velvet.

★ ★ ★

For Kanha's wild animals the hard times are over. Food is plentiful again. The heat has relented. The rains will continue, on and off, till the end of September. For the next six months the jungles will be benevolent places of plenty.

After another week or so the superherds of chital will break up. The tigers will disperse, away from the creeks and rivers, and will be at their most elusive. The elephants are already at their rest camp. Any day excessively heavy rain can come in from the southwest, flooding rivers, sweeping away bridges, and undermining roads. We could be marooned for weeks. Our chances of seeing tigers in Kanha will be nonexistent until the park reopens after the monsoon. It is time to see what is happening in Ranthambhore.

[CHAPTER 16]

ABU THE SUPERTIGER AND RANTHAMBHORE'S GOLDEN AGE

Ranthambhore Tiger Reserve— 21 August

There is a high thin cloud that diffuses the sun to a bright yet shadowless light on this monsoon day. Belinda has stopped the Jeep on a track on top of a ridge about a kilometer from Rajbagh. She thinks it a good place to see a tiger. She has an at times uncanny instinct about that. On our right, totally unexpected for there have been no alarm calls, a tiger materializes out of the green. His coat is a brilliant yellow-orange. When he sees us he stops and looks directly at us, not threateningly but with curiosity, his ears pricked and turned toward the front. Not slowly or cautiously, as is usual with tigers when they approach something unfamiliar, but boldly, he walks toward the open Jeep. No matter how long and how often you have been watching tigers, an approach like that raises a flicker, not so much of fear for I have never felt real fear in the jungle, but of excitement about what may happen next. Four meters from the Jeep the tiger stops and again looks us straight in the eyes. He is a powerful yet athletic mature male without the extraheavy muscles that make some older males slow and ponderous. In his summer pelt he is sleek, lacking the shaggy neck ruff he may have in winter. He yawns in our faces, displaying enormous canines, walks on, and vanishes behind a curtain of weeping dhauk branches. Belinda got enough photographs of his face to prepare an identity card for him. We call him Abu after a friend.

18 February

It's winter and Ranthambhore has changed its colors to gold and silver with a tinge of purple on the dhauk trees. A few touches of green remain around the lakes. It is cold this morning with frost on the grasses and other ground plants. The clear skies, however, promise a warm day. We drive slowly along the trail beneath the fort, now looking dark and forbidding against the reddening sky. All the familiar birds from flycatchers to woodpeckers and from storks to geese are around us. The proximity of so many trusting animals is a great lift to our spirits.

When we reach Malik Talao, the furthest lake, the sun spills its warmth over the horizon. The yellow tall grass drips with the melting rime. There is no sign whatever of any deer or wild pigs, which usually congregate here. It seems likely that a tiger has caused the evacuation and remains hidden in the tall grass. We drive to a vantage point to watch and to listen. Tree pies congregate in a small ber tree in the middle of a patch of grass and look intently at something below them. Searching through binoculars we see just a tiger's tail, lashing in annoyance.

Slowly we drive toward the tree. When we are seated in the completely open Jeep, the grass reaches above our heads. Under the tree the grass is shorter and we see the tigress with a freshly killed yearling chital. To get a clear view of her we must creep just a little closer. She takes exception to this and comes rushing out, hissing and snarling, her perfect canines bared. Belinda, who is driving, anticipates the charge and takes a few photographs. When about six meters from us the tigress stops, stares at us for a few seconds, and retires to her kill. She takes no further notice of us.

This meeting with a tiger on our first day back in Ranthambhore augurs well for our filming prospects. While we love the forests and tigers of Kanha, the dense cover makes it difficult to see the tiger for long, uninterrupted periods. Also we can only keep the elephants out for four or five hours at a time. Ranthambhore's habitat, being in the semiarid zone, is more open and the terrain is for the most part negotiable by Jeep. Tigers are more easily seen here and once found it is often possible to stay with them all day. There are many aspects of the tiger's lives we could not see in Kanha but especially the stalking and striking down of prey. We have come to Ranthambhore for that.

We call the tigress who rushed us Links because the black markings at the base of her tail resemble links in a chain.

20 February

At the western end of Jogi Mahal Lake is a ravine half hidden under a canopy of giant fig trees laden with fruit. We stop to film some monkeys eating the figs. The langurs' hands seem as cold as ours for they are unusually clumsy. I have gone only a few steps when a peacock giving his alarm call, "kok, kok, kok, kok," explodes out of the undergrowth. A tiger must be nearby. We quickly jump back into the Jeep. Belinda drives slowly to where the undergrowth opens out. A tiger lies regally on a rock about thirty meters away. It is a male, and Belinda soon works

out that we have seen him before, but only once. He is the same tiger who came so unnervingly close during the monsoon in the hills about five kilometers east of here. Without Belinda's drawings of his facial markings we would never have recognized him. He is now thickly furred with a pronounced ruff. Even his color seems to have changed—he looks more orange and less yellow in the rays of the early sun. This is Abu.

After looking at us benignly for a few minutes, Abu yawns prodigiously. Twice more he yawns then slowly, lazily, he gets up and stretches. He walks toward us. When he is only a few meters from the Jeep he turns down a bouldery slope and disappears into the ravine.

Soon the sounds of cracking bones and of shearing teeth cutting through tough skin comes from a clump of bushes hidden from our view by a rock outcrop. Abu is on a kill. He had left his hiding place, scaring the peacock, to see if we were a threat to his prey.

We assume he does not regard us as such. Belinda maneuvers the Jeep down the bouldery slope, squeezing the small vehicle between rocks and trees and coaxing it down amazing drops. The bottom of the ravine is open, almost parklike, with green grass and shrubs under the spreading trees. Beneath the largest shrub lies Abu. He looks at us over his kill, a chital stag. A shaft of sunlight catches his face. His eyes glitter and blood drips from his jaw. Suddenly he does not look so benign. Jammed as we are between rocks, we cannot possibly make a quick getaway. We can but wait. Slowly Abu returns to his meal.

This small pocket of forest is full of animals and despite the big predator's presence all is calm and peaceful. A party of langur monkeys is feeding nearby. Many are on the ground and the adolescents play their roughhouse games all around. A male magpie robin, plumaged in shining black and immaculate

We first see Abu the supertiger in a dhauk forest during the monsoon.

white, sits on the chital carcass and snaps up a fly here and there. Parakeets converse in quiet voices as they feed on the figs, occasionally dropping a half-eaten fruit on our heads. A coppersmith hammers out his song. Peafowl scratch noisily in the leaflitter. Unless the tiger is perceived to be hunting he is ignored rather than feared.

But then a mongoose peers over the ravine's edge. Its pink nose twitches and its intense, intelligent brown eyes take in every detail. Squirming between rocks, running and leaping among the boulders then pausing, the mongoose moves closer and closer to the tiger's prey; the scent of meat drawing it inexorably forward. The mongoose reaches the place where the chital was actually killed and licks the blood that has pooled in some leaves. Abu has long since finished eating and lies on his side, panting from the quantity he has eaten. His ears twitch; he can hear the mongoose's approach. A few me-

ters from the kill the small animal jumps on a log and stares hard at the tiger. The mongoose approaches closer but hearing the pitter patter on the dry leaves Abu raises his head. The mongoose runs off. Time and again this scene repeats itself. Finally Abu gets tired of this and ignores the approaching footfalls. Just as the mongoose is about to sink his teeth into the chital, however, Abu leaps up with a roar and dashes after the pestering animal. The mongoose runs straight in front of our Jeep, Abu leaps after him his tail almost brushing the bumper. Abu stops about three meters away, turns around, and snarls at us as well.

With Abu's roar and charge the peace is shattered. Monkeys race up the trees and now bark and chatter in consternation. Parakeets and pigeons leave the grove in a noisy rush of wings. Peafowl scatter. There is complete silence as Abu once more settles down at his kill.

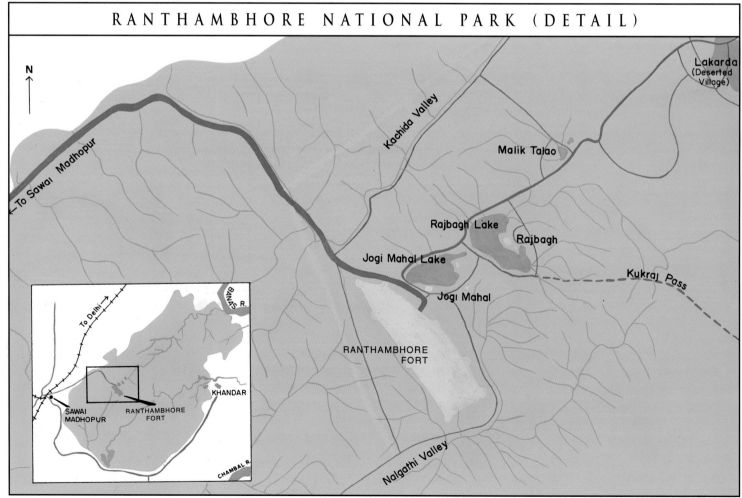

RANTHAMBHORE NATIONAL PARK (DETAIL)

Not to scale.

21 February

Rounding a bend in the trail near Malik Talao, I see a tiger lie down surreptitiously behind a grass tussock. We stop. Soon two more tigers walk through the forest and join the first. The three move sinuously around each other, rubbing faces. They are young animals, a large, pale-colored male, a smaller, dark male, and a compact, athletic female. The female keeps looking at us and slowly moves closer and closer. She pauses here and there and bites small twigs off trees and bushes—never taking her eyes off us. When only about a meter from the Jeep she turns back.

We drive on in the vibrant afternoon light to a meadow just beyond the lake. An adult tigress we soon recognize as Links paces about restlessly, moaning and growling to herself. She is quite thin and must be hungry; she may have missed making a kill.

She stops pacing and with face alert stalks through a patch of fine-leafed grass—sniffing the air delicately. Raising one front foot, her tail held horizontally in the classic pose of a pointer dog, she concentrates on a spot just to one side of the Jeep. Her tail suddenly goes straight up and, ears pricked, she leaps in long, graceful, loping bounds over the grass—and scatters a flock of gray partridges.

Moments later a single chital alarm call and the urgent sounds of distress of several peafowl come from a small stand of dhauk trees about 150 meters away. Like us, Links is instantly watchful. She walks slowly and cautiously toward the disturbance. We follow at a distance. She moves faster now, trotting along in a half crouch. The calls of the peafowl intensify. Links runs to the grove of trees and as she arrives a jungle cat dashes out from the other side. When we catch up with Links we find her standing over a freshly killed peahen—no doubt caught by the jungle cat. Links lies down with the peahen between her front paws. She plucks the bird with her teeth and spits out the feathers with what seems an expression of distaste on her face. She is not comfortable where she is and, picking up the carcass in her jaws, gets up. As she does one of the peahen's wings unfolds right across Links' face—blindfolding her. The tigress does not know what to do. She walks backward, forward, to this side and that, but whichever way she turns she blunders into the trees. She jerks her head back and forth anxiously. When she finally drops her stolen prey her eyes are wild and panicky. But only for a moment—she soon crunches through the peahen, leaving only a few bunches of feathers.

In the late afternoon, on our way back to Jogi Mahal, we stop at an area of short green grass on the shore of Rajbagh Lake. To one side is a patch of tall grass. Both chital and sambar graze close to it. Belinda is convinced a tiger is lying in ambush in the tall grass and gets her camera ready. We wait and wait. Just a few grass blades move. Another half hour passes. We are about to leave when a tigress explodes out of the grass in a horizontal streak—claws extended. Deer scatter in panic, and escape.

It is dark by the time we arrive at Jogi Mahal. The fire is already burning under the banyan tree. Fateh Singh arrives from a long drive through the park and joins us. In what has become a daily ritual, we relate our adventures with tigers over drinks and dinner. Fateh tells us about the four tigers he saw in another part of Ranthambhore. Between us we saw nine different tigers today—all in daylight. These are extraordinary times.

26 and 27 February

The night is cold and moonless. We sit around the comforting fire and have just started our dinner when a tiger's full-throated roar comes from across the lake and reverberates off the fort's wall. Again and again the tiger roars "aroom, aroom" with a tremendous booming force in the final "oom." In keeping with their solitary habits, tigers are rarely vocal and when they do call it is usually for only a few minutes at a time. But this powerful voice continues and comes steadily closer. Belinda grabs her tape recorder and I get the Jeep started. In less than a minute we are off. We are ill-prepared for this foray. The Jeep's battery is almost dead so we can use our headlights only sparingly. Our only flashlight shows no more than a glimmer. The tiger is still roaring as we race off, but soon he falls silent.

We stop where we think he last called and Belinda sets up the tape recorder. Only the stars, blazing in the cold sky, give us light—but we are surprised how much we can see. However, we hear rather than see the first tiger. By chance we have stopped the Jeep only ten or fifteen meters from him where he is hidden by some bushes. Now he roars with full force in our direction—a thundering sound that makes our hair stand on end and our blood run cold. The dim light and the echoes rolling off the fort walls add to the eeriness, the power of the experience.

The tiger keeps roaring, and I literally feel the forest shake with its force. As suddenly as the roaring began, it stops. In the quiet, our senses heightened, we can hear the faintest cricket chirp. An owl calling softly overhead startles us unreasonably.

The crackling of footsteps on dry leaves comes from the direction of the tiger. Our eyes are accustomed to the faint light and we see him emerge from the undergrowth. Walking steadily and purposefully he advances toward us. When he is close, seven meters perhaps, we use our feeble flashlight. There is just enough light to identify the tiger. Abu again. He walks on without a glance at us. Before we have time to gather our wits we hear lighter footsteps on our other side. Another tiger, a female. A quick look with the flashlight and we can see it is Links. She follows Abu for a short distance, lies down in some grass and rolls sensuously on her back, meowing softly. Abu has moved on and now roars again. Links gets up and walks off in his direction.

For four hours Abu walks around the lakes and roars, never diminishing the strength of his voice. At dawn we find his pug marks; they lead to the south, away from Jogi Mahal and the lakes. We follow them for about ten kilometers then lose them.

2 and 3 March

The sun is just setting and the air becomes refreshingly cool when we reach the Lakarda rock pool. The warmth of the day still glows in the cliff-face above the pool and the last light turns it to fire. The fine tracery of the dhauk trees' branches is etched in black against the darkening sky. Nightjars circle and swoop overhead and call in creaking voices. And then we see her—a tigress lying serenely out in the open on a rock outcrop overlooking the pool. She has appeared silently and without the herald of alarm calls. She looks calmly down at the pool, the soft breeze stirring her neck ruff. There is just enough light for Belinda to identify her. It is Lakshmi, a tigress we have seen just once before and that was here, at this same pool. Only a slight orange glow lingers in the sky when she gets up and walks off into the tall grass. A few minutes later we hear chital alarm calls. In the distance a jackal howls.

Just as the sun rises over the hills, we pick up Lakshmi's pug marks on a trail close to where we saw her last night. They lead down from the plateau at Lakarda along a steep track to the narrow, cold Kachida valley. Because the valley is

closely shut in by hills, the sun does not penetrate here till midmorning. Lakshmi's prints leave the trail and move toward a dry, rocky streambed. Four tree pies and two crows hop around in the bushes, intent on something still hidden from our view. Bouncing over boulders we move the Jeep closer and soon have a view of the streambed. The birds are peering at Lakshmi standing over a freshly killed sambar doe. The tigress' face is bloody. Belinda guides the Jeep over the stones to within six or seven meters of Lakshmi and her kill. The tiger ignores us, but not the adventurous birds. Testing her resolve, the tree pies and crows hop closer and closer to the carcass and try to snatch pieces of meat. Lakshmi hates the intruders. She growls and snarls and time and again rushes at them. But the birds never give up.

Normally Lakshmi would drag her catch away from the scavengers or cover it with dry leaves or grass. But the stream's bed is too steepsided and the sambar is probably too heavy, heavier by far than the lightly built tigress. Obeying instinct rather than reason she tries to rake stones over the carcass with sweeping motions of her paws. But it is ineffective. In the end she lies down almost on top of the kill, using the sambar's head as her pillow. Now she sleeps uninterruptedly.

The sun warms the valley. It is getting hot and after the exertions of the hunt and her subsequent feeding Lakshmi needs to drink. She moves experimentally down the nulla toward a pool a few hundred meters downstream. But whenever she moves away the tree pies and crows, who now number about fifteen, descend en masse and she rushes back. By midafternoon she tries another strategy. Pulling with all her strength she attempts to drag the carcass *toward* us. Does she think she can stash it under the Jeep or does she want us to mind it for her? But the heavy prey is wedged solidly between rocks. She must drink and finally she turns her back on the birds and strides down the nulla. The birds descend immediately, pulling pieces off the sambar. The crows are the smartest. They tear off chunks of meat as fast as they can and cache these in various hiding places; under stones or in tree hollows. One bird puts some under one of the Jeep's front wheels. After twenty minutes Lakshmi returns, still dripping from her cooling dip. We wish we could follow her example—the sun has become fierce.

The tigress has not mellowed. She chases the birds with angry growls and hisses. She is hungry again. Cutting through bone and skin she opens up the carcass and has another prodi-

Mario, who stole Lakshmi's sambar kill.

gious meal. After a while she pauses and looks straight at us. She snarls and growls then rushes toward the Jeep. More puzzled than frightened by this change in behavior, we are slow to realize her aggression is not directed at us, but at a crow. The bird, in trying to retrieve the scraps of meat it had stashed under our front wheel, has come too close. When we leave Lakshmi at dusk, there is enough left of the sambar to keep her fed for another two or even three days. We feel cramped and stiff after having sat in the tiny Jeep for eleven hours.

4 March

Lakshmi is not at her kill this morning. She lies on her back about twenty meters away on the grassy bank of the nulla. On the streambed with the remains of the sambar literally clutched to his chest lies Mario. He is a large, muscular male tiger with a scarred nose and one of his canine teeth broken off. He has eaten so much that he lies uncomfortably, panting, on the bed of stone. We can only imagine the roaring and hissing that went on while he drove Lakshmi from her kill during the night.

All day Mario tries to get comfortable, lying first this way then that. Panting and groaning, he constantly shifts his weight but he never manages to relax. Poetic justice perhaps.

During the night, Mario—it must have been him by the amount he has devoured—has eaten most of the viscera and in the process had turned the carcass inside out. The sambar's stomach has been removed and the spine severed above the pelvis. The leg bones lie discarded down the nulla.

There is nothing left on them even for the crows. Mario does not have another meal till late afternoon. Then he eats the ribs with much noisy cracking of bones. The body cavity of the carcass is not yet emptied and time and again Mario pulls great mouthfuls from it, his face dripping with blood. On and on he eats. As neatly as if he used a sharp knife he opens the sambar's stomach. He dumps the contents but eats the stomach itself. A cloud of flies buzzes constantly around his face.

Lakshmi stays in the vicinity all morning but never approaches Mario or tries to take possession of her kill. Wisely, perhaps, as male tigers do not hesitate to attack others of their kind when what they consider *their* kill is threatened. And Mario is far larger and stronger than Lakshmi. Often when more than one tiger has been observed at a kill the animals take turns to feed. But not Mario, he keeps Lakshmi's kill to himself to the end.

5 March

The next morning Mario is still with the sambar. Only some of the forequarters, the neck, and head remain. Shortly after we arrive, at the same time as the annoying birds, Mario picks up what is left of the carcass and carries it about half a kilometer and then drags it into a patch of dense prickly bushes. Moments later a tree pie arrives, then a crow.

Alarm calls of a chital and then a peacock alert Mario. He sees the other tiger before we do. A deep slow rumble starts deep in his chest. He curls his lips back. The approaching tigress sits down at this warning and waits.

Perhaps as a displacement activity, perhaps to try to finish his prey, Mario begins to eat. The sounds of cracking bones and tearing flesh are too much for the tigress and she comes closer. Mario leaps to his feet and comes roaring out of the scrub. The tigress turns slowly away and walks off. We follow her as Mario goes back to embrace the now stinking remains of Lakshmi's kill.

The female is thin, obviously hungry. She turns and stands broadside-on to us. I cannot help an involuntary recoil—she looks awful. Her right flank is a red raw wound. A piece of skin, at least fifteen by fifteen centimeters in size, has been ripped off and hangs down in a loose flap. The wound weeps. Maybe, unlike Lakshmi, this tigress did try to fight over a kill. Certainly the wound was inflicted by the ripping action of another tiger's claws. Antlers, teeth, or hooves of prey species could slash or puncture but not peel off such a swath of skin. Slowly, painfully, she turns and licks it clean. Walking stiffly but not too uncomfortably she makes for the old kill site. Vultures and a score of crows have moved in to clean up what is left of the hindlegs and much of the spine. Scattering the scavengers, the tigress sniffs at the meager leftovers, picks up a leg bone in her jaws, then despondently drops it again. She walks to a small pool and after drinking she lies down in the water and rests. The cooling water seems to have stiffened her for when she finally gets up and walks on she stumbles and drags one leg. Mario in the meantime has completely finished the sambar leaving only the shoulder blades and jaw bones.

★ ★ ★

In the early weeks of March the weather rapidly warms up. Many streams are reduced to water holes. Little nutrition remains in the hill and forest grasses. On the edges of the lakes, however, green grass continues to flourish and in the lakes themselves water lilies, lotuses, and other plants proliferate; many flower. Before the chital and sambar can reach these riches they must go through a fringe of three-meter-high, dry grass that encircles each lake.

The sambar are compulsive lake visitors by mid-March. Herds of up to thirty animals leave the hills two or even three times a day to drink and to feed urgently and nervously on the water plants. The deer wade up to their necks into water to reach the delicacies. Fawns often flounder in the deeper water and must stay in the shallows on their own. Several times a day the deer negotiate the fringe of tall grass where they are vulnerable to attack from tigers in ambush. As we watch these sambar go to the lakes, I often think that if I were a tiger I would specialize in ambushing deer in these places. Taking all three lakes into consideration, about 250 sambar cross the danger area at least once every day.

Abu, who has returned from the far reaches of his territory, becomes that specialist. Sambar wade into the lakes only during daylight hours, and Abu becomes a daylight hunter. After all the years we have been watching tigers we have only rarely seen them make a kill. We had seen it only in Kanha in the semidark of the dense forest or at dusk. So just as Abu concentrates all his efforts on the deer, we concentrate ours on Abu.

For six weeks we virtually live with him and we come to know him so well that often we can predict his movements and behavior. Never have we worked with such intense concentration. Many days are spent in the increasingly hot sun, first to find Abu then to stay with him till he makes his move. We become so attuned to him that we begin to think like a tiger, assessing the movements of sambar, the direction of the wind, the quality of cover, which individual deer would be the easiest to catch. More often than not our choices coincide with Abu's. Soon we need to see only a few of his pug marks in the dust to know where he is headed and what his intentions are. We need to see only some grass stems move to know where he lies in ambush and which deer he will chase. Abu for his part tolerates our presence without any signs of hostility. As with Saja in Kanha we have a special rapport with him. More than once he uses our Jeep as cover to stalk a sambar, chital, or even a peacock. If we are parked in the shade of a particular tree he often comes over and lies near the Jeep, even though there is plenty of other shade. It seems Belinda and I and Abu have become one. Even so, there are occasions during our vigil when Abu just vanishes from under our noses as if he had been spirited away by magic.

14 March

The sun is already up by the time we leave Jogi Mahal. Just as we climb into the Jeep, alarm calls of chital and langur come from the forest near Rajbagh. We have only gone about one kilometer when we see Abu walking through the woodlands—graceful and lithe, his head lowered and his mouth partly open, a typical tiger's walk. Without glancing in our direction he crosses the trail and walks into the hills. It is his shortcut to Rajbagh. We cannot follow him but make a small detour to position ourselves where we think he will come out. In a few minutes he appears from the nulla, crosses our path again, and walks to the water's edge. He splashes through the shallows, scattering countless small frogs. A basking crocodile slides off the grass into the water. The langurs in the Rajbagh garden are frantic as the tiger enters their domain, but he does not pause. At the northeastern corner of the lake he lies down to drink, lapping for a minute or more. Water dripping from his mouth, he looks up and surveys his surroundings. Soon he is up again and walks into the tall grass. Here he lies down at the edge, his shaggy head barely visible,

Early one morning we find Abu sitting on the edge of Jogi Mahal lake.

Abu snarls at mugger crocodiles that seem to have taken the sambar he has caught.

the water, still some 200 meters away, Abu sneaked back into the tall grass and we lost sight of him. We expect him to creep slowly, carefully through the grass, unseen, until he is within striking distance. He pinpoints the deer's whereabouts by the sounds of their splashings as they pull the lilies from the water. Then we see Abu, crouching at the very edge of the tall grass. But the deer are still more than a hundred meters from him. If he bursts from cover the sambar might run out of the water, which would give the tiger a chance. If they go into deeper water away from the shore and then swim to the other side, Abu would have no hope of catching one.

his eyes glittering in the early sun. It is already hot and as there are no deer in sight we return to the shade of a mango tree some hundred meters away. Abu dozes.

Shortly after midday the first herd of sambar slowly walks down the hill. There are twenty-three of them; a mixture of big stags, does, yearlings, and fawns. The leading doe stops about forty meters from the tall grass and tests the light breeze. But Abu is still 250 meters away and whatever light wind there is, is in his favor. He has seen the sambar and stares at them fixedly.

We move into a position where we can get a clear view should Abu try to make a kill. We have to move now, while the sambar are still a good distance away, for they are so tense and nervous that should we so much as sneeze when they are near us they would stampede.

The leading doe moves several paces forward, stamps her foot, raises her tail, and is ready for instant flight. Painfully slowly she edges towards a spot where the fringing high grass is only a few meters wide. For more than half an hour she stands and waits—listening, sniffing. The others wait patiently and quietly but take no part in testing for danger. Suddenly the doe walks toward the grass and then trots through to the lake's edge. Without questioning her judgment the rest of the herd follows. Soon they wade out and begin eating the lily leaves. They brush past a group of crocodiles basking in the sun on rocks jutting out of the water. As the sambar entered

For hours he watches and waits as the crocodiles tear at his prey.

Slowly Abu goes into a crouch then explosively uncoils himself and hurtles from cover. He bounds through the shallows. Most of the herd make for the shore.

Abu—in the fastest, longest run we have ever seen from a tiger—puts on extra pace and is gaining on a yearling male. Just as we think Abu will trip the sambar by knocking one hindleg from under him, the deer leaps up the lake's bank and escapes. Abu, without slowing, changes course, trying for another stag running in the shallow water. The stag evades Abu's teeth by a desperate jump into deeper water where he can swim faster than the tiger. Even Abu is not invincible.

For a while Abu swims slowly in the lake and then returns to shore. A large crocodile approaches him. Lifting its head the big reptile snaps its jaws at the tiger. Abu, not to be intimidated shows *his* big teeth as he growls and hisses.

16 March

The first light is just creeping over the lake when we hear the sound of a score of sambar bellowing in alarm and rushing out of the lake. Abu must have made a charge.

No more than 150 meters from Jogi Mahal we find him sitting on the lake's edge, staring intently at a spot in the water plants. We follow his gaze but can see nothing unusual. But Abu is infuriated. He walks into the water, bares his teeth, growls, and hisses fearsomely. He rushes forward and lunges at something in front of him. We cannot see what it is. Did he make a kill this morning? And if so did it get entangled in the waterweeds and sink or did the crocodiles grab his prey and pull it under?

After some more lunges at the unseen foe, Abu slowly walks out of the lake and lies down at the water's edge. If the place had no interest for him he would enter the tall grass and lie down and sleep, but he stays in the open, wide awake. When the sun rises, it becomes hot. Still Abu, now panting, keeps watch. Once again I scan the water plants and now I see it: just

Finally Abu plucks up courage and strides out to retrieve his catch…and drags it back to shore.

an ear of a sambar sticking up out of the plants. I grab Belinda by the shoulder and point it out to her. As we watch, the ear bobs up and down as though being pulled from underneath.

Slowly more of the sambar becomes visible, the head and

the bloated ribcage. The snouts of two crocodiles surface near the kill. Several gigantic turtles pull at the sambar's skin. Time and again the larger crocodile (we guess him to be about three meters long) grabs the carcass by a haunch or the neck and pulls and rolls in the water, splashing noisily. Abu stares and stares. Even when a herd of sambar comes down to the lake to drink, unaware of the tiger's presence and perhaps just within range, Abu does not even glance in its direction.

The crocodiles and turtles continue to tear at the sambar, which we now think must have been killed by Abu; otherwise he would not stay with it so closely for so long. By the time the sun begins to go down and a cool breeze fans our hot faces, it seems nothing much can be left of the sambar below the waterline and we expect Abu to move off soon. We have positioned ourselves under a small tree beside the lake. After about nine hours of sitting in one place, Abu gets up, walks around the edge of the lake, and settles in the shade of the same tree we are under. Soon he is up again. Slowly he wades out, snarling and hissing. The water becomes deeper and he now has to swim. For the last twenty meters he must force his way through the tangle of water plants. Slashing with his mighty paws, he soon reaches the sambar. Savagely he grabs it by the neck and gives it a tremendous heave, turning the deer over so its legs point in the air. To our great surprise the carcass is intact. The crocodiles have been unable to take a single bite out of it. Unlike the tiger's teeth, which can cut through the toughest skin like a pair of shears, the crocodiles' teeth are rows of interlocking cones designed to seize and hold prey, not to cut through it.

Now comes Abu's greatest test of strength: he must drag the 100-kilogram carcass while swimming through the plants. Grunting with the effort, he strikes out for the shore. Twice he pauses and looks around challengingly, as if daring any crocodile to come near. When he has struggled out of the water plants he inexplicably drops the sambar and swims toward the bank. Did a crocodile make him lose his nerve? For half an hour Abu sits up to his neck in water and waits. With even greater determination he then swims back. He grabs the sambar by the neck with such force that both disappear under the water. Then Abu erupts out of the lake in a burst of power. He pauses only briefly at the shore to shake himself, then he drags the kill into the forest. We see the puncture marks in the sambar's throat. Abu did kill it.

We are keen to film the end of the story. It takes us about five minutes to make the detour and find where Abu has dragged his prize. But already he has opened up the hindquarters and is bolting down big pieces of meat. Sensing that this is not a good time to go close to Abu, we stop about fifteen meters away. It is the farthest away we can be in the

Abu, seconds before he charges us.

thicket and still get a clear view. I begin to film and Belinda is taking still pictures with her large 400-millimeter lens. Abu continues to eat, but glares with hostile eyes. He growls. Without warning he leaps at us, ears back, teeth bared, roaring in a full charge. We have no time to think—though it flashes through both our minds that finally this is it! We scream as loudly as we can to try to scare the tiger off. Belinda raises the large lens high above her head ready to hit out with it. I quickly grab the white cloth I use to protect the camera from the heat and lean as far forward as I can, waving it in the tiger's hissing spitting face—about a meter and a half from ours. Belinda has enough presence of mind not to actually hit Abu, which would probably enrage him even further. Abu comes to a stop beside the Jeep—but continues to hiss and snarl—and we continue to yell at the tops of our voices. Then he slowly returns to his kill. When Abu is with his prey again, Belinda quickly starts the Jeep—after a silent prayer this will not be one of the many occasions the starter or battery malfunctions—and we back off.

★ ★ ★

Abu is with this kill for three days and we stay well clear of him. We watch him from a distance for another two days, steadily going closer. He shows no signs of belligerence and on the third day, after he finishes his kill, we reestablish our old rapport with him. As so many times before, he comes up to our Jeep and lies in the shade a few meters away. As he walks toward us on this occasion, however, we have to suppress the impulse to start the Jeep and keep our distance.

22 March

Last night we heard Abu roar repeatedly across the lake from Jogi Mahal and this morning we soon find his giant footprints. They disappear down a stony nulla that leads to Rajbagh. But at Rajbagh all is peace; monkeys forage in the treetops, chital and sambar feed along the lake confident and unafraid. There are no pug marks here. Maybe Abu continued on to the third lake.

We search all the trails around Malik Talao. Nothing. But knowing the tiger's habits, we think he must be here, hidden in the tall grass. Once again we search the trails. Belinda, who is especially skilled in tracking, finds a single, barely visible pug mark. It is unmistakably Abu's broad print and it points

Abu and Links mating.

the neck. With one powerful bite he severs the spinal cord. Trotting back, the fawn in his jaws, he soon vanishes from view into the tall grass. After waiting for five hours the action is over in a few seconds. Moments later the birds sing again, the monkeys play in the trees above us. Other deer come walking toward the lake to drink.

★ ★ ★

This is the pattern of Abu's reign of terror. The sambar and chital at this time of year *must* come to the lakes to feed and to drink, and at one of them Abu will lie in wait. Usually he catches the fawns and it seems he will wipe out a whole generation. So fierce is the tiger's hunting that even when he has made a kill, he rushes out again if more deer come to the lake. On one occasion he catches two sambar fawns in one afternoon. He eats both of them.

The end of March and early April—the beginning of summer—is very hot this year. Every day the temperature rises to 38 degrees Celsius or more in the shade. Dust storms tear in from the northwest and raise whitecaps on the lakes. Banyan and flame of the forest trees are shedding their leaves and the storms scatter them in great showers. The banyans replace the old leaves with new immediately but the flame of the forest are soon bare. The sky remains hazy with dust and the light is diffused.

directly to the tall grass where we had thought he might be.

We position ourselves in a strategic spot and wait. By midday the first group of sambar tentatively approaches the lake but the deer hesitate uneasily. As the afternoon wears on more and more deer arrive and with an increase in numbers they gain in confidence. Walking through the shallows, nibbling at waterweeds, the fifty or so deer slowly move to the bank of tall grass where we think Abu might be lying in wait. Belinda nudges me and points silently. Abu creeps slowly toward the sambar. He lies down. We can see him clearly but the deer cannot and they gradually move toward the danger. When they are about twenty meters from the tiger, a doe with a fawn at heel senses the tiger—a slight shift in the breeze has brought his scent. She barks in alarm. But before the sound is out of her throat Abu charges out of the grass, chasing the herd into deeper water. In four gigantic bounds Abu has the small fawn, pushes it under water, and grabs it by

15 April

Abu's tracks were on all the trails around the lakes this morning but we could not find him. This afternoon, when it is still stingingly hot, we drive to Malik Talao. There are sambar in the lake. We pause to discuss what to do next. As Belinda switches off the engine, Abu charges out and races after the sambar—through the shallows, up an embankment, and down into a meadow. In an extrapowerful leap he reaches the rump of a small stag. The deer goes down and Abu has it by the throat in a split second. With a mighty heave of his shoulders Abu twists the animal's neck, breaking it.

We are breathless and speechless. Few tigers would have charged in this heat, fewer still would have chased their prey for 300 meters, none but Abu would have had the tenacity and speed to overtake a sambar in full flight and bring it down. For a minute or so Abu keeps his jaws clamped over the sambar's throat. Then he releases it and stands there panting.

He looks in our direction and glares, snarling. We are ready to beat a retreat. But before we do, for he is some distance away, we look to see if this wrath may be directed at someone else. It is. A tigress comes trotting toward him. Links. She stops about ten meters from the male. But it is too close for Abu. With a frightening roar he lashes out at the tigress. She leaps out of his way. Abu picks up the kill and drags it into the tall grass. Links follows at a distance. She looks very thin.

17 April

A dusty and warm dawn promises to develop into a scorching day. Driving along the northwestern end of Rajbagh Lake we spot Links lying in a small clearing. A few meters away we can just make out Abu's muscular form. After about half an hour Links walks over to Abu. Hesitantly they make nose to nose contact, then the two mate, half-hidden by the grass. As a final flourish Abu leaps away with a deafening roar. He walks to the northeast corner of Jogi Mahal lake where he lies down in the shade and sleeps. After two hours Links reappears. She too is hot and she lies down in the water. Finally she gets up and once again she approaches Abu. Sometimes tender, sometimes violent, they mate again, in full sunlight, and right in front of our cameras.

Four more times during the next thirty minutes the tigers mate, then each goes its own way, Abu east along Jogi Mahal Lake and Links back to Rajbagh.

After two and a half years, we finally have a tiger film—the last scenes being of Abu and Links mating. The anticipated release of all the pressures of filmmaking, combined with the sheer beauty of the scene, overwhelms us.

19 April

It was too hot to sleep indoors in Jogi Mahal. We dragged our beds from our room and slept on the verandah. Our bags and cases are already packed for an early departure. At dawn we sip our tea and watch a group of about twenty-five sambar come down to the lake. The dust has cleared and the light seems to be extraluminous. The sambar enter the water. Almost by reflex we pick up our binoculars to see if Abu is there with designs on the deer. He is. Soon we see the flame of his colors flicker in the grass then burst forth as he speeds after the herd. The sambar are so closely bunched together that they bump into each other. The fractional slowing down is fatal for a three-quarter-grown doe. The last we see of Abu is him dragging his latest victim into deep cover.

★   ★   ★

During our weeks in Ranthambhore we saw tigers every day, sometimes even in groups of three or four. Their pug marks were all over the roads and trails. All the wildlife, from tigers to the tiniest birds, was unconstrained by fear of humans; they were open, trusting even. The ruins of ancient buildings, now inhabited by wild animals, added to the notion that humanity can be one with nature; it does not always have to be the destroyer. They also showed that nature can reclaim an area once inhabited by people, even after a thousand years. The 1980s in Ranthambhore were a truly golden age in the relationship between tigers and humans.

Much of the credit for creating this heaven on earth has to go to Fateh Singh Rathore. It is due to his dedication and his uncompromising protection that the jewel that is Ranthambhore shone.

Those weeks were the pinnacle not only of our days with tigers, but of the total of our wildlife experiences in India. For us the ideal is to move among wild animals without causing fear or being afraid of them, to be neither threat nor prey. Only in Keoladeo and, even more, in Ranthambhore, have we found this ideal, have we daily been closely surrounded by wildlife. When these experiences are in a place where the wildlife is both numerous and diverse, and are drenched in the sunlight of a semiarid climate, then they do not come any better, any more exciting and stimulating. And when the tiger is the dominant animal—then that is our Garden of Eden.

[CHAPTER 17]

"LAND OF THE TIGER" COMPLETED

Two weeks after the last time we saw Abu terrorize the sambar, in April 1984, we arrived in Los Angeles to edit our film. We called it "Land of the Tiger." National Geographic executive producers met us at the international airport, said, "Welcome to L.A.," gave us the keys to a rental car, and said, "See you at the office tomorrow." After two years in the Indian jungles we suddenly had to deal with Los Angeles' freeways, find a place to live for six months, and try to cope with life in a mostly windowless building, one riven with office politics. Welcome to L.A. indeed. But putting the images and sounds together, and seeing the story we had envisaged take shape, was an exciting experience.

"Land of the Tiger" had its television premiere on Public Broadcasting Service on Wednesday, 16 January 1985. It was well-received and won many international awards.

We returned to India from Los Angeles a few days after India's prime minister, Indira Gandhi, was assassinated on 31 October 1984. For several days after she was killed, mobs rampaged through Delhi. Our neighbor's house was set on fire by rioters. Further down the road a family of five was burnt to death. A mob gathered at the gate of our small farm. Police drove the rioters away by firing over their heads just as they were about to overpower our watchman, cook, and gardener, whom we had left in charge. When we got back home, all was quiet again. Blackened houses and burntout buses and trucks just down the road were the only evidence of the disturbance.

For me India was never the same after that; a certain innocence and a basic good-naturedness had been shattered. Life became more circumscribed by more and more bureaucratic hassles.

After a time, Belinda and I decided we would settle in Australia. We bought sixty hectares of tropical rain forest in the country's northeast and planned to build a house there. Before we did we returned to India, to Kanha and Ranthambhore, for two months in the winter of 1988 to 1989. In Kanha we had an extraordinary experience that showed us there was still a lot to learn about tigers.

Kanha National Park—15 December 1988

Shivaji bears us majestically along a nulla filled with tussocks of grass topped with tall white plumes. The meadow grass has turned russet with the cold of winter. We enter a sal and bamboo forest where dappled light falls on a dense covering of seedling trees about a meter high.

A shaft of light illuminates a patch of orange among the green: the longish fur of a tiger cub perhaps nine months old. Almost immediately we see the second cub a few meters

The regal Ranthambhore tiger we called Bako.

away. The two look at us steadily through reddish brown eyes. Shivaji noisily and roughly pulls down some bamboo stems to eat. The cubs, both males, take no notice. Sabir urges Shivaji on as we cast about in a wide circle looking for other tigers.

In the meantime the cubs walk up a nulla filled with smooth black stones and shaded by bamboos. They climb onto a large boulder and nuzzle each other. One makes quiet calls of "ow," mouthing the sounds with his lips peeled back. Upstream along the nulla a tiger roars; it sounds like a female. The cub continues to "ow" softly. From an area to our right comes the deep-throated roar of an adult male tiger. Shivaji, made to hurry, strides off in that direction and soon we come upon the tiger. But he is smallish and young, perhaps no more than three years old, and not big enough to have produced the mighty roar we have heard. The young male walks off into the direction of the cubs. He gives a long, plaintive-sounding call, more a howl than a roar. From our right, in answer and quite close, come three tremendous roars. Slowly we move toward a grassy clearing and see a large male tiger walking purposefully toward the nulla. He is lithe yet powerful and muscular.

Within a few seconds the big male and the three-year-old meet—not in the nulla but on a patch of lush grass among bamboo. The younger tiger drops down on his haunches, then slowly rises again. The two circle while rubbing against each other. Finally they stand face to face and nuzzle one cheek then the other. The younger one briefly touches the larger, heavier tiger on his shoulder with his paw. All the while their voices rumble deep in their throats. Now and again they make friendly "prrrt, prrrt" sounds by blowing through their lips. They lie down about three meters apart. The sun has gone down but a green twilight hovers in the small clearing.

The cubs come bounding up and greet the large male by rubbing against him and walking under his chin. "Prrrt, prrrt," he greets them. The young tigers play and leap all over and around the big fellow. Then one comes walking playfully toward us. The young adult stares at us and snarls. Sabir thinks he might charge us. A few weeks ago this tiger attacked another elephant who had gone too close to the cubs and lacerated its trunk. But we have faith in Shivaji being able to thwart any assault and we stay where we are.

In fact the cubs are not interested in us, but in the tigress who walks up from behind the elephant. She joins the others. The cubs and the three-year-old rush toward her. There is much mewing, rumbling, and "prrrt, prrrt." The larger tigers rub faces while the cubs try to get between them.

It is almost dark when we leave. Belinda identifies the female as Chota Madi, meaning "little female," who now, however, is strong and robust. We have seen her just once, six years ago, when she was small and diffident and lived in the shadow of a large and experienced tigress.

We wonder how this group came to be together. Tigers are thought to be solitary animals who join others only to mate. Mothers with cubs were believed to be the only social groupings. Males especially were characterized as antagonistic to each other. Yet here were four males of three generations showing only affection for one another. Fateh Singh has recently seen similar groupings in Ranthambhore.

Sabir explains the relationships in this way: Sabir had seen Chota Madi mating in October 1985. The cubs, a male and a female, would have been born in late January of 1986. He saw the tigress carry her small young in her mouth to a new hiding place only a few weeks after that. When these cubs were fifteen months old the female one was killed by the same large male who is with the family now. Sabir easily recognizes him by the fine striping along his hindquarters. The three-year-old male is the surviving cub of the 1985 mating. The large male is the father of the nine-month-old cubs, but not of the three-year-old. Chota Madi and the three younger males are constantly together, the three-year-old, according to Sabir, even baby-sitting while the female goes hunting. The big male comes and goes. It is most unusual for a young tiger to stay with its mother for more than two years, even rarer for it to be tolerated near her next litter.

Sabir tells us of many other intriguing observations and says we should never have left Kanha. Imagine, he adds, what we could have discovered about the tigers if you had stayed.

★ ★ ★

In late January 1989 we arrived back in Australia, but Belinda could not settle down. India drew her back, as deep-down I knew it would. Being a person who does not thrive on constant crises, hustle, and bustle, I decided to stay in Australia and build my house in the rain forest. It has proven to be a wonderfully stimulating environment and I still live there.

It took Belinda a few years to find her feet. Just when she had found her equilibrium and an inner peace, she was overtaken by events that turned her life upside down. They also ruptured forever our innocent, untainted involvement with wild tigers and other Indian wildlife.

[CHAPTER 18]

RETURN TO KANHA AND BUILDING SHERGARH

Kanha National Park—23 March 1995

Since arriving at Shergarh, about a week ago, Belinda has been busy with meetings with the police, Kanha park officials, and conservationists. Not until today do we have a chance to go into the national park purely for the pleasure of being in the jungle.

We pass an enigmatic sign just before the entrance gate that says:

Do not disturb wild Animal.
Do not make horn.
Dot not use surch light in the
night. During checking do not
Fleel but coaperat in low
processor.
THANKS

Once we have entered our life histories in three or four enormous ledgers and have been issued with a fistful of tickets, our compulsory guide joins us and we are off. At first I do not recognize this young man with the shy smile. Belinda has to jog my memory. It is Harish Chand, Gunpath's grandson.

In the forest, the bamboos, the sal trees, the birdsong, the monkeys, the deer, and a lone gaur bull combine to bring back a rush of memories and inexpressible emotions. For several kilometers we follow the pug marks of two tigers, a male and a female that walked along a dusty road. We stop the Jeep in a particu-

larly beautiful spot shaded by huge sal trees. We ask Harish how Gunpath and all the other elephant people are and what the elephants have been up to. Belinda has heard some horrific reports. Harish gives us the good news first. Gunpath is enjoying his retirement. Bundh Devi, his old elephant and our favorite during our filming days, has had a calf just five days ago. Shivaji is its father. Last year, Harish says, Tara killed her grass cutter. No one knows exactly what happened. She and her grass cutter had gone down as usual to bathe in a water hole. Tara came back on her own, quite calmly, and lined up for her food with the other elephants as usual. People soon realized her grass cutter had not returned. They found him face down in the water with his ribcage crushed.

Shivaji, in so many ways the pride and joy of the elephant village, is also guilty of murder. He killed a forester out in the national park two months ago. We ask Harish if he knows just what had happened. Harish suggests he tell us the story exactly where it happened.

The road winds through forest for several kilometers. Harish tells us to stop at an enormous sal tree beside the road. There is a large bulge in the tree about two meters above the ground and below it are two perfectly round holes, each about four centimeters in diameter, through the bark and deep into the wood. The holes were made by Shivaji driving his tusks into the tree. The track winds on for another 400 meters and crosses a dry stream. On the far bank is an idyllic forest scene. A man, bare-chested and wearing a *dhoti,* draws water from a well. Beside the well is a trough full of water where wild animals come to drink. Beyond the well is a small, neat, whitewashed building roofed with terracotta tiles. Around it grow spreading saja and jamun trees. A fence of woven split bamboo encloses the house and trees. Smoke from a cooking fire rises slowly in the warm air. Washing dries on the fence. A steep hill covered in large, black boulders rises directly behind the house, which in fact is the Kopa Dubri guard outpost. It was here Shivaji went berserk on 23 January.

There were signs that something was amiss with Shivaji about a month before this, Harish explains, when he started attacking Jung Bahadur, another large tusker. Sabir was still "sitting on Shivaji" then. On 3 January Sabir was sent to take part in rounding up wild elephants that had left the forest and were terrorizing villages in the north of the state. Shivaji was fine for the next two weeks in the care of his grass cutter. But then the elephant came into musth properly and he went mad. Neither his grass cutter nor the other *mahouts* could control him. Shivaji broke the enormous chains that shackled him, dragging a length of chain on one of his hind legs, and took off into the jungle. He took all the female elephants and their calves with him. The *mahouts* and grass cutters followed them and left food for the elephants at a distance, afraid to go near their charges. Shivaji became angrier and angrier. The elephant men caught two female elephants, our old friends Bundh Devi and Tara, by offering food and by shouting commands at them, Harish says.

Shivaji moved menacingly toward a village at the edge of the park, threatening to demolish it and to destroy the crops. Riding the two female elephants, the *mahouts* tried to head Shivaji off. But holding his head high, flapping his ears wildly, thrusting with his tusks, rampaging and screaming and trumpeting, Shivaji tore the *howdahs* from the female elephants and

attacked the *mahouts*. They leapt to the ground and ran for their lives. But Shivaji was diverted from the village.

Three nights later, on a bright moonlit night, Shivaji with other elephants approached the guard outpost. They came silently. Three men were asleep inside, two laborers and a forester called Bagwan Das Patel.

Bagwan Das had come to Kanha only three months before. He was a stout man in his fifties with a large, black mustache and graying hair.

The men woke between one and two in the morning to the sounds of Shivaji tearing the back of the house apart. Other elephants surrounded the place. The two laborers, experienced jungle men, ran up the steep slope behind the house. The elephants chased them but could not climb the rocky hill. Shivaji returned to the house and pushed the walls in with his forehead. Bagwan Das ran out of the other side and down the road. Shivaji ran after him.

The two laborers heard Bagwan Das scream twice. They ran through the night to the next guard outpost, where they stayed until dawn. When they returned next morning they saw Shivaji standing over Bagwan Das' inert body with the other elephants close around him. The laborers went on to the elephant village and raised the alarm. The *mahouts* rushed to the scene in a Jeep. The elephants had gone. First they found Bagwan Das' towel. Then they saw the marks of Shivaji's tusks in the sal tree with the bulge on it. Bagwan Das' body was on the other side of the tree, literally torn limb from limb.

A violent and sudden death like that, says Harish, is like dying before you are married; your soul is not at rest. The outpost has been rebuilt and repainted and has a new fence, but Bagwan Das' ghost still haunts it. His spirit is often heard as he sighs and moans, rustles the leaves and beats on the tree trunks. Harish says that Bagwan Das liked to smoke *bidis* and that they left some lighted ones for him under the sal tree. After that his ghost was at rest for a while.

Shivaji next made his way toward the elephant people's village at Kisli, and there was a real fear that he might cause mayhem there too. Before he reached there Sabir arrived back. He walked up to Shivaji, talked to him, shouted at him, caught him, and brought him back to the village. He is bathed and fed there every day now and is no trouble. Everyone agrees Shivaji cannot help what he did. He went mad and did not know what he was doing, Harish concludes.

Sabir, the *mahout*, with his elephant Shivaji, who is in musth. A year earlier Shivaji killed a forester.

We drive on to the elephant village at Kisli. We go up to Shivaji, who is standing there with a heavy chain tied to one back leg. Sabir walks up and joins us. We stroke Shivaji's trunk and his heavy, polished tusks. He has grown enormously powerful in the years since we filmed tigers from his back. His grass cutter comes and leads Shivaji slowly out into the forest to forage. Sabir is sad and upset about the incident and says he should not have been sent away when his elephant came into musth.

We look in at Gunpath, old and somewhat frail now, but as cheerful as ever and full of extravagant and richly embroidered tales about our filming days.

Shergarh near Kanha National Park— 24 March 1995

Belinda and I leave Shergarh early to take a long walk into the forest. In the past, whenever we were in the jungle we were always attuned to signs of tigers, listening for alarm calls, looking for pug marks and other signs. We were always instantly ready to act on the information and to look for the tiger. More often than not we would find it. Since coming back to Kanha this time, I do not feel this compelling urge to see tigers. I am content to know from the signs that they are there and to enjoy the jungle as we find it. I have noticed that Belinda does not feel the same eagerness to see the tiger either. I ask her about it. She says:

I think the more you get to know an animal, even one as elusive and unpredictable as the tiger, the more you can visualize in your mind what it is doing by looking at the signs. When you see a group of vultures sitting in a tree, for example, you can imagine a tiger lying with its kill. By looking at the habitat you have a fair idea what that kill is and so on. That is not to say that if you did follow things up there wouldn't be a few surprises. But I no longer feel the driving necessity to actually see a tiger. Another reason I'm no longer constantly looking for tigers is that nowadays the park is so full of people busting a gut to see them, and being so obnoxious about it, that I don't want to join them. I treasure my memories.

And as you well know we worked with the tiger at the best possible time, between 1974 and 1989, before the upsurge in poaching. It is quite extraordinary that those fifteen or so years, those glorious years, when we spent so much time with tigers, were in fact the peak years for watching wild tigers. That can never be repeated.

When I look back on those years when you and I were filming and photographing, I marvel at how we fitted it all in. It's difficult to work and travel in India as we did. It was rough and uncomfortable. I'm just so glad we did it when we were young. Not a day goes by when I don't use some of the knowledge that we gathered. Because of this I probably have a better understanding of the problems and what is at stake than any other active conservationist in India, with the exception of Ranjitsinh and one or two other people. I've seen most of wild India—tigers in all kinds of habitats, Manas in its heyday, Kaziranga and the rhino poaching problem, the parks of south India, and so on.

I'm still amazed at our Land Rover days. If someone gave me an open Land Rover as basic as that one today and said, here are the funds to drive around India for a year and a half to photograph wildlife, I don't think I could do it.

And you know wherever we went the first thing we'd say was, "Wow, look at this bird, or that habitat, or how this insect lives." Now I go with a completely different mental attitude. I'm looking for trouble; the first thing I think now is, "What poaching is there here and who's the bastard who chopped those trees down?" There's no longer that sense of wonder we had.

You ask if I think our films made a difference? They undoubtedly did and still do. With the Keoladeo film it was plain and simple. Two weeks after Mrs. Gandhi saw the film for the second time, with her family, Keoladeo was declared a national park. That was a direct result of the film. She, of course, had other people working toward it, but sometimes you need more than words and factual reports to get a message across. What was needed for the final push was a visual statement of all that Keoladeo stood for and what the problems were. Our film did that very powerfully.

What the tiger film did was slightly different, I think. It brought an enormous amount of understanding and sympathy for the tigers at a perfect time. Wherever you go where there's television, everybody has seen the film, not just once but many, many times. It is a film that small children have seen and that grandparents have seen. It's made a really incredible difference to people's respect for the tiger, to their admiration for it. It has almost become a cult film. The other day I was at Howrah Station in Calcutta to catch a train when suddenly I heard these familiar sounds—and there it was on television monitors all over the station.

People you meet want to shake your hand because you made "Land of the Tiger." Everyone is spellbound by the tiger. This could never have been done any other way, I believe, nor could it be done again. You cannot do it with words alone nor with still pictures. Still pictures put you at a distance, as a distant observer. But a film with the animal looking you straight in the eye, and hunting, suckling its young, mating, drinking—that is what brings the tiger and its jungle alive.

The positive effect of the film, as just one factor in saving the tiger, would have continued and grown. But then another factor entered the equation, and it is not one anybody could have predicted. And this is the poaching and trading in tiger parts—mostly bones. This element is fueled by greed and big money and the people you're up against are extremely cunning, professional criminals. And they are tipping the balance against the tiger, the rhino, and others.

★ ★ ★

We cross the sandy creek and from habit look for tracks. We see those of a jackal, some chital, and, surprisingly, those of a striped hyena. The trail leads through bamboo thickets to a chattan with gigantic granite boulders. For many years a tiger had its lair here in a cavern among the rocks. We climb to the summit and sit beside the silky white trunk of a kulu tree. All around, for as far as we can see, there is forest. Young langurs play on a ledge directly below us. I ask Belinda why and how she came to build her house here, right next to Kanha.

I initially leased the land, only about six hectares, simply to protect it. It was for sale but the owner was going to cut down all the trees and sell them first. So I offered to lease the land—trees and all—and he agreed. Then in 1992 I knew a huge battle to save Kanha and other places was brewing and I suddenly had a tremendous sense of urgency to build here. I needed some space and time to think.

As you know, I've always loved and been totally enamored by the old forest bungalows, the forest rest houses, that were built during the British times. They were always built in magnificent places, not necessarily with grand views, but magic spots in the forest like in Kanha and also Kaziranga. I wanted to build something like that, something that had the same atmosphere. This certainly is a magic spot. I wanted a house that was not ostentatious but was roomy, comfortable, and had a soul. I wanted to put the house into place without disturbing anything and for it to look as though it had always been there. I didn't want a wide driveway or to plant an avenue of trees, I just wanted the house to look part of the forest.

I really loved building the house, it was one of the most creative things I've ever done. Even though the house looks very simple, it was a real challenge to build.

From day one the langurs thought this house was built just for them. In summer the whole troop, about thirty of them, sit in the shade of the verandah with their legs dangling over the side as though they own the place. When I walk out, the troop's male, who is usually quite *friendly, glares at me as if to say, "Hey, this is my place, what are you doing here?"*

★ ★ ★

Back at Shergarh, messages have arrived about more poaching in Ranthambhore and from other people who have information they want Belinda to act on. Urgent reports are needed by the Ministry of the Environment in New Delhi.

Another reason we have come to Shergarh and Kanha is for some uninterrupted time so Belinda can tell me in detail how she came to be so deeply involved in Indian conservation issues and about her work in trying to stop poachers. In Delhi or on the road we never have enough time for Belinda to gather her thoughts and tell her stories fully. During our excursions into Kanha and walks around Shergarh she has slowly unwound. For the first time in months she is rested and fresh.

We sit and talk under a large hara tree that still has a few leaves on it. Even at the

A sal tree on the edge of the Kanha meadows early on a winter's morning.

The following chapters are about what she told me that night in her own words. It is an extraordinary story of overcoming personal crises, of courage, and of total commitment to the conservation of Indian wildlife, especially the tiger. During the early years, from 1991 to mid-1994, Belinda worked completely on her own, unfunded, and without support of any kind. No one was particularly interested in or concerned about the things she discovered, not the authorities, not the conservationists. They mostly preferred to pretend nothing was wrong. It is more comfortable that way. It was also much easier to harass Belinda and to try to discredit her than to face disturbing facts. This unexpected hostility and lack of support for a time undermined her confidence and forced her to examine her motives, her commitment, and what course of action to take. To think these things through, Belinda came here to Shergarh at the end of 1993 and stayed for four months.

house there would be frequent interruptions from nearby Kipling Camp. It is late afternoon and no longer so very hot. We have to shoo resting langurs from the table and seats. They do not go far and are soon feeding in the trees around us. Drongos and tree pies sing and call close by.

I start the tape recorder and, prompted by a few questions, Belinda begins to talk. Thoughtful friends and staff at Kipling Camp quietly bring us afternoon tea and, as we continue, drinks followed much later by dinner. When it becomes dark they bring lighted candles. Belinda keeps on talking as owls call and a lone leopard "saws" in the distance.

At the end of that period she emerged calm and determined, with a clear vision of what was needed and what she would do. She was also considerably disillusioned and increasingly concerned about who she could trust.

There are two interwoven strands to Belinda's personal and lonely early struggle. One concerns the threatened destruction of Bhitarkanika Sanctuary, including its mangroves and its breeding grounds for hundreds of thousands of marine turtles. The other is about Kanha and Belinda's efforts to have poaching there recognized as a problem, let alone stopped.

[PART V]
FIRE ON ALL SIDES—TRYING TO SAVE THE TIGER

There is fire on all sides.

Mamta Sharma, DFO, commenting on
the pressures from poachers when she was
in charge of Rajaji National Park, 1995

India has ... effectively destroyed in twenty years of

freedom what nature had endowed her as a result

of millions of years of organic evolution.

M. S. Mani in
Ecology and Biogeography in India, 1974

CHAPTER 19

THE NIGHT OF
THE SEA TURTLES

Bhitarkanika Sanctuary—
20 March 1992

On this bright moonlit night, after six hours in the small, narrow boat with its hard seats, we slid onto the beach of the island. We were on the landward side. I was glad to see my friend and colleague Shekar Dattatri was already there. There were hatchling turtles everywhere.

An olive ridley hatchling reaches the surf.

We walked up the dune that forms the tiny island. From the top we looked down on the sea. Low waves were breaking. The whole beach for as far as we could see was littered with enormous, glistening olive ridley turtles heaving themselves out of the water. The trails the turtles left on the wet sand made the most beautiful patterns in the moonlight.

Shekar and I went about halfway down the dune and just stood there, overawed. The turtles were so determined to come ashore that they were in fact unstoppable. If you stood or sat in front of them, they just barged on—pushing you aside or trying to get over the top of you. The hatchlings were also possessed of a determination to keep pushing on, but in the opposite direction, trying to reach the sea. All around us adult turtles were excavating nest holes, laying eggs, and filling in their nests. It was a wild free-for-all.

*That first experience of the mass nesting of the turtles was one of the most moving, most extraordinary sights I've ever seen in my life—these incredible animals had so much energy. We estimated that about 100,000 turtles came ashore to lay that night. This phenomenon of mass nesting is called the **arribada**, which is Spanish for "the arrival."*

*Experiencing the **arribada** was like adding a whole new dimension to my life. It was truly awe-inspiring and utterly unlike anything else I've ever experienced. You did not see the classical beauty of nature there as you would in, say, a flower or a tiger gliding through the bamboo. It was elemental, powerful, violent even. The weather was turbulent, the setting barren—and then this miracle happened as all these animals rose out of the sea.*

★ ★ ★

The olive ridley turtle is the smallest and also the most enigmatic of the marine turtles. It is the only species known to gather in *arribadas,* though not all ridleys nest in this manner. Herpetologists now generally agree that there is just one species of ridley turtle, called the olive ridley, *Lepidochelys olivacea.* Olive ridleys are found throughout the tropical seas and small numbers are known to nest on the beaches of Australia, southern Asia, west Africa, and the Americas.

Long after the life histories of the other marine turtles had been documented, that of the olive ridley remained a mystery. It was thought that maybe it did not lay eggs at all but produced live young, as some other reptiles—but no other turtles—do. Then some hatchlings were found near a beach in the Gulf

Right: olive ridley laying eggs.
Opposite: an olive ridley turtle comes ashore to lay her eggs.

Preceding pages: the tigress Nikku snarls at us after we have come upon her in tall grass.

of Mexico. But still no nesting sites were found despite exhaustive searches on both the Atlantic and Pacific shores of Central America where ridleys were numerous.

The answer came to the attention of herpetologists in the 1960s in the form of a film made in 1947 by a Mexican industrialist. It showed an *arribada* of some 40,000 ridleys on an isolated beach on the Atlantic coast of Mexico. What one turtle researcher had called the most mysterious of living animals was suddenly not so mysterious anymore. Stranger still, perhaps, than the great numbers of nesting ridleys, was the fact that they nested during the day. Two other *arribadas* were discovered along the Pacific coast of Costa Rica.

The first known Mexican *arribada,* the one that was filmed in 1947, had been reduced to just a few hundred turtles by 1961, the year the film came to the notice of the world at large. Excessive egg collecting and the slaughter of turtles for meat and leather were the cause. Other *arribadas* in Mexico have suffered a similar fate.

The *arribada* at Bhitarkanika on the Bay of Bengal in the state of Orissa was first recorded in the scientific literature in the early 1970s. But the news barely made a ripple and even today it is a little-known phenomenon. It is one of only two *arribadas* known outside the Americas and is by far the largest.★ In March 1991, exactly a year before Belinda and Shekar were at Bhitarkanika, 610,000 ridleys came ashore to lay while millions of hatchlings of the earlier nesting emerged. Some people calculated that about fifty million hatchlings were produced that year.

Besides the ridley turtles, Bhitarkanika is home to vast numbers of other animals. The largest flock of overwintering bar-headed geese comes here every year. Some 50,000 openbill storks nest in the mangroves during the monsoon. Considerable numbers of saltwater crocodiles, many seven meters and more in length, cruise the waterways. In the trees live enormous lizards, the mangrove monitors, some of them two

---

★In March 1994, a second large *arribada* site was discovered about 275 km south of Bhitarkanika.

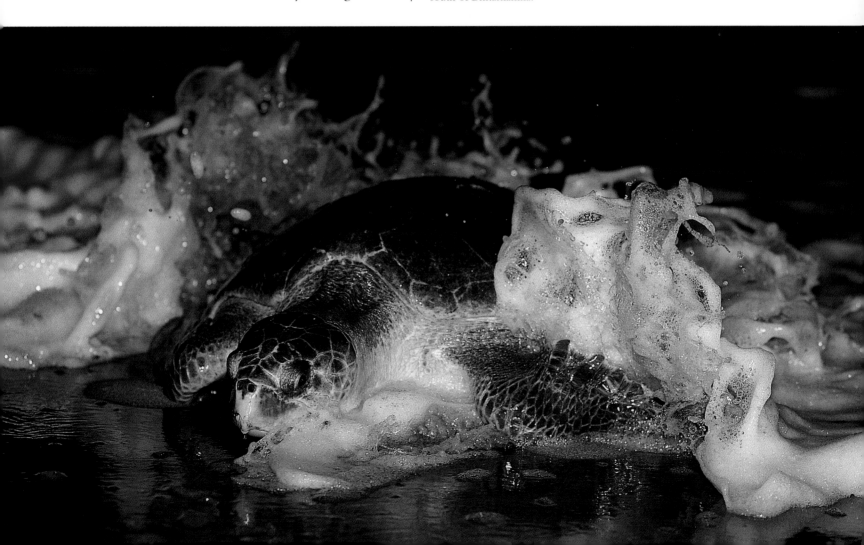

and a half meters long. The endangered Indian python, king cobra, and fishing cat occur there in significant numbers.

All these multitudes reflect that mangrove forests are among the most productive of habitats. And of all the mangrove forest remaining in India, and possibly the world, Bhitarkanika has the greatest diversity of mangrove trees. The sanctuary is also a vital breeding ground for the shrimp and fish that are the mainstay of the local people and commercial fisheries. By all these criteria, Bhitarkanika is one of the most critically important nature reserves. This was recognized in 1975 when it was made into a wildlife sanctuary.

The onslaught that threatens to destroy Bhitarkanika began in 1992, under the banner of much-needed development for this underdeveloped area. The plan calls for the building of sixteen large jetties in the region to accommodate many hundreds of trawlers; the building of ice factories; and the alienation of land to build ponds for shrimp farming. This last project is to be on a grand scale, mostly financed by the World Bank. All the proposed developments break India's environmental laws.

★ ★ ★

Belinda continues:

An olive ridley turtle heads back to the sea.

*It was because of my powerful and strange experience at the **arribada** that I became determined to do all I could to save Bhitarkanika. The first thing I did was to draw up a document that stated clearly and dramatically what was at stake at Bhitarkanika. Through friends at the Madras Crocodile Bank, a private herpetological institution, I sent letters to turtle experts and conservationists in India and around the world asking them to write to both the Indian and Orissa governments objecting to the building of the jetty and other proposed development at Bhitarkanika. I persuaded magazines and newspapers everywhere to publish illustrated stories about the fate of Bhitarkanika and the olive ridley. I didn't really know what else to do at that stage.*

*In 1993, the first jetty, an ice factory, and a road cutting a great swath through the mangroves were built. Hundreds of trawlers fished close to the **arribada** island, flouting all the safeguards and regulations that had been put in place. Hundreds if not thousands of turtles were killed. When I returned to Bhubaneswar, Orissa's capital, to talk to government officials and a growing band of local conservationists, I was followed by plainclothes police, who shadowed me very clumsily in cycle-rickshaws. I was refused permission to go to Bhitarkanika by the government. But I went anyway.*

In 1994 the State Government announced in Parliament that they planned to "denotify" Bhitarkanika—that is, they would strip it even of its sanctuary status. I felt very depressed. The problems in Kanha were also mounting. If anything, they were worse than those at Bhitarkanika.

Adult turtles coming ashore to lay eggs crush many hatchlings going in the opposite direction.

[CHAPTER 20]
POACHING AND PERSECUTION AT KANHA

Odds and ends of information about poaching used to come my way. I am good friends with some of the forest guards, the Baiga tribals, and people in the villages. Over the years they have come to trust me and they tell me about things that worry them or they think are not right. They wouldn't dream of talking to the police or forest department officials, either of whom would brush the villagers aside or even arrest them for the things they said were going on. I came to hear that chital were being shot and their meat and skins sold. Several people told me that sambar had been poisoned inside the park. Then I got news that five tigers and three leopards had been poached in and around Kanha and that six or seven people had been arrested. The Forest Department vehemently denied this or talked around the subject in meaningless generalities. I heard shots on the edge of the park and found a dead sambar with a bullet hole in it. In places where I used to see tigers, suddenly there were none. I had this terrible feeling that things were going wrong, that all the good work in Kahna was about to fall apart.

The forest department authorities claimed that Naxalites were responsible for the poaching in Kanha. Naxalites are a violent offshoot of the Communist Party; they first came to prominence as terrorists in the Naxalbari district in West Bengal. That was in 1970. Since then they have moved, mostly to Andhra Pradesh in central India, where they are still very active, and also here to Madhya Pradesh.

The Naxalites in these forests are rather mysterious figures. They are said to steal from the rich and corrupt and distribute these goods to the poor. They're well-educated. Many of them are women and they are well-armed with AK-47s and hand grenades. They're the champions of the poor, and the villagers and forest tribal people hide them and give them food.

In the summer of 1991, when I was staying at Kipling Camp, Naxalites actually came into Kanha's core area. Before and since, they have operated mostly on the periphery. When they came into the core area they targeted one or two corrupt officers who apparently regularly pocketed half the wages of the tribal laborers. Two of the officials were beaten, literally to within an inch of their lives, by the Naxalites, who made no secret of why they were beating them. Also they put up posters in all the villages telling the people not to tolerate corrupt officials. These in effect said, "If you have a problem let us know and we'll deal with it." This had two immediate effects: everyone was paid fairly (and still is); and the forest department staff fled the park. There were no guards in Kanha. It was deserted. The barriers were left open and there was nobody, absolutely nobody, in the park, staff or visitors.

You never saw the Naxalites, but they had this presence in the forest. Everyone was very frightened. It was suddenly like having a man-eating tiger around. So the Forest Department blamed the Naxalites for

Baiga people have lived for generations as hunter-gatherers in and around Kanha. These are the same forests in which Rudyard Kipling set his *Jungle Book* stories. This Baiga boy evokes Kipling's Mowgli.

everything that went wrong in the park—tiger poaching, fires, unexplained dead animals. Even long after they left, the Naxalites were blamed for all these kinds of things. I've since asked the opinion of the police, who consider the Naxalites their archenemies and who suffer heavy casualties at their hands, and they said that the Naxalites would protect the wildlife, if anything. I've talked to the Baiga and other forest people and they say the same.

So during that summer no visitors came, for it was in all the newspapers that Kanha had been taken over by Naxalites. But it was mostly panic and rumor.

As you well remember, the Baiga are wonderful people to be in the forest with and they have a great sense of humor. One evening at the park's entrance gate, after the visitors had left, I overheard one of the Baigas talk about me to a group of forest guards, guides, and drivers. He said, "Belinda can call up the spirit of the tiger and cast a spell on you"—as if to say, "be careful." No one laughed and I'm still not sure if he was serious or having people on. Maybe this is how even more bizarre stories got around. One day a well-dressed man of middle age came rushing up to me and asked if I was Belinda Wright. I said I was. "Oh good," he said. "I've been told you call up tigers and then wrestle with them. I've come all the way from Bombay to see that."

These were some of the few lighthearted moments in what turned out to be a grim year—from the summer of 1993 to the summer of 1994.

Time and again I talked to the local officials and also to the conservationists in New Delhi about the poaching. They all said I was wrong; that I was a troublemaker, stirring up problems where there were none. The message everywhere was, "Go away, you're a nuisance." Everywhere, that was, except at the central government. The Minister for the Environment, Kamal Nath, who comes from Madhya Pradesh, believed and supported me. He gave me letters saying the park authorities should cooperate and investigate the information that had come to light. That only seemed to inflame the Kanha officers even more. They became obstructive and even abusive.

The various authorities began to harass me. The police seized my vehicle, our old Land Rover, under the pretext that the registration was not in order—which it was. I had to give a policeman 2,000 rupees [$65] to get the vehicle back. The Forest Department came with a search warrant, signed by a former field director we both knew well, to see if I had any illegal wood for building my house. I'd been scrupulous in getting receipts from legal sawmills for all of it, so instead they picked on the building contractor, saying that the wood he had used to make his ladders was stolen from the forest. The poor man could not prove otherwise so he was fined.

They came again and again, saying that my visa was out of order and that Kipling Camp's resident elephant was kept illegally. The officials were aggressive, some looking me up and down with nasty expressions on their faces. These things get to you after a while—which, of course, they're meant to do.

But I kept on saying to myself, "I'm right and I won't budge. Something is very wrong here and I'll get to the bottom of it." The Minister for the Environment in Delhi again sent letters to the local officials, telling them to leave me alone. But they didn't.

In the summer of 1993, in the midst of all this unpleasantness, I had a confrontation with a local leopard, a large male who was the terror of the local dogs. This same leopard had taken one of the dogs: just a soft plaintive "yip" from the dog and it was gone, taken from between two people sitting by the fire. The fellows ran after the leopard with sticks and torches, but he just vanished without a further sound.

Summers are very hot at Shergarh and the only way I can get some rest is to take my bed outside and sleep under the stars. The Camp's grounds were part of the leopard's territory, but so far it had not been a problem. One night when I was really tired I heard chital alarm calls close by. I was already dozing off and I remember thinking, "Oh dear, the leopard's close tonight." But I just fell asleep.

In my sleep I heard something, presumably a snarl from the leopard. I shot up in bed, suddenly wide awake. There was the leopard crouched just centimeters from my foot. I could see him clearly in the moonlight. I screamed at the top of my voice, and the leopard jumped into the air, roaring, and ran off. The langurs must have woken, for they too gave their distress calls. I sat there for many minutes, unable to move or make any sound, let alone speak. That's only the second time in my life that I have been literally stunned. The first was in Ranthambhore when Abu charged us. I still slept outside after that, but always under a mosquito net. It was enough to keep the leopard away.

Things were getting worse in Bhitarkanika: more jetties planned; more World Bank–funded shrimp projects; more mangroves cleared; more threats of denotification. I became increasingly distressed by this and the continuing threats and harassment in Kanha. I felt totally powerless and alone, a voice blown away by the wind of indifference. I went back to Bhubaneswar, the capital of Orissa, to see what was happening at Bhitarkanika. That visit was an important turning point for me in all this.

It is vital that local people take up conservation issues, for they are on the spot and so can gather information more readily and keep the pressure on the governments and organizations that pose the threats. When I got to Bhubaneswar, I met with a group of students who had taken up the Bhitarkanika cause and were doing good work. Cracks were

Baiga women in a ceremonial dance in their village near Kanha.

*beginning to appear in the government's determination and plans. I also met the opposition party's spokesman for the environment in the Orissa Parliament, Banka Behary Das. He said, "I'm so happy to meet you. You are a hero of Orissa. I can't thank you enough for bringing the Bhitarkanika issue to the notice of so many people." While this was music to my ears after all the earlier frustrations, I had to remind myself this was a politician speaking. But I found him a sincere man, a real conservation warrior. Already he had sown the seeds of dissent and stirred up trouble in the Orissa Parliament on the denotification move. I also discovered that all the information I'd prepared and sent all around the world with photographs of the **arribada** had not fallen on deaf ears. Substantial stories, all condemning the Orissa government's moves, appeared in newspapers and magazines in India, and abroad in such periodicals as the **Boston Globe** and **New Scientist**. The government had been inundated with faxes and letters.*

I was incredibly touched and thrilled by these responses. I suddenly realized that my efforts, including the information I'd so painstakingly gathered, were having an effect. Bhitarkanika was becoming a major conservation issue. Very few people knew that I was the instigator. That too gave me a kick. It was an absolute watershed in my life. And it didn't even involve tigers! It wasn't pleasure I felt, more satisfaction I suppose. I didn't want to waste my life beating my head against a brick wall.

Up to then I'd been trying to make a film on cobras for the National Geographic Society as well as working on the conservation issues. I was only concentrating on the film in bursts, but fortunately my coproducer Shekar Dattatri was very understanding. When I was at my lowest ebb, I felt I was failing in Bhitarkanika and Kanha, failing as a filmmaker and as a person. Then suddenly things turned around at Bhitarkanika. I hadn't solved the problem but I had succeeded in motivating people to stand up and say, "We must save Bhitarkanika!" It was like lighting a

There was a leopard around Belinda's house during the summer of 1994.

flame and, after watching it splutter and splutter, seeing it suddenly take hold and burn brightly.

This gave me heart to tackle the Kanha poaching business head on. I went to Delhi to attend a Cat Specialist Group meeting and let the convener know I wanted to say something. I started in a quavering voice, "I'm sorry to have to tell you this but things are not right in Kanha. There is poaching of tigers and other animals," and then outlined what I knew.

There was a stunned silence. Kanha was supposed to be the one place where nothing could ever happen to the tiger. It was too remote, the forests were too big, the tigers too numerous. After that initial nervous announcement I felt stronger and stronger and was able to point out the problems lucidly and logically. I still got into trouble with some people, but thankfully enough were convinced.

I suddenly realized that I really had nothing to lose. My detractors had tried everything to frighten me: harassing me; taking away my vehicle; taking away our elephant—all without real effect. I returned to Shergarh completely at peace with the world. I was no less determined about the problems, but now I knew that, slowly and steadily, I **would** get somewhere. At last I knew that I was not wasting my time. Before, it was all frustration: I was getting no results. Now at least I knew that if I did my best I could contribute something. My tenacity, my character, whatever it is, would make a difference. I also thought I should become a bit bolder.

Then, on the afternoon of 30 April 1994, there was a knock on the door. There I found a strange man with a bag in his hand who'd just stumbled off the bus.

[C H A P T E R 2 1]

TIGER POACHING EXPOSED

As I opened the door to this stranger, he said, "Hello Belinda, how nice to see you again," and kissed me on the cheek. Later, he introduced himself as Firoz and told me that he had come in response to a message I'd sent to Ashok Kumar, adviser to the Minister for the Environment. He turned out to be the same Firoz who had been instrumental in the seizure of 400 kilograms of tiger bones in Delhi in 1993. We had not met before. He apologized for the earlier familiarity, but as there were other people in the house, he wanted to give the impression that he was a friend who'd dropped in.

The information that brought Firoz to Shergarh was that someone had tiger skins and bones for sale in Baihar, a small town bordering Kanha's buffer zone and only about thirty kilometers from Shergarh. I had come on this information quite by chance. Little hole-in-the-wall telephone booths have sprung up everywhere since India modernized its telephone system. I have no phone here so I had made a rare visit to Baihar to make some calls. When I'd finished the calls, the man owning the booth started up a conversation. "Are you going to Delhi soon?" he asked. I said I was. Then he said, "I've got some-

The telephone booth and *paan* shop in Baihar near Kanha where Belinda was offered tiger skins in April 1994.

thing I want to talk to you about." At first I thought he wanted a favor done, and I was inclined to ignore him. But there was a look on his face that made me curious, and I started playing for time. I made some more calls and did some shopping. I was about to leave when he called me over and took me aside. He said, "I've four tiger skins for sale, do you know anyone who wants to buy them?" Almost instinctively, I knew what to do. I stayed very cool, appearing not at all surprised, and said, "Oh, that's very interesting. I personally don't want to buy them, but I think I know somebody who might. Could you just keep them for a few days?" And then I asked casually, "Where did you get these skins from?" "From around here," he said. "It's very easy. I get them from the tribals."

I immediately sent a coded message to Ashok Kumar. From past experience there seemed no point in giving the information to the local authorities, and I didn't want to try to handle the case myself and blow my cover so close to Kanha. Forty-eight hours later, there was Firoz.

I gave him the information I had, a description of the man, where he was, and what he had said. Firoz left straight away. Another forty-eight hours later, he came back, just smiled, and said, "Well, I did the job." He added, "That was the most accurate information I've ever received and as a result the quickest and easiest job I've ever done."

Firoz had gone to see the man at the telephone booth and gotten into conversation with him. He then accompanied the man to his house, where he showed Firoz one tiger skin. Firoz then took the information to the police, who arrested the man and seized the tiger skin. Another man involved in it all, and probably the owner of the other three skins, ran away and was never caught. After the police interrogated the telephone booth man, four other people were arrested, including one of the men who actually killed the tiger. At last we had proof of tiger poaching going on near Kanha—and it was not something the authorities could hide.

Firoz and I talked all night. I told him about all the other problems and rumors that were going around. In the end I said that these seizures and arrests are fantastic, but just to walk away from them and never to know the whole story was a tragedy. Here was an opportunity to really find out everything all the way down the line—how the tigers were killed, where they were killed and by whom, how the traders established their network, and where the tiger skins and bones finished up. By the early morning I had persuaded Firoz to help me take up this particular case as a test, and see how far we could take it. That is what we did for the next ten days.

We began with the man at the phone booth, who was still in custody at Baihar police station. He was in a small cell, in chains, in this brick block of a building that burned under the summer sun with no trees to shade it. From him we learned who actually killed the tiger. It was a group of four people, only one of whom was caught. That man had been taken to a proper jail in a larger town called Balaghat about 100 kilometers to the southwest.

I really surprised myself by how quickly I became immersed in this world of police stations and jails. Like most people I was intimidated by the police and avoided them at all costs. But suddenly I found I had a knack for dealing with them and the criminals they had in custody. I found that my anger, determination, and passion for the tiger overcame my misgivings about people in uniform.

The prison in Balaghat was originally built by the British sixty or more years ago and is a more agreeable place than the Baihar police station. There are shady trees all around, some even inside the prison

A tiger poacher under arrest near Baihar.

walls. The prisoners are not shackled and they look well-fed. We passed through many locked and barred gates and eventually found our way to the superintendent's office. He was a clean-shaven man with a large belly, wearing a khaki uniform. The superintendant liked to bark his instructions and reinforce them by hitting a wooden table with a stick.

The prisoner was a fairly young man with a mop of thick hair. I had some sympathy for him. He was a very different kind of person to the telephone booth man. The latter was an opportunist who tried to make some easy money by trading in tigers, which he knew to be illegal. The actual poacher was a Gond tribal, a poor subsistence farmer living in a tiny village deep in the forest. He and his family had very little. The tiger killed a buffalo, a valuable animal. So he and his accomplices cut a hole in the dead buffalo and filled it with poison—an insecticide supplied by a middleman. The tiger died that night after eating the poisoned carcass. It was a slow and horrible death.

The poacher was brought into the office in handcuffs and made to sit on the floor. I sat down beside him, offering him a cigarette. I talked to him, in Hindi, at length.

I asked him why the village people had not reported the buffalo's death to the Forest Department and put in a claim for compensation. There is a scheme whereby people who lose livestock to tigers are reimbursed for their losses; it is an effort to stop people from killing the predators. The poacher scoffed at that. "Nobody reports anything to the Forest Department," he said, "for everyone is corrupt. The forest guard will not even come and look at your dead cow or buffalo unless you pay him a bribe. There is another bribe to be paid for him to sign the form. This involves hundreds of rupees. We simply do not have this money and even if we did, there is no guarantee we will get the compensation—some government person will pocket it most of the time." He told me the same goes for poaching. "If you're caught with a jungle fowl you pay the forest guard 25 rupees [80 cents] and he'll keep quiet. If you have a chital stag it costs you 100 rupees and a sambar 200 rupees. There is a set figure for everything. That is why poaching cases are never registered—the guards make money instead—and that is why officials say that there is no poaching. Some even believe it."

For the villagers it is not a matter of real choice. They cannot deal with the authorities yet they need the money to buy new cows or buffaloes so they fall into the hands of the traders in illegal skins and bones. These people supply the poison for free and pay pretty good money for dead tigers. The amount varies enormously from just a few hundred rupees to several thousand. This man and his three accomplices got 3,000 rupees [$100] for just the skin. He said they'd buried the tiger carcass without removing the bones. "Then I had to go away for my younger brother's wedding." In his own eyes and the eyes of the people in his village, he had not committed a crime—he had merely protected his property and his livelihood.

I asked the poacher if he would show us the place where they'd buried the tiger carcass. He agreed. Two policemen came with us; both had rifles and the prisoner was chained to one of them. That visit was quite a moving experience. We went to a tiny village of about fifteen to twenty houses, called Bariya. It is just outside Kanha's buffer zone. Immediately around it is farmland that is surrounded by tall forest. The road in was used almost exclusively by bullock carts and was very rough. It was a hot, dry day and altogether most uncomfortable in my small hardtop Land Rover.

The row of neat houses made of mud and grass with tiled roofs was crowded along a central lane and shaded by huge fig trees. When we arrived, the whole village came out and greeted the young man, who was shackled. His wife and his aunt asked us if we would like to eat. That was an amazing gesture, for these are very poor people. We went inside their house, which was totally without furniture. We all sat on the earth floor. There was a pile of onions in one corner and a grain bin made of woven bamboo in the other. There was a ladder up to a loft where everyone slept.

The prisoner was given his food first while we and his family

Digging up the tiger carcass.

looked on. It was a simple meal of rice and dal. When he had finished, his wife cleared things away and helped him wash his manacled hands. Then we were given our food. It was all done with great dignity and unbowed courtesy. Chickens kept walking in and out and a goat tried to get into the already crowded room. A buffalo pushed its head through a window.

We left for the site where the tiger had been buried. His family said goodbye to the prisoner, touching his feet in respect and giving him a clean shirt. We drove through the forest for some distance but had to walk the last three kilometers in intense heat. We could smell the carcass long before we reached the spot where it was buried. The prisoner, still in chains, dug it up. The stench was indescribable. One of the policemen vomited. There were large chunks of rotting flesh, but no bones. The poacher looked genuinely surprised and said the bones had been there after he'd helped skin the tiger. I believed him. It seems his accomplices had left him to take the blame and then made off with the more valuable bones. We took the poacher back to jail and spent several days trying to find the others.

Somehow this whole saga appeared, totally garbled, in the local press. The officials at Kanha were embarrassed and on the verge of panic. None of them knew who Firoz was and why he was here, nor that the arrests were made as a result of information I had supplied.

The forest officer who was charged with the job of investigating the reports came to see me at Shergarh. I've known him for years and find him a likeable person with a genuine desire to stop poaching. He was one of the few people who were willing to admit that poaching was going on and he was keen to do something about it. We sat on the verandah here, the three of us. I remember sitting there while the forest officer and Firoz chatted, thinking about the implications of this case. It was just a few minutes but my entire life flashed through my

A tigress in a steel trap near Raipur in Madhya Pradesh.

mind—my past life, our work together, my involvement with tigers and conservation, and also what I hoped my future life would be. I was looking forward to slowing down a little so that I could spend more time in my wonderful new house. I would do conservation work around Kanha, make the odd film, and involve myself more in the life of the Baiga people. I was looking forward to a peaceful life, without always being in a rush. I planned to form some kind of society, "Friends of Kanha" or something like that, that would act as a watchdog.

I knew that once I told the Forest Department that it was I who had given the information, there would be no going back. My whole life would change. It may seem strange that this would make such a pro-

found difference, but I had a sense of impending doom should I go down that road. I knew my privacy and the way of life I had chosen would be gone forever. If I revealed my involvement, I knew I would have to take up the battle full-time and that my days of observing wildlife in tranquility would be gone. I would become an angry person. In the last few days I'd seen enough to know that poaching was far more widespread than anybody suspected and that it **had** to be documented and exposed. So far nobody had tried to get to the root of the problem, to analyze exactly what was going on. In those few minutes, or seconds it seemed—it was an extraordinary experience—I also knew I was the one who had to do it.

The forest officer, in the meantime, kept asking Firoz again and again, "Who gave this information? Who?" Firoz did not want to give me away and his answers were evasive. Suddenly I interrupted and said, "I gave the information." The officer's mouth fell open; he couldn't believe it. But no one was more surprised than Firoz. We'd talked about it earlier and he didn't think I would choose that kind of life — being permanently on the run, always under stress.

After the forest officer left, I suggested to Firoz that he and I should just vanish for two months and do a huge undercover operation in central India, in Madhya Pradesh, the place with the most tigers in the world. I told him that people always point to Madhya Pradesh as being the safest place for tigers, but that I kept getting information that it wasn't, and that poaching was becoming a serious problem. So far it was all rumors and circumstantial evidence. It was time to find out what was really going on. Firoz agreed.

So for two months, June and July, we traveled the length and breadth of the state in my small Land Rover. No one knew where we were or what we were doing. We stopped everywhere in our wanderings. We'd enquire about skins and bones. To my horror, we were offered the skins and bones of tigers or leopards in every city and town we investigated throughout Madhya Pradesh. We found that the Forest Department had little idea of what was going on. Sometimes it was a case of not wanting to know, but for the most part they just hadn't a clue.

Raipur, a city to the southeast of Kanha, is a classic example. An old friend of mine had a senior position at the Forest Department there and we went to see him. We had credentials from the Ministry of the Environment in Delhi and we told the forest officials in Raipur that we were looking into the possibility of tiger poaching. My friend and his colleagues said, quite sincerely, "You know, we're so fortunate: unlike so many other places, we have absolutely no poaching here. We're just so lucky — none whatsoever." After the meeting we walked out of the gate and down the road. There was a cycle-rickshaw driver there. Firoz walked up to him and said, "I'm here to buy tiger skins and leopard skins, do you know of any?" The man said, "Sure, fine, I'll take you to meet someone." Ten minutes later we were talking to a dealer in skins. We found another two such contacts in Raipur within twenty-four hours.

To begin with, our objective was only to gather information. We had to find out what was going on and how far-reaching the problem was. At the end of the two months we were in Jabalpur. We became friends there with the most senior policeman and passed on to him all the information that could be acted on. Shortly afterwards the police, sometimes with us, sometimes on their own, went bang, bang, bang and carried out a num-

ber of raids and arrests. It sounds simple but we had many exciting and interesting adventures.

One tiger poaching case became very public. It was near Raipur, the place they were so lucky not to have any tiger poaching. We visited the city's small zoo, where we were shown a tigress, looking miserable in a tiny cage. Half of her left front paw was missing. The editor of the local newspaper told us her story.

Six months before, the tigress had been caught in a steel trap in the Manipur forest in the Raipur district. Her roars and screams were heard by a forest guard who informed the district forest officer. The DFO immediately contacted Kanha, where the only tranquilizer gun in Madhya Pradesh is kept. The Kanha officials told him they didn't have the funds or a vehicle to send the gun. A Jeep was sent from Raipur and seventy-two hours later a man and tranquilizer gun arrived. In the meantime, the Manipur people proved ingenious and compassionate. They filled a child's homemade toy cart with food and water and pushed it toward the tigress with a long stick. She ate and drank and stayed alive. This was in front of a crowd that swelled to about 8,000 people. Eventually the tigress was tranquilized and taken to the zoo, where veterinarians amputated half her paw.

Back at Shergarh, I wrote the report of our two months' work, complete with names of poachers and traders, where they lived, and what they offered. In the summary I wrote:

"In the past two months the authors have positively identified forty-two tiger and leopard poachers in Madhya Pradesh and thirty-two traders in skins and bones. The skins or bones of thirty-nine freshly killed tigers were in one way or another offered at different locations to the authors during their investigations. There was talk of the whereabouts, in five towns, of a further forty-five tiger and leopard skins."

Many of the poachers and traders were arrested and quantities of skins and bones confiscated. All of the people arrested, however, are now out on bail. None have been convicted by the courts. In fact only one or perhaps two people have *ever* been convicted and sent to prison for tiger poaching in India. The laws have no teeth and the courts are too slow and unwieldy.

There is no doubt that the report is the most important contemporary document on the problem of tiger poaching in India. It stunned everyone who saw it, from the Minister for the Environment downward. The World Wide Fund for Nature–India, which controls TRAFFIC, sacked Firoz, and their tiger trade investigations ground to a halt.

Toward the end of our two months, something else happened that had far-reaching implications. Firoz had gone to investigate the whereabouts of a tiger bone trader. I stayed behind in Jabalpur at a fairly basic hotel. Just before he left, Firoz asked me to telephone a friend of his, Samir Thapar in New Delhi, about information he had about someone keeping tiger cubs. Samir was a buddy of Firoz's. They'd met socially not long before, and Samir, realizing Firoz wasn't making much money, invited him to stay at his company's guest house in New Delhi. Samir has an abiding interest in wildlife and was once a hunter of deer and wild pigs. He is also a member of one of India's wealthiest families: The Thapar Group, their group of companies, of which his uncle Lalit Mohan Thapar is chairman, is the fourth largest in India.

Up to now we had been operating on Firoz's pay from TRAFFIC—a derisory amount—and what money I had with me when Firoz arrived at Shergarh. Firoz left with most of the remaining funds for an indefinite journey. I had the equivalent of about five dollars left. Not enough even for a meal. The hotel bill alone would come to hundreds of dollars, and a telephone call to Delhi would add to that. "Ah well," I thought, "in for a penny, in for a pound."

So I rang Samir and explained who I was and asked if he had that information about the tiger cubs. I thought it would just be a short call, yes or no and that would be it. Samir said no, he hadn't any more information. Then we started chatting, and I suddenly realized that Samir had no idea what Firoz was doing. So as we talked I told him about our work in Madhya Pradesh. Occasionally I'd look at my watch, thinking, "How am I going to pay for this?" In the end we talked for an hour. I told him about my aims and objectives, the sort of life I'd been leading during the past two months. Samir is young, about thirty I'd guess, and he

was intrigued by the cops and robbers excitement of it all. He just could not believe what we were doing. Then he asked, "Who's paying for all this?" I said, "As a matter of fact, nobody, because WWF/TRAFFIC has just terminated Firoz's investigation contract. Right at a critical juncture. I have exactly 137 rupees, which will not even cover my meals for the day. I'm about to contact my father in Calcutta and ask if he can send some money." To which Samir said, "How much do you need?" "Twenty thousand rupees [$650]." "When by?" he said. "Tomorrow." Then he said, "I want to help you. There will be a man knocking at your door tomorrow." And there was; he handed me 20,000 rupees and walked away.

Since then, Samir has generously helped me in many ways. On the telephone, and again when we later met in New Delhi, I talked to Samir about forming a society that would employ people to follow up leads, gather information, and also train investigators—that is, to organize this whole business of detecting wildlife poaching and trading and devising methods to combat it. Things really got off the ground when Samir took me to meet his uncle. I'd met Lalit Thapar before and he has known my parents for years and years.

I met with Lalit Thapar at his gorgeous residence in New Delhi, a large house with a beautiful garden of green lawns and big trees, located in the best part of town. He was in his midsixties; he was eloquent, extremely wise, and clearly had impeccable taste. A very elegant, urbane man, he was dressed on that day in a perfectly tailored suit. A black Labrador dog pattered behind him wherever he went. He had an aura around him of someone who had succeeded and who was very com-

Belinda at Baihar police station in May 1994 with the skins of a tiger and a chital killed near Kanha. The skins were seized in her first successful operation against poachers.

fortable with his success, his wisdom, and his power. There was a comfortable, relaxed atmosphere in his house.

I told him with great passion about what I had been doing and how I would like him to get involved and be the president of a society. I would call it the Wildlife Protection Society of India. Mr. Thapar's reaction was fascinating. He listened intently to everything I was saying and I could tell by his eyes that his interest had been aroused. When I had finished he sat back, took a drag at his cigarette and, after a long pause, said, "What you told me is amazing, it's riveting. I cannot express in words how much I admire what you're doing. There's obviously a problem out there, and what you've done so far is spectacular. But why should a society like you're proposing make a difference? You've told me facts and figures that I find distressing and alarming, but I'm not convinced that such an organization can make a difference. Come back to me when you think you can convince me."

It was the best thing that ever happened. I went home with my tail between my legs. I thought I was a kind of hero and could just drift along and everyone would throw money at me. I needed his comments to jolt me back to reality. So I went away and I wrote two papers, "The Tiger Crisis in India" and "The Wildlife Protection Society of India." In the second one I set out specific ways such an organization could make a difference. I was forced to sit down and think it all through. At the end I came to the conclusion that if we did A, B, C, and D we might just be able to lick this.

I took these documents to Lalit Thapar and he agreed not only to be the president of the Wildlife Protection Society of India, but to give the society office accommodation at his corporate headquarters. From the beginning I was honest with him and said we could never compromise on trying to save the tiger, no matter who was involved in its destruction. He understood that. He just wanted someone to get on with the job and he trusted me.

I felt there was another reason for his involvement. We never talked about this but I can see it in his eyes sometimes. People like him, when they were young, probably had some of the best experiences of their lives in the jungles of India. I'm not talking about hunting and killing animals, but just being deep in the forest in a remote bungalow with campfires and oil lamps and having wonderful conversations with friends: that whole atmosphere of being in the jungle and being really honest with one another, of sensing the fresh air and hearing the birds and perhaps the roar of a tiger. To someone like Lalit Thapar, perhaps, this is the real India: the India he treasures. I have the feeling sometimes that he lends his support to save those memories and that way of life—a bit of them anyway.

A few months later, in September 1994, the society was formed. Ashok Kumar, the founder and director of TRAFFIC-India, joined WPSI and we took on a small staff. I was incredibly lucky to have the support of a man of Ashok's experience and caliber. In the mid-1970s he had joined my mother Anne in stalking tiger-skin traders in the back streets of Calcutta. During an eleven-year stint working in the Middle East, he had continued his interest in trying to expose the illegal wildlife trade. He has been a leading light in the conservation movement ever since.

In between the tasks involved in setting up the society, Firoz and I continued to investigate reports of poaching and trading. We next went to the northern state of Uttar Pradesh, where Billy Arjan Singh was worried about tiger poaching in Dudhwa. Like me, he'd alerted the Forest Department to the possibilities and had given them what information he had. And, like me, he'd gotten nowhere.

To begin with, I was a bit hesitant in going there. In comparison to Uttar Pradesh, Madhya Pradesh is paradise. I knew we would have to deal with hardened criminals in Uttar Pradesh. It would be nasty, dangerous, and sleazy.

How Many Tigers in India?

Right profile of tiger (T-004); this photograph was taken by one of Dr. Ullas Karanth's camera traps.

Every four to five years a comprehensive tiger census is conducted throughout India. The numbers arrived at have been highly significant for the tiger's fortunes. In the first census, in 1972, tigers were said to number 1,827. This alarming and unexpected low count was a signal event in starting Project Tiger and other conservation measures. The 1989 census claimed that India's tiger numbers had risen to 4,334. This spectacular increase led to self-congratulations at Project Tiger's headquarters and among park managers, and complacency in the country at large. But in the 1993 census tiger numbers were said to have declined to only 3,750. To conservationists it came as a final warning, especially as it coincided with the detection of wide-scale tiger poaching for the trade in their bones. Unfortunately, park managers and the people of India remained complacent.

But just how accurate are these figures? They were arrived at through inaccurate and highly subjective methods. No rigorously tested scientific program was, or is, used by park management to determine the populations of wild tigers.

In the mid-1980s, Dr. Ullas Karanth analyzed the methods and their results. He looked at census figures of tigers as well as those of their prey species and found both to be inaccurate—in some cases wildly so. From long-term ecological studies by Dr. Karanth in India and by American and Nepali scientists in Chitwan National Park, the optimum density of tigers—that is, the number of tigers per hundred square kilometers of a given habitat—is known. The minimum number of prey animals required to sustain them has also been established. The census figures given for some reserves were far greater than any possible density of tigers. In others the number of tigers reported would consume the entire estimated prey in one year. It has been demonstrated that tiger populations are remarkably stable after rapidly attaining saturation densities and do not continuously increase. Yet many reserves recorded an increase at every census, sometimes in dramatic numbers.

The census method used throughout India is for park staff to disperse throughout the reserve and to trace a sample of each discrete set of pug marks onto a piece of glass. It is assumed that each tiger has unique paw imprints and that the differences between them can be recognized by the census takers. However, except for a few individual tigers who may have misshapen or injured feet, pug marks are difficult to tell apart. Also the tracks of the same tiger in, say, sand, look very different to those in mud. The speed at which a tiger moves also alters the imprint. As a consequence the same tiger is often counted many times.

When Dr. Karanth presented a number of experienced census operators with thirty-three pug marks from four zoo tigers, they identified between six and twenty-three different tigers. On the other hand, soil conditions in many reserves are not conducive to getting any prints at all. Therefore both underestimates and overestimates of tiger numbers are inevitable, but no one can say by how much.

To count all the tigers in India is like trying to count all the fish in the sea—it is impossi-

The top photograph is a left profile of a tiger (T-004), below is a left profile of a tigress (T-005). Note the difference in stripe patterns between the same profiles of these different individuals and also between the right and left profiles of the same tiger (see opposite page). Photographs taken by Dr. Ullas Karanth's camera traps.

move about mostly at night, other techniques are required. For small animals such as rodents, the classic census method is known as capture-mark-recapture. Individuals are trapped, marked in some way so that they can be recognized again, and released. The population density can be accurately assessed by setting lines of traps along transects over a period of time.

This method would not work for the tiger. But an innovative adaptation of it, perfected by Dr. Karanth, is elegant in its simplicity. Tigers move through the jungles along well-known trails. They like to walk along forest roads, for example. By setting up lines of camera "traps" that are connected to an infrared device that the tigers themselves trigger, the animals are "captured" and "recaptured" on film along their trails. Each tiger is uniquely marked by its stripes and facial markings and no two tigers have the same pattern along their sides, so no two tigers are counted twice this way. From these "trapped" tigers, population densities can be worked out, population trends noted, and some indication of the true status of the tiger established.

However, Project Tiger and the Forest Departments of the various states still eschew these simple, accurate scientific techniques. They say they are expensive and time-consuming and instead persist with the inaccurate and logistically complex method of the pug mark tracings.

ble and whatever figures are arrived at are of little value. What can be established, using comparatively simple, well-proven scientific field techniques, is the population densities of both the tiger and its prey. Deer, antelope, wild pigs, gaur, and monkeys—animals that move

about during the day—can be counted along measured transects through their habitats. From this information, accurate and useful estimates can be made of the numbers of these animals in a given area.

For shy animals that remain hidden or that

[CHAPTER 22]
TIGERS IN TRAPS—AGAIN

Billy had set up the Billy Arjan Singh Tiger Foundation "to provide assistance for the deteriorating status of Dudhwa National Park." He also recruited several informants who gave good intelligence about tiger and leopard bones and skins being sold in the nearby towns of Palia and Lakhimpur-Kheri. Some of the animals were killed in Dudhwa itself. The police had seized some bones and skins. Billy confronted the park's field director with this evidence, but the official refused to act and, in Billy's words, "brazenly stated that there was no wildlife crime in the area." The tigers and leopards seized, the field director said, had come from Nepal, which has a common border with Dudhwa. But, as Billy pointed out, there is no forest and there are no tigers on the Nepal side of Dudhwa.

In September 1994, things were so bad—there were so many reports of poaching—that Billy asked Firoz and me to see what we could find out. This time we had with us a police guard armed with an AK-47. His cover was that he was our driver. We contacted four or five different groups (gangs of criminals really) who were operating in the area, posing as wealthy buyers of tiger and leopard bones and skins.

The first gang we contacted was in a village, whose name I forget, near Dudhwa and almost on the Nepal border. They asked us to meet them in the dead of night, which we did. I've seldom felt more uncomfortable. The people were very nervous and suspicious and said they would talk to only one person. So Firoz went off on his own, about half a kilometer on foot, and met three of the ringleaders. They said they could deliver twenty-one tiger skins, six leopard skins, some rhino horns, and other contraband. They didn't show Firoz anything. They just wanted to see his money and take a big advance. We couldn't get anywhere with them and suspected the skins and bones—if they really existed—were stashed over the border in Nepal.

Over the next few days we tried to work out who the other gangs were and if there were any links between them, where they were getting the tigers and leopards, and who they were selling them to. We had a ghastly time in a truly dreadful hotel in Lakhimpur. The rooms were

cement cells painted a sickly green, with two beds in the middle. They were full of mosquitoes. The bathrooms stank and the water leaked and dripped constantly.

A trader with one of his henchmen came to meet us there. They saw we had whisky and polished off the entire bottle. It was all we had with us and I was furious. But we had to be jolly with these people, of course, to win their confidence. We slapped them on the back and asked if they wanted anything to eat—always speaking in English and pretending I couldn't speak a word of Hindi. The trader and his mate talked to each other in Hindi all the time and I got a lot of good information that way.

The main trader was a local lawyer, very suspicious, very cunning and quick-witted, and smartly dressed in a suit. His companion was also a quite senior man in the community. He was dressed in kurta-pajamas. They were really disgusting people. We ordered some food, which they ate slurping and burping and yelling for more whisky. They kept looking me up and down lecherously. To try to speed things up and also act out our cover, I played the part of a whining wife. I kept saying, "Oh, sweetheart, I don't like it here. I want to go back to Delhi. I've got so much shopping to do, please, can we finish all this quickly." Firoz would then turn to the trader and say exasperatedly, "What can I do, we must get this business over and done with." Then they'd giggle and laugh. It was horrible. They offered us four tiger skins and produced two leopard skins. The trader said he also had rhino horns.

The next day we suggested to a senior forest department official that he make the arrests when we had everything set up. His first reaction was to go into a rage and shout, "This kind of thing will bring disrepute to Dudhwa and the Forest Department." He didn't even want to know the details. When he calmed down he said he would do it, and then vanished—just left the place.

The third group of criminals contacted us many times but never came to the hotel when they said they would. Finally they came at three o'clock in the morning. They knocked on my door, I opened it, and they started talking business. There were three of them. The leader was cross-eyed and had a big mustache. He was quite young, shifty, and suspicious, and very, very greedy. They said they had two or three tiger skins, but we'd have to wait another day for them to be collected.

We met one or two other gangs. They all wanted money. They would say they needed it so they could buy the skins and then sell them to us. But as usual we were adamant about not giving any money. It hurts them even more if the traders themselves put up the money, so when they are arrested they lose their money and their goods. They are also put in jail, for a while at least, where they are interrogated—vigorously at times. No one trusted anyone else and everyone was trying to outsmart the others. This went on for about ten days.

During this time our local contacts were muddling things up in their eagerness for us to seize the maximum number of bones and skins and arrest as many gangs as possible. It was beocming increasingly messy and complicated and we had to make our move. We decided to concentrate first on the gang led by the cross-eyed man. We agreed to meet him down a narrow lane in the middle of the night.

It was the worst kind of place. That side of Lakhimpur-Kheri is the pits. It has in abundance all the things that are distressing in India, and it is one enormous slum. The roads are potholed and rutted. Raw sewage runs down the gutters past stinking, ramshackle hovels. At night all you see is pigs, snorting and groveling through the sewage, eating human feces. Yowling dogs covered in skin diseases trot up and down.

We sat in the car in this horrible, stinking place and waited. There were funny squeaking sounds and rats running

hither and thither. Clouds of mosquitoes whined around us—I've never been bitten so much in my life. Nobody came. We got out of the car and stretched our legs. Then a motorcycle went by, ridden by one of the traders, and after a while two cycle-rickshaws came up with the traders' accomplices in them. We said, "You're late." They said, "Yeah, but we don't want to do the deal here." We'd agreed to buy their tiger skins. "We want to do it down this road, you'll see some shutters and a light on. Go there," they said and took off. After a few moments we followed them in the car and found the place—a shop with the shutters open and a light on in the room. It was part of a row of car-repair workshops. The burned out skeletons of buses and trucks stood abandoned along the already narrow street. We parked next to one of them.

Our driver/policeman got out, and leaning against the car he looked into the lighted room. I was in the driver's seat and suddenly he said to me, "I can see them loading a pistol." I said, "Oh, don't worry, let them load a pistol. Tell them that we've waited long enough." He shouted this information across to them and they shouted back, "We're coming, we're coming."

Five people came out of the shack. They told us to meet them at a certain temple and gave us directions. It was another dreadful, narrow lane with big piles of stinking rubbish from the town and again lots of pigs, howling mangy dogs, and swarms of rats. One man came up and asked us if we had the money with us. We said we had. He went away

The bones and skin of an entire tiger. This huge ten-foot-long male tiger was caught in a steel trap set by the poachers near their village. They said they had heard it roaring with pain all night and the following morning had returned to the forest and beaten the exhausted tiger to death with sticks.

again. We were sort of trapped there and when no one returned we got suspicious. It looked like we were being set up for a robbery.

At about 1:30 we decided it wasn't safe to wait any longer. I started the car, drove on a bit, and turned around. We couldn't see anyone. I continued to drive on very, very slowly. Two policemen on bicycles went by. A little farther on, two people suddenly appeared in front of us. We recognized them as two of the traders. Our "driver," who spoke Hindi, said to them, "Quick, quick, there are policemen here, so these people don't want to hang about. If you want to do the deal do it now." At that stage another person walked forward with a large bag in his hand. We said, "Have you got the goods?" He said, "Yes." "Well come on, hurry up and get in," we urged him. Two of the traders—including the one with the bag—squeezed into the front seat with me. The third, the squinting leader, got into the back and sat between Firoz and our "driver."

I took off, fast. They yelled, "What are you doing?" Firoz said, with the "driver" translating, "What in the hell do you think? We're not going to do business in a place like this. We're not going to hand over all this money where we know all your people are. We're not that stupid! We'll go up the road a bit, somewhere where it's safe, and hand over the money." To them that was fairly logical: don't trust anybody.

In my mind, I'd already plotted our route to both the police station and the house of the superintendent of police. As it was close to two o'clock in the morning, there'd be no one at the police station, so I headed for the superintendent's house. I drove in that direction, not too fast. Here the houses were spacious and the roads paved, and there was no sewage in the gutters. The traders kept saying, "Why don't we stop here?" Firoz kept saying, "No, no, I don't like this place." We came to a fork in the road. The traders were getting a bit suspicious now. One of

them said, "Go straight, go straight." I went straight on but at the last minute swerved right, because that was the direction of the superintendent's house. As soon as I did that, they knew something was wrong.

Out of the corner of my eye, I saw the man next to me reach surreptitiously into the bag. I yelled to Firoz, "He's reaching for a gun." Quick as a flash, Firoz leaned forward and got both men in the front seat in a headlock with one arm and pulled hard. With his other hand he grappled with the man with the pistol. There was some pushing and shoving in the back seat between our "driver" and the chief trader, the one with the squint. Firoz had his hands full but he could see that the man with the squint was lunging forward, so he jabbed him hard with his elbow. The trader slumped sideways but he had time to plunge a knife with an eighteen-centimeter blade into the top of the driver's seat. It missed my neck by five centimeters. Our "driver," in the meantime, had been struggling to get his AK-47 out and had finally managed to do so. It was chaos. We were all crammed into the car and there wasn't much room to move.

I accelerated down the road, nearly racing past the superintendent's house. Firoz cried out, "It's on the left" just in time. I saw two armed guards at the superintendent's house and swung the car toward the closed iron gates. I flashed my lights, sounded the horn, and yelled, in Hindi, "Open up, open up." And they just did. With everybody struggling in the car I roared into the compound of this beautiful, well-kept old bungalow. I stopped in front of the porch in a screech of brakes, flung open the car door, and threw myself out. It was getting very violent in the car with everyone struggling with guns and knives. The policeman/driver also jumped out trying to keep his gun trained, while Firoz was left inside with these three, now very frightened, men.

The two guards came running from the gate and another from inside the house. It's a wonder we didn't all get shot, for nobody knew we were coming. I ran towards the guards yelling, "Quickly, quickly, help the sahib in the back of the car with those three thieves and robbers." The police surrounded the car and got them and their bag out without further incident. We were taken into a small reception room inside the house. There was another policeman there. He just stared at me, openmouthed. I said to him, "Please wake the superintendent sahib immediately."

The next thing I saw was two fluffy Pomeranian dogs prancing out of the door followed by superintendent A.D. Mishra. He was a charming and handsome man—tall, slim, quite young, dressed in his night attire of crisp, white kurta-pajamas. He wore dark-rimmed spectacles. Despite what was happening, he was very calm. He saw us and said—

Caravans of yaks like these in Ladakh smuggle tiger bones from India into China.

in English—"Aha, you'd better tell me what's going on here."

I quickly explained the situation, and it turned out he had heard of our work against poachers and traders. The three traders had by now been arrested. The superintendent came outside, looked inside the bag and found one tiger skin, a pistol and two .315 bullets. The flick-knife was also retrieved. The pistol was homemade, or "country-made" as they say here. Mishra went to his radio in the reception area. He was amazingly calm and efficient. He called up five mobile units, saying, "If you're not here within five minutes I'll need a very good explanation." Then he looked at us and said, "I don't know how you two do this." "What do you mean?" we said. With a smile he answered, "We can't go into those areas. You must be mad, do you realize how dangerous it is? Do you realize what you're doing?" We said, "Yes, but it's the only way we could get these people." He just shook his head and then the mobile units arrived.

Mishra sent them out to pick up the other people we had met and to search their houses. Our three prisoners were interrogated, and they gave more names. Those people were also picked up. The dreadful lawyer's house was empty; he must have gotten suspicious or been tipped off. The squinty leader kept looking at me with hate in his eyes. He and his accomplices could go to prison for some time, not because they had an illegal tiger skin, but because they had unlicensed weapons.

By this time it was getting light and we had to go on to another job. We'd arranged to meet a young man in the forest near Dudhwa. He had promised tiger skins and bones and had connections in the village of criminals near the Nepal border. We wanted to keep the appointment, because before long news of these arrests would be common knowledge and we would not be able to do anything further.

As we were leaving Mishra said, "You know, the work you're doing is quite extraordinary—is there anything else I can do?" "Well, yes," I said. "We're going to try to do another job and we need a note for the officer in charge of the police station at Palia." He wrote a note, in green ink, on a small strip of paper. He addressed it to the appropriate officer and wrote, "These people are doing a noble job. Please give all possible help and protection to the bearers of this letter if they bring you some problem," and signed it. We thanked him and drove off. We were in extremely high spirits, because we'd been successful but also out of relief at having survived so many dangers. But it wasn't over yet.

Firoz drove like a madman to keep our appointment, and we arrived with a few minutes to spare. Sure enough, there was the man standing beside the road in the forest, just beyond the railway crossing where he said he would be. He whispered something to our "driver," who in turn told us that they wanted us to go to a spot up the road a bit. We drove there. The trees and bushes were very close to the road, so again it was the perfect place for an ambush. Time dragged on and nobody came. Finally two people walked up to us, one an old man, the other middle-aged. They looked at me then disappeared again. This went on and on, people kept coming and going, but nobody talked to us directly. They were all just looking. We were getting a bit worried about the number of people appearing and disappearing.

After more than an hour the fellow we'd met beyond the railway crossing came up and said that Kansar, the older man and the leader, wouldn't come and talk to us. But he wanted to see our money. To which we said, "If he wants to see the money he'll have to come here, because the money is in the car." I was still sitting in the car with the money beside me in a bag, as if I were guarding it. Firoz and the driver/policeman were walking about outside. These were quite different people than the ones we had dealt with during the night. They were unsophisticated village people, people who actually did the poaching. They were not experienced in "dealing" with the likes of us. We insisted Kansar come to the car. After another long interval, the younger man came back again and took our "driver" to meet Kansar. Our "driver" said to the old man, "If you want to see the money you'll have to go to the car." Kansar said, "Why?" To which the "driver" replied, "I'm only the hire car driver, but I've been working with these people for a while and they don't trust anyone; they've had some bad experiences." This turned out to be a smart thing to say.

The villagers went into a huddle again and people kept popping out of the bushes all around us. We were in fact surrounded. Firoz shouted to the driver, "Tell them to hurry up, I don't have the patience to keep on waiting." At that, we drove up the road a bit to a more open place. A few minutes later, Kansar came to the car. We'd borrowed the equivalent of about $1,000 from a friend of Billy's the day before. This was quite a stack of notes and we'd enlarged some of the bundles with cut-up paper. The real money was on top. I opened the bag and showed Kansar the pile of money. I lifted a bundle of 10,000 rupees in 100-rupee notes and fanned it out under his nose. I could see by his face that he was completely bewitched by the sight of all this cash.

Just seconds after that, in the rearview mirror of the car, I saw a man coming up the road pushing a bicycle with a huge sack strapped to it. The "driver" went to the back of the car, opened the trunk, and said to the man, "Put it in." He did, quite meekly, as though used to obeying orders—which no doubt he was. He probably had not meant to hand it over then and there. Firoz now jumped in the front seat—I was driving—and I said to the men waiting to be paid, "Get in, get in, we'll pay you over there," pointing up the road. They didn't know what to do; they all talked at once, our "driver" translating back and forth. Finally

the "driver" said, "Do you think they'd be so foolish as to give you the money here where they're surrounded by your people?" We virtually pulled two of them into the car, the original poacher and another rather mean-looking man. At that I gunned the engine and took off. Lots of people came running out of the bushes onto the road, looking rather astonished as we raced off. I slowed after a while. The two said, "Stop now and pay us." I shook my head and said, "Let's go a little farther and we'll check the goods." I kept going till we were well out of range of the others, then stopped. Firoz got out and opened the trunk. He ripped open the sack and saw a perfect and huge tiger skin and a complete skeleton. He slammed the trunk shut, got back in, and I took off again. "What are you doing?" they said.

We were still driving through forest, beautiful sal forest, on the edge of Dudhwa—perfect tiger habitat. The two were perplexed rather than alarmed. I broke into Hindi, which they didn't even notice, and said, "Look, we want to do business with you people for a long time. We are very interested in these sorts of things, we pay good money, so let's go and make friends, get to know each other better. You tell us about your work, we'll tell you how we can set up a supply route. So let's go to Palia, let's celebrate a bit, we'll have something to eat and drink."

We felt terrific and were very jovial. This was our second success of the day. The two men fell in with our mood and soon we were all laughing and joking as we drove towards Palia. Firoz leaned out of the car window slapping buffaloes on their backsides and shouting compliments at the pretty girls. The poachers thought it was hysterically funny.

I said to them as we drove along, "We want really clean skins; is this a clean skin?" They said, "Oh yes, it doesn't have a mark on it." "That's great because bullet holes and things make the skins less valuable," I added. "How do you do it, do you use poison?" "Oh no, no," they answered in unison. "It's much easier than that—we just put out a trap. We know where the tigers are, what their favorite trails are. They live very close to our village. We simply buried the trap under a thin layer of soil, on the tiger's trail, and chained it to a tree. This tiger then walked along and he caught his foot in the trap. We could hear his roars in the village. He roared and screamed. All night we heard him. Toward the early morning he was quiet. So the two of us and two friends went to the tiger and found him lying there, exhausted. He was huge. We had heavy wooden sticks with us and we beat the tiger to death. When he was dead we skinned him and cleaned the bones."

They said that they had the large trap made by a nomadic black-smith for 300 rupees ($10), which is a considerable sum for them. They thought the trap was wonderful because they could use it over and over again—and apparently had.

Still laughing and joking, we drove into Palia. "Oh good," I said. "We can go and have some food." Instead, I drove to the police station. Those police were pretty surprised to see us. The station was one of those hideous concrete buildings, painted yellow and with a verandah. There was a large tree in the compound and we parked in its shade.

The poachers weren't armed—we didn't think they had been—and they went to be arrested and charged meek as lambs. They cried real tears.

Firoz and I went into the office of the most senior officer. They had no idea what we were on about. They didn't even seem to know that tiger poaching was illegal. And this is in Palia, right beside Dudhwa Tiger Reserve, where there's been so much poaching reported. I showed the officer the note from the superintendent of Lakhimpur-Kheri, and the poachers were locked up. We tried to persuade the police to go to the village and pick up the other people. They did eventually go, but it was too late—the poachers had run off. We went back to Billy at Tiger Haven, which is quite close, and returned the money.

I had come full circle. Twenty-three years ago I had found a tigress in a trap right here in Dudhwa. Today Firoz and I had apprehended two people who had caught, and killed, a tiger in a trap—if not in Dudhwa, then very close to it.

These were just two of the operations I did with Firoz. There have been many others. Firoz set up a spectacular seizure in Kashmir in November 1994 while I was away in America finishing the cobra film. It was the largest seizure of skins ever made and included those of tigers, leopards, snow leopards, clouded leopards, and others—1,366 skins in all, with a value of more than one million U.S. dollars.

The flick-knife and homemade gun with which poachers tried to attack Belinda. They are shown on the skin of the tiger killed by the poachers.

When I finally turn the tape recorder off it is quite cool under the hara tree. There is a glimmer of light on the eastern horizon and a coucal gives its first booming call of the day. We have talked all night.

I cannot help thinking how Kanha has changed over just three generations, often with the involvement of Belinda and her family. In 1924 Kanha was a reserved forest on a vast forested plateau where Belinda's grandfather, then a colonial administrator, had reluctantly helped organize a tiger hunt for the Viceroy of India, the country's British ruler. Seven tigers were killed at a time when tigers were abundant. Forty-nine years later his daughter Anne was deeply involved in setting up Project Tiger, whose reserves included Kanha, by then a National Park. Now Belinda, his granddaughter, is helping to uncover the forces that threaten to destroy the last of Kanha's, and India's, tigers.

Belinda's anti–tiger poaching work in Madhya Pradesh, Uttar Pradesh, and Rajasthan has led to many positive developments. The publicity her work has received has spread a general awareness throughout India and other parts of the world that the tiger is in serious trouble, the victim of a highly organized assault: something that was not known before. The Forest Departments of the various states and other government agencies have had to acknowledge there is a serious conservation problem with tigers, and one they must squarely face. Some are doing so, most are not. Ignorance never was an excuse for allowing the tiger to slip towards extinction. Now it is part of the crime.

[CHAPTER 23]
FRIENDS REDUCED TO SKIN AND BONES

Kanha to Balaghat—3 April 1995

During the two months' investigation in Madhya Pradesh in the summer of 1994, Belinda befriended two very special policemen stationed not far from Kanha. Both officers had personal and genuine interests in wildlife, and even though their prime objective was to hunt down Naxalites in the forests, they had done some effective undercover work on wildlife cases. As a result they arrested a number of traders and poachers and seized quantities of contraband skins and bones. Today we drive down to Balaghat to talk with the policemen and to see what has been seized. One of their raids had been at Mocha village—within sight of Shergarh—and tiger and leopard parts were recovered from there.

Most of the 100-kilometer journey to Balaghat is through wooded hills. Here and there, small villages and their croplands have been carved out of the forest. People gather the fallen waxy flowers of mohwa trees by the bucketful. They will dry the flowers and then distill them into a most palatable and potent liquor of the same name. Monkeys and chital also gather the mohwa harvest. The villages have immaculate two-story houses with neat courtyards where pale gray cattle and black buffaloes chew their cud. Boys and girls lead herds of goats out to graze in the forest.

Belinda drives, and we make good progress on the virtually empty roads. We pass through Baihar, where the same man who offered Belinda tiger skins is

back at his telephone booth. As we drive along, Belinda tells me a little about the two policemen and how she came to be involved with them.

We got great cooperation from the police right from the start. There were lots of reasons for this. In some cases, the interest in wildlife was quite genuine. Chasing poachers was also a break from boring routine and a way of getting good publicity. At first the police had really no idea that poaching was such a big issue. It was not on their list of priorities.

We also made an interesting discovery. Police deal with murderers, people in the drug trade, gangs of thieves, gun runners, terrorists—any and all major and minor criminals you can imagine. These are exactly the kind of people who are in the illegal wildlife trade—in other words, the very people that the police deal with all the time. They're also people the Forest Department do not often run into—and, to do them justice, are not really equipped to deal with. It meant the police had information about poaching and traders and didn't know the significance of it till we started putting two and two together and pointed it out to them.

One result of this was that Mukesh Gupta, the superintendent of police at Balaghat—who you'll meet soon—was able to make the arrests and seizures he did—three tiger skins, five tiger skeletons, six leopard skins, and two leopard skeletons. He was offered many more skins and skeletons but some poachers slipped through the net. He and his associates arrested forty-five poachers and traders. By the number of people arrested, the contraband obviously passes through the hands of lots of middlemen.

A suitcase full of tiger bones that traders tried to sell in Jabalpur in central India.

Also the police are there to uphold the law, so when people like us come along with clear evidence of law-breaking, with all the details, they act. Why shouldn't they? I always like to think the police act because they want to protect the tiger, but on the whole they are rather unimaginative about that. They're pragmatic first and foremost.

Anyway, let me tell you about Mukesh Gupta. I met him during the two months' work here. He's a young man, just over thirty, and he'd only just been posted to Balaghat. Senior police do not stay long in Balaghat, for it is in the heart of Naxalite country. Their main job is to pursue Naxalites and that is dangerous work. Gupta had just completed an operation in which four Naxalites, including a woman, were gunned down by police. The police had produced a rather grisly poster showing a photograph of each of the bodies—blood, bullet wounds, and all—as a warning to others. That poster was widely distributed in the area.

The man I met, however, was not at all the sort of person you would think would do that. Maybe it comes with the job, for he has a reputation for being a fair-minded policeman. He was absolutely straightforward, but also showed a dry, quiet sense of humor. He had a picture of a tiger in his office. After I explained what I was doing, he looked directly at me and said, "I haven't been here very long, and wildlife is not anything I'm directly concerned with, but I can tell you poaching is rampant here. We're dealing with Naxalites and we use informers from among the villagers and forest people all the time. Through them I know for a fact that there is a lot of poaching, including tigers and leopards." That was the first time I'd heard an official say outright that there was poaching. And so close to Kanha. I quoted him saying that—"poaching is rampant"—in the report. My critics seized on that more than anything else and said I was exaggerating—I **must** be. How could poaching be **rampant** in Madhya Pradesh of all places? But as Mukesh's recent arrests have shown, it is true, and if you plot the places where he made the arrests on a map, you see that they neatly encircle Kanha. They're like a noose around the tiger's neck.

The other policeman who has become a friend of mine is quite different. His full name is Prashant Katlam but everyone calls him just Katlam. He's of a more junior rank, and was in charge of a small police station in the forest whose main responsibilities center around catching Naxalites. Katlam is a tribal, a handsome young man, also about thirty years of age. I first met him in the Baihar police station. He sized up pretty quickly what I was trying to do and he gave me a lot of good information. He acted out of a love for wildlife; perhaps because he is tribal he has a greater affinity with nature.

Not long after I first met Katlam, I dropped in at his police station a few hours after dark. I swung the car into the driveway and apparently

someone shouted, "Halt." I didn't hear it and drove on. Immediately people came running from all directions, rifles and machine guns at the ready: you have to be alert in Naxalite country. I stopped very quickly. I found Katlam in high spirits: they'd raided a Naxalite hideout, arrested someone, and recovered arms, ammunition, explosives, and food supplies.

Shortly afterward the Naxalites got their revenge—perhaps for the raid, perhaps for the four of their associates who were killed. The truck that Katlam and sixteen of his men were driving in was blown up along a forest road. All sixteen men were killed. Katlam was thrown clear and, though injured, was alive. The Naxalites fired at him and wounded him further before they escaped with the arms and supplies the truck had been carrying. Katlam survived but was in the hospital for six months. I hope we'll see him this afternoon.

The road meanders through thick forest that is on good, well-watered soil and is therefore still green. We pass beautiful forest rest houses set among the trees. Several have been blown up by the Naxalites. We detour around an old stone bridge—also blown up, or perhaps it just collapsed. We pass Katlam's police station, neat and painted white, inside a perimeter fence.

Balaghat must once have been in the middle of the forest in a wide, fertile valley. But the forest has long since retreated in the face of the outward march of agricultural land. It is a small, dusty place, the downtown area devoid of trees and very hot. We go out of town a little way, pass the jail, and reach the police station. It is part of a cluster of buildings that also includes the courthouse and other government offices. Large pipal trees shade the parking area and a single arrow-straight silk cotton tree has showered its flowers over parked police vehicles.

The police station itself consists of two buildings, painted a yellow ocher, with elegantly curved roofs covered in terracotta tiles, stained black with the mold of decades of monsoons. They are joined by a covered walkway. We enter by this whitewashed corridor. There are rooms on either side where policemen go about their business. We go to the very end where we meet a polite, smiling young man in a khaki uniform with a magnificent red sash from shoulder to waist and an equally impressive, shining brass belt buckle. Belinda says we wish to see superintendent sahib Mukesh Gupta. The red sash man disappears behind a curtain and reappears moments later to usher us into Gupta's office. Belinda and he greet each other like old friends. He shakes my hand with a firm grip and smilingly looks me in the face; his eyes, enlarged by spectacle lenses, shine with humor and intelligence. Like most senior officers, he does not wear a uniform but is dressed in a pale blue sports shirt, faded blue jeans, and brown suede shoes. His hair is a spiky crew cut and he has a thin mustache. He is tall and fit-looking with broad shoulders. His large hands have strong and supple fingers.

Mukesh's office is spacious with a high ceiling where fans whir away. The furniture is spartan—an imitation wood desk facing eight steel chairs with worn plastic seats. On the wall behind his desk are three boards that list all of Balaghat's superintendents of police. Number one was an Englishman, Superintendent Fairweather, who was here in 1908. Number sixty-two is Mukesh Gupta—who arrived in April 1994. Huge, colorful maps adorn the other walls. Tucked between them is one of the gruesome posters of the dead Naxalites.

After a few preliminaries I ask Mukesh why he is interested in catching poachers.

"Before the Tiger Cell [a special anti-poaching unit formed after Belinda's report on poaching in Madhya Pradesh in July of last year] was formed in the police force it was not part of our mission," he says. "Now it is. Every day our inspector general rings up to ask what we are doing about poachers. But we are busy with so many things. In the morning it may be Naxalites, then undercover work with poachers until the middle of the night, then other things. We get no sleep. I would not be doing it but for Belinda and Firoz: they showed us the problem and stimulated our interest. There is a lot of poaching in this area, which is close to Kanha. It is not just the tiger, but also leopards, chital, sambar, even wild boar. We are offered all of them in our undercover work. Even allowing for the exaggeration, there are many, many tiger bones available. And that is just in this district. We see only the tip of the iceberg.

"Naxalites are *not* poachers. They will not allow even a tree to be cut down. The Forest Department say it is the Naxalites that do this thing to cover their own inefficiencies.

"The catching of the poachers a few months ago was like a performance. We all had to playact and not look like policemen. I posed as a big shot from Bombay, so I had to talk and even walk like such a man. I'd just been on a pilgrimage and my head was shaved. The officer in charge of Baihar police station had a French-cut beard [we never discovered what that is] and hair down to his shoulders. R.S. Saket, my additional superintendent, is a strange-looking fellow with wavy hair and silver earrings. So we did not look like policemen; and neither could our men talk to us as though we were. One operation by the Forest Department failed because one of the forest guards called his officer 'sir.'

"We also used very unpolicelike techniques. We brought one group of middlemen to a hotel. We'd been talking to them for a day or more and they told us all kinds of things about how they operate. We learned many of their secrets. We all got on very well. When in the end we revealed to them that we were police, we all smiled at each other: they recognized they had been outwitted. That too was very unpolicelike—but it was a good feeling for us. It wasn't messy with handcuffs and things, and getting so angry you cannot control yourself. I liked this operation. It was successful. It was like a drama."

Belinda laments the fact that Mukesh and his team found three tiger skeletons concealed in a house in Mocha village, "Right under my nose, so distressing," she says. Mukesh laughs and replies, "Don't worry, things happen right under my nose all the time."

It is dark by the time Prashant Katlam, the heroic station officer whose men were killed, walks into the room. Belinda has a great affection for this young man. She told me how he used to be full of confidence and high spirits, throwing back his head with laughter just for the joy of it. Today he still has a smile that lights up the room, yet it is a sad smile, and there is a pained and faraway look in his eyes. He's been back on duty for only three days and still wears a back brace because of his spinal injuries.

R.S. Saket, the additional superintendent and the second member of the undercover team, also joins us. He is just a little older than Mukesh, heavier, less sophisticated, but also with a twinkle in his eyes. It is a poignant, and also an historic moment for me to see these four disparate people together: an English woman of privileged background whose family has been deeply involved with the area for three generations; a highly intelligent and well-educated senior police officer; a tribal man; and a man from the country. They are joined in a bond of affection and friendship and in a common commitment to saving the tiger in this small town carved out of the jungle. The talk is now about Katlam's recovery and his traumatic experience. Each, in his or her own way, is trying to reassure him, to draw him back into everyday life—sometimes awkwardly, sometimes with piercing insight.

A junior officer, having spotted Belinda, suddenly puts his head around the door and with a wide smile says, "Worry not about this poaching and all. We've got our thumb on the pulse and soon we'll have the rascals under a barrel," and he is off again.

Mukesh and Katlam walk us to our car. The seized tiger

and leopard skins and bones are held in the Baihar police station. Mukesh says he will phone his colleague there and arrange for us to inspect them tomorrow. It is quite late and we have to drive through the night. "Be careful of the Naxalites," says Mukesh and laughs.

Baihar Police Station—4 April 1995

Baihar is a much smaller version of Balaghat, right on the edge of Kanha's buffer zone. The jungle is closer, there is no congestion. The pace of life is leisurely. The town center is a pleasant place shaded by huge trees. Belinda wants to make a telephone call to Delhi. We try at the post office, which is a small concrete building. In the trees above it are hundreds of flying foxes—huge fruit bats that flap and quarrel, or swing, sleeping with folded wings, in the gentle breeze. It is dark and dingy inside the post office, where a ceiling fan wheezes overhead and dusty files flutter on stone shelves. People sit sorting mail into pigeonholes black with age. There is a special nostalgia about this post office for Belinda: it was from here in the early 1920s that her grandfather, then a junior administrator, sent a telegram proposing to her grandmother, who was back in England. Little seems to have changed since then. I ask the postmaster if they still use Morse code to send telegrams. "Oh yes," he says, but the "machine" is out of order just now so they use the telephone. Unfortunately, the telephone is also out of order.

At the entrance to the police station stands a sentry with an ancient .303 rifle chained to his waist. The policeman in charge is in his office, a small cell-like room, with a desk piled high with files facing some wooden chairs. The windows are barred. Baihar comes under the Balaghat district and Mukesh Gupta is this officer's immediate superior. The young man's name is also Gupta, Rajesh Gupta, but no relation. I think he's in his late twenties, dressed in crisply pressed gray trousers and an immaculate pale blue shirt. He wears gold-rimmed spectacles and has a small mustache. His hair has been cut short and stands almost straight up. No sign of the "French" beard or long hair of this third member of the undercover team. Though a younger man, he looks less fit than Mukesh, more academically inclined, though also with a quiet wit. He gives a constrained smile where Mukesh would laugh out loud. He was the gold medal winner in his final exams for the Indian Forest Service. But instead of joining the Forest Department, he completed a Ph.D. at the Indian Institute of Technology in Delhi. Then he joined the Indian Police Service. When at the Institute of Technology he also was India's national debating champion. He is so well-educated that he's either vastly overqualified for a tiny jungle police station, or he's earmarked for rapid promotion. He has an enviable command of the English language and speaks very, very fast. Baihar is his first posting—the undercover work was his first operation.

On Mukesh's orders, Rajesh planned the operation, which took twenty-five days to complete. In the end it was simple, he says. "You just say, we want these tiger bones and skins now, and show them a big bundle of money. It is the greed, you see, that gets most of them."

Rajesh also had evidence that tiger poaching does go on right inside Kanha. When they came to "settle up" with one trader, he sent a man on a bicycle about two kilometers inside the park. He returned after some time with a tiger skeleton in a sack strapped to the back of his cycle. It is time to look at the skins and bones.

A line of policemen bring out a large number of sacks, suitcases, and cardboard boxes, and spread their contents out in front of a parked police bus. One suitcase contains the skins of two small tiger cubs—pathetic and obscene at the same time. Rajesh says that the poachers told him that they had killed the cubs' mother. When the cubs stayed around, they shot one and clubbed the other

Kanjar tribal women trying to sell fake tiger claws and musk pods in Srinagar in Uttar Pradesh.

The police officer Rajesh Gupta (center, in white shirt) and his men with the tiger and leopard skins and bones they confiscated from illegal traders around Kanha.

to death. Belinda takes a particular interest in the consignment from Mocha village. One of the skeletons, judging by the skull and perfect large teeth, is that of a large male tiger in the prime of life. Belinda photographed a male in just such a condition and of such a size at Kisli. Not long after that this tiger disappeared. According to Rajesh's information, this tiger skull came from the Kisli area. The same tiger? It seems likely. There is also the skin of a male leopard. Is it the one that Belinda saw at the foot of her bed? That animal disappeared as well.

The sun is now merciless. A terrible stench comes from the bones and skins. Some of them are still very fresh. A crowd has gathered at the gate. They've come to look at the skins and at this strange woman who caused so many people to be put in jail. Some policemen with rifles go and lock the gate and push the people back, shouting at them. The flying foxes in the tall trees suddenly take to the wing. Huge black bats, screeching, fill the air. They appear sinister to me—which is strange, for I love these intelligent, harmless animals. I feel nauseous and have to rush into the police station to be sick.

The skins and skeletons are returned to their bags and boxes and we take our leave. We're soon in the cool jungle of Kanha's buffer zone, and we stop. We sit on a rock under a pipal tree and I slowly regain my composure. Storm clouds come rolling in from the southwest. It is almost dark when fierce winds tear at the trees. Heavy rain and hail hammer on the car's roof. Lightning illuminates the drenched forest. Thunder cracks directly overhead.

★ ★ ★

Belinda and I want to visit some special jungles and also return to such favorite places as Ranthambhore and Kaziranga. But this is not a good time of year and I go back to Australia for a few months.

[CHAPTER 24]

THE RISE AND FALL OF RANTHAMBHORE

After an unusually hot summer, India's monsoon has been generous and when I return to New Delhi on 17 November 1995, the countryside is still green. The air, however, is as polluted as ever.

Since I left in early April, Belinda and the Wildlife Protection Society of India (which she founded a year ago) have continued their groundbreaking work. WPSI is now internationally recognized as being a "cutting-edge organization for conservation in India." Belinda, as honorary executive director and Ashok Kumar as honorary vice president, and a paid staff of seven, have moved mountains.

Belinda continued her investigative work, which led to the arrest of numerous poachers and traders and the seizure of their goods. Over the months Belinda and Firoz increasingly disagreed about the methods they should use to arrest the traders in tiger skins and bones. Belinda adhered strictly to the principle that traders were *never* to be given a cash advance and that if a trader had even a single tiger bone, he should be arrested immediately. By giving money and waiting to arrest the trader until he has accumulated more bones and skins, which he invariably promises, there is a real danger that poachers will be sent out to kill tigers to fulfill the investigators' "requests." Firoz increasingly wanted to change the rules by giving cash advances and waiting to have traders arrested in the belief that more skins and bones would be seized. The

A red lotus in the main lake at Ranthambhore National Park.

danger then is that the investigator could be thought of as a trader. In September 1995 Belinda and Firoz agreed not to work together anymore.

Our first journey is to Ranthambhore to talk to Fateh Singh Rathore and to see what the park is now like. After being excluded for more than three years from the reserve that is largely his creation, Fateh can once more patrol Ranthambhore. It is not through some rapprochement with the Rajasthan Forest Department. They are still quite hostile to him over disagreements about management and poaching. Fateh has the authority to enter Ranthambhore because he has been appointed to a high-powered central government committee that is investigating the management of national parks throughout India.

Ranthambhore Tiger Reserve— 24 November 1995

At the first gate nothing has changed. A lone forest guard lounges at the medieval archway. At the base of the fort, however, the courtyard that was usually deserted is crowded and noisy with Jeeps, scooters, trucks, a few buses, and a throng of people. Because we are with Fateh, who can enter any time, we drive straight through the ancient gateway into the park. The guards and other staff, some from Fateh's days, bow with folded hands and obsequious smiles. Fateh acknowledges them with an imperious nod.

A tigress eats a chital fawn.

Once through the gate we move back eleven years in time, to our visits during Ranthambhore's golden age. The lakes are full and the forests around the ruins lush. On the hills the grass is golden and the dhauk trees are beginning to turn purple. There are sambar, including some large stags, in the lakes. Among the chital there are many fawns. The deer seem fewer but the wild pigs, round and prosperous looking, are numerous. Just as I am thinking it, Belinda says that every few meters there is a place we associate with a tiger—where we saw Abu for the first time in winter, where we saw him and Links mating, where Lakshmi tried to cover her kill with loose stones. But around the lakes there are no tiger pug marks and no alarm calls.

Farther afield in the dhauk forest at Lakarda we see the footprints of a tigress, in the same place where we used to see those of Lakshmi. They lead down into the Kachida Valley. We feel a flickering of the old reflexes and instincts as we study the prints and strain our ears for the sounds warning of the presence of a predator.

On the road that runs parallel to the stream, leading deep into the valley, there are more pug marks—those of a male. We follow them slowly. They leave the road into dense cover. The three of us see the tiger almost simultaneously. He is only about fifteen meters away with his back toward us. He is stalking. Slowly, with infinite care, he places one foot after another. He creeps forward for a few paces then sits on his haunches. A sambar, close but hidden from us, barks in alarm. The tiger

gets up immediately and strides off into the forest, followed by a stream of calls from chital and langurs. All the animals, from tigers to partridges and from mongooses to hawk eagles, are as approachable as ever.

Belinda says that Ranthambhore's heart is still there. Fateh agrees. Its heart maybe, but for me something of its soul, its spirit, is missing. Is it Fateh's spirit? Or was it something in us, in those days in the 1980s when we were so full of verve and passion for the tiger, that is now missing? Is it our dashed enthusiasm and optimism that makes us feel a little sad and subdued on this glorious and mellow afternoon? The cattle we see grazing and the trees we hear being cut down are not reassuring for the future.

The area around the lakes Lakarda and Kachida is much as it was eleven years ago. There are even a few tigers. These 160 square kilometers are the only area where visitors are allowed to go—but it is only a little more than one-third of the park. The rest, Fateh says, is as bare as the devastated wasteland we drove through to reach the park, with as many cows, goats, and camels eating it into oblivion and with as many people carrying off its trees.

We reach Jogi Mahal just as the last sunlight touches the treetops. It is deserted. The banyan tree, graffiti carved into some of its stems, looks forlorn without Fateh sitting by the campfire waiting for us to return with tiger tales.

Fateh, perhaps prompted by the sight of dilapidated and desolate Jogi Mahal, tells us about the time when he moved several villages out of the park. Everyone was sad, he says. People hugged the trees. Others said they wanted to die there. Most were in tears. Fateh himself was close to crying, but he fought it back. If he had given way to his emotions he was sure the people would not have moved that day, and if not that day, not ever. So he put on a stern exterior and the people moved to a new life. Fateh says, "You cannot cry for things that have passed."

25 November

At his farm in the shadow of Ranthambhore's cliffs, where he has a spacious and comfortable house, Fateh still likes to sit by a fire out under the stars in the evening. On this moonless night, while a leopard or perhaps a tiger elicits occasional

A tigress keeps watch from ruins in Ranthambhore National Park.

alarm calls from sambar and langurs, we sit by the fire. Fateh talks about how he tried to "return Ranthambhore to nature" and the disasters that befell it after he was forced to leave. It is a fascinating case history of the rise and fall of one of India's greatest national parks.

Fateh first came to Ranthambhore in 1960 when he was a very young man. In January of that year he assisted Kesri Singh, the noted Rajasthani hunter, in organizing the tiger shoot for Queen Elizabeth II and Prince Philip. In 1964 Fateh was transferred to another sanctuary but returned to Ranthambhore in 1970 and stayed there more or less continuously for the next seventeen years. In 1970, when he was in his thirties, he came as a range officer. He was promoted to field director in 1976. I ask Fateh what Ranthambhore looked like in those early days.

"There were no roads at all then," he says, "so there was little patrolling. A lot of villages, about twenty, were inside the park, and the people had their cows, buffaloes, and a few goats. A tribe of herdsmen, *gujjars,* lived in camps with their cattle throughout the sanctuary. People from outside villages also brought their cows to graze here. In those days when I stood on the highest hill at night I could see these graziers' fires on all the hilltops. The lakes you see now like Jogi Mahal, Malik Talao, and so on—they were not lakes at all then.

"There were trees, but they were all lopped and not a single blade of grass grew underneath them. People even used to sweep up the fallen leaves of the dhauk trees and take them away in bags for their cattle. The place was in terrible shape. We never saw sambar. Never. Chital we definitely used to see. Tigers were always there but we never saw them, only their pug marks sometimes.

"In 1969 I was picked to take a diploma course in

wildlife management in Dehra Dun. That training really changed me. Earlier I was just an ordinary forest officer. I did the routine work—going to the office, a little patrolling, and this kind of thing. I was not very serious about preservation or conservation. I had it not in mind at all. I was much more interested in riding my motorcycle and being a singing man or a dancing man. But this training under the director S. R. Choudhury, who was my guru really, changed the whole aspect of my future life.

"When I returned to Ranthambhore, Choudhury used to come and see what I was doing. The first thing I did was to stop the grazing around the three lakes. Next I repaired the dams so that the lakes could keep their water. But then it became an attraction for the people who brought more and more cattle to drink. So I stopped that. I didn't get much cooperation from my own department. I still remember the chief conservator of forests saying, 'The graziers are the voters and should not be prevented from grazing in the park. If you do it again you'll be in trouble.' But my guru Choudhury said, 'Go on—no problem, do it.' After I stopped the grazing, this whole lakes area, which covers about twenty square kilometers, began to change. I started seeing sambar coming out during the day. The whole place was *full* of wild animals.

"In 1972 parks and sanctuaries were being selected to be included in Project Tiger. Any place that was included would have bigger budgets, more equipment, and more staff. So I was very keen for that. Members of the selection committee and even the chairman of Project Tiger all came here and were very impressed. I said to the committee, 'Why are you only including those well-known parks like Kanha and Corbett? They already have a large budget. They have all the things. Try one like Ranthambhore that is not known to anybody and see what we can make out of it. I'm completely sure I can make it work.' So ultimately Ranthambhore was declared one of the first nine Project Tiger parks and it was the smallest.

"When Project Tiger was launched in 1973, I became the game warden here. The first field director, he was a zero in wildlife. He was not interested. He completely handed everything over to me and said, 'I'm going to sit in Jaipur. I need one staff member, one motorcycle, and a Jeep. It is all up to you what you're doing in Ranthambhore.'

"In 1974 and 1975 we made 270 kilometers of road so that we could patrol the whole park.

"Moving the villages out began in 1974 and took three years. It was difficult to persuade the people to move. The compensation the government offered was very good. Each family was given the equivalent of their land plus an extra

1½ acres (0.6 hectares). Anyone who had no land was also given 1½ acres. We gave compensation for the old houses. If they had a well, or special fruit trees, or whatever, we gave compensation for that also. We assisted in the building of people's new houses. We built a new village with a school, a hospital, and a temple. They wanted to go with their god, you see. Every village has a god. We had a very good district administration at that time, the police superintendent and the collector were both good men. We worked as a team. Everyone was treated fairly and received their compensation and land. In the end we were able to persuade people to go; we didn't have to force them.

"We shifted 1000 families, which is twelve villages, and excluded 10,000 cows and buffaloes. The people are happy now. They used to curse and abuse me, but now they are very happy and have my photograph in their temple, and say, 'You are the god.' Everybody has water and electricity now and there is a high school and a community center—none of which they had before. They're absolutely very prosperous.

"When I started seeing results in the park, when I saw the forests completely clean after the villages had gone, when the grasses were there again, the trees started flowering and flourishing and the tigers started coming out—then I really fell in love with Ranthambhore.

"My best times, I often think, were the early days and they did not necessarily have to do with tigers. Finally in my work I could use my wisdom, my vision, and all the power I could feel inside me. I had, you know, a complete cinemascope view of what I could do here. I realized, My God, this is the thing I can do in my life. So I enjoyed making roads, making guard outposts, I enjoyed every kind of thing. I used to dance around the campfire in the night with my road builders. I enjoyed living in the forest where every day you get a new sunrise.

"After nearly all the villages had gone in 1977 I began seeing tiger pug marks everywhere, but I saw tigers only about two or three times in a year. Then one day I saw the big pug marks of a tigress and all around it the small marks of her cubs—the tigress and her cubs were running and playing in the park, *my* park. I had tears in my eyes. Not long after that I found this tigress, which I called Padmini after my elder daughter.

"The villagers had left one lame buffalo behind. Over the years it became very large and not a single tiger was able to kill it. But finally this Padmini, she managed it. I found the dead buffalo under a tree. Foolishly I climbed up and sat in

another very small tree not far from her kill. I had a Pentax with a 200-millimeter lens hanging around my neck. When I saw Padmini come to her kill I clicked. She charged at me with full force, giving a great roar. I still remember the shiver in my body and cursing myself; I will die here, I thought. It took me about an hour to get back to normal. By that time

Padmini was sleeping near her kill. So I thought, Why not take one more picture. 'Click.' She just lifted her head for a moment and went back to sleep.

"In the afternoon I saw four cubs, then five, right at my tree. Once more I thought, this is the end of Fateh Singh, for surely she will charge again. While the cubs were under my tree I heard a jackal's call and looked up, for perhaps two seconds. When I looked down the cubs had gone, just vanished. What signal she gave them I don't know, for she just lay there asleep when I looked at her. I then took near about one roll of film—but Padmini lay there just like she was dead, never moved.

"I started following this tigress. At first she snarled and sometimes charged a little bit. But in a month's time she was completely familiar with my Jeep. That was the first tiger I got close to. Slowly, slowly her grown cubs got used to me also. Padmini's second litter and her third were born and all these things started happening about getting close to tigers. Padmini definitely made me into a tiger wallah. She's my hero.

"All this made me not the normal forest department officer; it made me completely involved in the progress of the park. I knew this is what I wanted and that I could do it. And I started enjoying every day.

"That all came to an end in 1987 when I resigned and later was transferred to Sariska, another Project Tiger Reserve in Rajasthan. If you change the man in charge, everything changes. In this country if you make a house that is green and somebody comes after you who doesn't like that color, he'll smash it all down and make it a red house. There is no rule how you have to proceed and what you have to continue. It all depends on your whims and wishes. Also, if you get really popular and successful, people don't like it.

"Then money started flowing toward this place, which actually didn't help. When I left in 1987 the budget for the whole park was only thirteen lakh rupees [$27,000]. With that I managed 200 people, all the maintenance, and all the patrolling. At the moment the annual budget is six crore rupees [$1,700,000]. I had three senior staff, now there are about ten gazetted officers sitting there with a staff of 400 and it is worse managed.

"I resigned because of an order issued by the local collector that all the cattle must be allowed to graze in Ranthambhore National Park. I could not stop it straightaway. So I resigned and cattle grazed, more than 20,000 of them. My whole life's work was gone, flop, completely. I had to resign. A new field director was appointed. The order to allow cattle to graze was challenged in court and ultimately the collector was suspended and removed from his post. For one and a half years while this was going on I lived here on my farm and was in the park nearly every day and watched tigers and photographed them. I saw some fantastic things and learned a lot about tigers.

"In 1988 the Rajasthan government said, No, we don't accept your resignation. Rajiv Gandhi, the prime minister, used to come to Ranthambhore and loved it. He had gone to Sariska and found it was in a mess. This was passed on to the Rajasthan Government with the message, 'Fateh Singh has done great things in Ranthambhore, now get him to take Sariska.' So the government told me, For God's sake do it and clean the place up. I went there in August 1988.

"I applied to return to Ranthambhore, but the post of field director there had been upgraded, and I had not been promoted. I challenged that in court and won my promotion. At the same time I was suspended because I had stopped mining and quarrying in Sariska. A lot of prominent people were making a lot of money out of that. I fought that in court too and won, but still I was not returned to Ranthambhore or Sariska. They made me sit in an office in Jaipur doing virtually nothing.

"I came to know about tigers being poached back in 1989 when I was in Sariska. I still had an informer in Ranthambhore and he came to see me. He said he knew of people who had three tiger skins. I immediately informed the chief wildlife warden and the new field director. They came to this farm and had breakfast with me. I said, This is the story and this is the man. Now send your staff and arrest those people. They said, 'Don't worry. We'll do it.' But what the field director did was to completely bash the informer—saying to him, 'How dare you inform those kinds of things. There are no tigers being killed in Ranthambhore.' They did not even try to catch the poachers.

"In 1991 I got to hear about a tiger being killed in Ranthambhore and I went straight to the police. And I was in big trouble again. When the poacher was eventually caught, in June 1992, he admitted to the police that he'd shot twenty-two tigers in Ranthambhore. He actually named the people he'd sent the bones and

A large male tiger found dead in Ranthambhore National Park during December 1994.

skins to. They were sent through the railways as children's toys. One of the people he said they were sent to was Sansar Chand in Delhi—a well-known trader in tiger parts. The police were pursuing their inquiries thoroughly and everything was going fine. But then the government thought it would give them a bad name and stopped the inquiries.

"Between 1988 and 1991 you could see the difference. I used to see tigers everywhere from Bakola to Nalgathi. I used to know most of them by name. There were four tigresses with cubs. The population was quite high. And suddenly you could see nothing, phut, it all collapsed; 1991 was a bad year.

"I saw the skin of the tiger that was confiscated from the poachers. Oh God, how beautiful a skin of such a huge tiger. I knew that tiger, it used to live at Bakola. I cried—the superintendent had to take me away. I thought it was that male, because the poacher told me when and where he shot it. He said he shot it at night, as he always did, and on foot, while walking in the Bakola area. He also said that he skinned many of the tigers he killed in front of the forest guards. He said he gave them money, shared his food with them. He even attended their marriages. They used to be my forest guards. They changed because they were given money. Money changes everything.

"Ranthambhore and the tigers even today can be saved. As long as the forest remains the tigers can remain. Poaching still has not taken all the tigers away. One or two are left, a male and female are still there. That is not the problem. The only thing is you must have control. If you just leave everything, leave your door open without any guards and say, 'Come and take everything,' then the tigers will go from Ranthambhore forever. That is what is happening today. But if you close your door, put your guards into place, Ranthambhore will come back. For sure. But what I see now when I go into the park is that after six o'clock most staff at the guard outposts are drunk. Another outpost is locked and there is no one there. When you go to the village they say they've not seen the man in charge for two months. He just comes to collect his pay and goes again.

"As you saw yesterday a lot of Ranthambhore is still marvelous. If in the next two or three years a good man will come, he can still save this park. But if it goes on like today when the managers are not even bothered to find out why a tiger has been shot, who is shooting it, where it was shot, and who is buying it, there is not much of a chance. If you are not bothered or concerned about the prime animal, the project animal, in your park while spending tens of millions of rupees for the sole purpose of protecting this animal, what's the use?

"I still love Ranthambore and I will remain here on my farm, close to the place to the end of my life. I'll do whatever I can to save the tiger and Ranthambhore."

★ ★ ★

In December 1995 the Cat Specialist Group of the International Union for the Conservation of Nature, based in Switzerland, issued a note about tiger conservation. The note explained that they had commissioned a computer simulation model that explored the effects of poaching on the viability of tiger populations. The model concluded that at high levels of poaching over a sustained period there was a good chance of the tiger becoming extinct in that area. Commenting on Ranthambhore, the note states, "This high level of poaching may have occurred at Ranthambhore Tiger Reserve in India where the population has reportedly declined from forty-four to forty-six tigers in 1991 to fifteen to twenty tigers in 1992. In our model this level of poaching leads to a 70 to 90 percent probability of extinction." It further said that the next three years would be critical. As both Belinda and Fateh have discovered, poaching did continue in the next three years. A poacher-turned-informer with a long and intimate knowledge of Ranthambhore estimates there are seven tigers left. Fateh estimates there are between eight and twelve.

For the tiger and other wildlife there was a brief golden age in Ranthambhore's recent history—a golden age made possible by Fateh's integrity, his vision, and his passion. That golden age has passed and there is only the smallest cushion from which it may perhaps bounce back. If the tiger does vanish from Ranthambhore it will be a great tragedy for both India and for Fateh Singh. But at least Fateh Singh will have demonstrated that great wild jungles *can* be maintained simply by implementing existing laws and guidelines. All it takes is courage and determination. In Ranthambhore, at least, it is not a lack of funds.

[CHAPTER 25]

RICH MAN, POOR MAN

Shergarh near Kanha National Park—
30 November 1995

During the summer, Belinda has continued her undercover work, making three significant discoveries. One of these involved her exposure of the trade in live animals from India to China via Nepal. Before she tells me about the other two, we travel to Kanha, to Shergarh, so we can sit and talk under the hara tree once again. In Delhi there are too many interruptions and Belinda is not in the right frame of mind to sit quietly and talk. She tells me about Sansar Chand, thought to be the evil genius of the tiger bone trade; about Mohammed Zayeed, an old man ruined by poachers and tortured by forest department and police officials; and about how she helped break an international rhino horn smuggling ring.

When Ashok Kumar started TRAFFIC-India in 1993, he collected information on court cases involving wildlife crimes. One name kept appearing as a prime accused, time and time again: Sansar Chand. After the seizure of 400 kilograms of tiger bones in August 1993, the people arrested all pointed to one man as the prime mover in the tiger bone trade—Sansar Chand. They said that he in fact owned the bones. Poachers arrested for killing tigers and leopards in Sariska, Ranthambhore, Kanha, Rajaji, and Dudhwa all said the skins and bones eventually ended up with Sansar Chand. They said it was Sansar Chand who organized the smuggling of tiger bones out of India. Ashok's dogged information-gathering revealed that Sansar Chand and his family orchestrated the bulk of the illegal wildlife trade in northern and central India. Yet the man himself remained a total enigma. Few people even knew what he looked like and his whereabouts and identity continued to mystify the police and the wildlife protection officials. Newspaper reports referred to Sansar as "the foremost wildlife criminal in the country," "the smuggler king" of wildlife, and "India's most notorious animal skin smuggler." So

far more than 30,000 skins of tigers, leopards, jackals, and snakes have been seized from him or his associates.

As Sansar Chand has probably been largely responsible for the decline in India's wildlife in a career spanning more than twenty-five years, we felt it was essential that he be exposed. The opportunity came when we managed to catch poachers with leopard skins in Haridwar and Rajaji National Park. Not unexpectedly, they said they were working for Sansar Chand. They gave us an address that matched the one we had from the 1993 tiger bone case. A police watch was kept on the house. An elderly police constable remembered what Sansar looked like and recognized him. Sansar was arrested carrying a parcel containing a leopard skin on 17 July 1995.

Not long after that Ashok and I had an opportunity to talk to Sansar Chand. We talked for about two hours and it was one of the most extraordinary experiences of my life. Sansar was dressed in white handloomed kurta-pajamas. He is quite good looking, quite magnetic in an evil sort of way. He seemed to be high on something and talked nonstop in a high-pitched, squeaky voice as his eyes constantly darted around the room. He perspired so profusely that his collar was damp. We sat in chairs across a table from him. He was cocky, and despite all the cases against him did not appear to think he was in any trouble. He knew a lot about everybody involved in the illegal wildlife trade. At all times he assured us that he himself, of course, did not take part in it in any way. The authorities were just trying to set him up, he claimed.

He knew the wildlife inspectors by name and said that all but one were corrupt, and that person had been transferred. He knew about the Kashmir operation. He told us that seized tiger skins had been stolen from government storerooms. He knew the people involved in tiger poaching in Ranthambhore and Sariska and what they had said to the police. He said about Ranthambhore, "Such a big case, so many goods seized, so many people caught, and yet they have all been let loose!"

Sansar Chand knew so much that I became convinced that if he changed sides, if he were on our side, we could reverse the threat to the tiger. Conservationists would win. Ashok put it to him. "Oh no!" he gasped. "My children—my son and daughter—will be killed. They will get the evil eye. My children curse you already because you are behind all my problems." To which Ashok said, "What about the animals, don't they curse you?" "Killing animals is a very bad thing," Sansar admitted, but he did not seem very contrite.

Sansar is actually a Khanjar tribal from Rajasthan. Many of them still live in or near the jungle where they are traditional hunters and trappers. They no doubt supply many animal skins and bones to the illegal trade.

To go back to the day he was arrested; before he could be interrogated, Sansar complained of chest pains and was taken to a nearby hospital. There he allegedly influenced the doctors to keep him in for endless checks. He was released, with a clean bill of health, an hour before he was due to appear in court. While he was in the hospital, officials in Uttar Pradesh, where he was wanted in three recent poaching cases, were called. All the newspapers were alerted and legal advice sought. We hired a film crew and, taking my own cameras, I photographed Sansar as he was led out of the hospital. He was livid and stood in front of me, glaring. Nobody has ever looked at me with such hate as he did then. I stood my ground and stared back at him, and actually moved forward and took more pictures.

When he got to court there were dozens of news cameramen flashing away at him. By that time Sansar Chand was surrounded by his womenfolk who screamed at the photographers and lashed out at his police escort. His wife, who is in local politics, was particularly noisy and aggressive and tried to cover his face with a cloth. A huge crowd had gathered by the time he was dragged into court followed by his five high-powered lawyers.

In the court the magistrate asked the wildlife inspector who was prosecuting the case if he would like the accused to be remanded in custody so more contraband could be searched for, and whether he opposed Sansar's bail application. To both these questions the wildlife inspector replied, "No"! In the meanwhile the Uttar Pradesh Forest Department arrived in force. The conservator of forests asked the magistrate if he could hand the accused over to him as he was wanted in three cases. The magistrate turned the request down and said the Forest Department was operating outside its jurisdiction. One experienced senior police officer turned to me and said, "I'm shocked beyond belief by their decisions."

One of Sansar Chand's lawyers then told the magistrate that his client feared for his life and demanded a police escort back to his house.

The magistrate agreed. There was a stunned silence. No one could believe what was happening—next day newspapers declared the court hearing a complete farce. Sansar Chand, protected by the same police who hours earlier had arrested him, walked out of the court a free man, straight back to his illegal trade. As Sansar Chand left the court, I was standing on a bench to get a better vantage point for photographs. Again, this time with his entire entourage, Sansar Chand came up to within about a meter, and stared at me. If looks could kill. . . .

The press conference that followed was more like a wake. No one could believe that India's most notorious wildlife criminal, who had been convicted in one case and was an accused in fourteen other cases, had gotten off scot-free.

The next day the story, particularly the magistrate's extraordinary behavior, received major front page coverage in just about every newspaper. Hours later the High Court, in an unprecedented legal move, brought a **suo motu** notice to the magistrate and Sansar Chand. They demanded to know why the bail application was not rejected when he had so many cases pending against him.

For a while the Uttar Pradesh Forest Department pursued their cases, but Sansar Chand could not be found. Then, on 11 August, the Uttar Pradesh government transferred all the officials who had been handling the Sansar Chand investigations and prosecution to other places and other duties.

The incredibly sad thing about all this is that wildlife criminals will now flout the law more than ever. They know they can get away with it. It is a major blow against the survival of the tiger. But at least Sansar Chand has been exposed and has had his photograph plastered over the front page of the newspapers. Maybe it will slow him down.

★ ★ ★

Despite his protestations of being a poor man, Sansar Chand has considerable resources. His numerous lawyers charge high fees and the bribes he allegedly pays out run into hundreds of thousands of rupees. Mohammed Zayeed, on the other hand, is a truly poor man. He has nothing except the few threadbare clothes he wears. He is seventy-two years old, very thin with gray hair and a gray mustache. From an early age, long before the present crisis, he alerted the authorities to the poaching of tigers, leopards, and elephants. He has suffered, and continues to suffer greatly, for his principles. Once he and his family had a small house and he made a reasonable living. Now he wanders around alone, sleeping where he can and finding laboring jobs in the area around Rajaji National Park north of Delhi. Mohammed Zayeed, because of his longevity and his persistence, is well-known to conservationists and poachers in the region. One of Belinda's friends from Haridwar told her about him and she went to see him.

Mohammed Zayeed told me that he has had an interest in wildlife since early childhood. He comes from a poor Muslim village and has had no formal education whatsoever. He cannot read or write. Because

he lived close to Rajaji he was aware of poachers operating in the national park. He said to me that this poaching is very wrong, especially in an area reserved for wildlife. From the time he was a young man he has fought a lone battle against it. Sixteen years ago Zayeed reported to the Forest Department that two

Wildlife trader Sansar Chand under arrest in Delhi on 18 July 1995.

poachers had killed a tiger. The men were caught and arrested, but as usual were given bail.

After about a year these poachers, accompanied by a group of henchmen, came to Zayeed's village. He lived with his wife, son, and three daughters in a simple mud house with a thatched roof. Thinking Zayeed was inside, the poachers barricaded all the doors and windows from the outside, doused the roof with kerosene, and set it alight. Zayeed was not there at the time, but when he returned home he found that his entire family had been burned to death. The people who did this were never caught.

Ever since that day Zayeed has spent his time roaming the forests in and around Rajaji looking for poachers. He told me he soon realized that it was futile to take his information to the local authorities. They would either brusquely tell him to get lost or arrest him and beat and torture him to try to get more information. The Forest Department is just not used to people, off the street as it were, coming to them with information about poachers. They think he must be involved or has some score to settle and therefore must know more.

So he changed his tactics. He now pays a streetside professional scribe to write letters for him giving all the poaching details. He writes to the Prime Minister, the Chief Minister of the state, and the Forest Minis-

ter. He signs his letters with his thumbprint. He has been doing this for years and has now added my name to the list. He has received a few replies, including several from Indira Gandhi. He carries some of these letters wrapped in a cloth tied around his waist.

Zayeed is very passionate about stopping poaching. He tends to talk on and on about how dreadful people are and how this person does this and those people do that. His information, however, is very accurate. That surprised me, because good information is always hard to come by.

He goes from village to village. People know what he does and they all gossip to him. When he picks up some interesting information he follows it up. He works as a day laborer, still at his age, and when he hears that some poachers are operating in an area he'll start working on the roads there or help in a tea shop—both of which are great places to pick up gossip. He'll just watch and listen and when he knows he's onto something he'll go off and write his letters.

He has no belongings. Many of the local people look after him, give him food and a place to sleep. I was surprised by how many people sympathize with him, especially young people—students and social workers, people like that.

The poachers also know him, of course, and he has frequently been beaten up by them and shot at. In early 1995 he was shot in the shoulder by leopard poachers in Rajaji. Luckily it was only a superficial wound and it healed quickly.

He has been quite effective. In early October 1995 he gave information about the poaching of three leopards near Rajaji. As a result the local forest authorities seized one leopard skin and caught two poachers in the process of skinning another two leopards. A gun was also recovered from them. Two weeks later Zayeed found a leopard that had been caught in a trap. Forest guards were able to free the leopard and release it back into the forest.

Shortly after the second incident, Zayeed was picked up by the forest authorities. As before, he was interrogated, beaten, and tortured. Ashok and I immediately got in touch with them and had him released.

But even so, Zayeed was picked up yet again in February 1996. His "crime" was that he had correctly identified several forest guards involved in poaching in Rajaji. This time a group of sympathizers arranged for him to stay hidden at a remote farm house, for they feel sure that if he is not protected he will sooner or later be killed.

[CHAPTER 26]
FIGHTING FOR THE RHINO

Shergarh—1 December 1995

In our second conversation under the hara tree, Belinda tells me how she tracked down an international gang of rhino horn smugglers and traders.

The Indian rhinoceros is possibly under even greater threat than the tiger, simply because it now lives in only a few small reserves. Rhinos, too, are a special concern to Belinda and the Wildlife Protection Society of India. This story began in March 1993.

When I think of Kaziranga, I of course think of rhinos. But also of a very special wild place with tigers, elephants, hoolock gibbons, and so on. The people there, too, were always kind and helpful. We had great adventures there, and I have very happy and exciting memories of it.

For one reason or another I never got back to Kaziranga, though I always very much wanted to. Then in March of 1993 Manju Barua, an Assamese friend of mine, invited me to join a group of conservationists on a trip to Kaziranga. He had organized for all of us to go by boat from Guwahati, up the Brahmaputra. I jumped at the chance.

For a whole day, in glorious sunshine, we sat on this boat and discussed the problems passionately. It was all very stirring and the Assamese people were greatly concerned about what was happening to the jungles and the animals—especially in Manas,

which is still under a cloud. Strangely enough, nearly all of them were senior government people—divisional forest officers, conservators of forest, a magistrate. A few were junior forest officers. What was so refreshing was that they did not talk like government people—all guarded and cautious. They were ready for action. And the place was magical. We glided along the Brahmaputra, which in most places is two or three kilometers wide. There were birds everywhere, people fishing, farmers busy in their fields on the bank. But I do get tired of discussions and hearing about the same old problems and lack of funds, over and over again. Discussions are no longer good enough.

When I eventually reached Kaziranga, after all these years, I was quite overcome. There were still many of the friendly forest department faces of the 1970s. And because of our film, which is still being shown nearly every day, and my long history there, I was greeted very warmly.

Baguri, one of the park's four ranges, was always a favorite of ours so I arranged to spend a day there. The range officer, Pankaj Sharma, was definitely a leading light in Kaziranga, though still a young man, about thirty I would say. He was well-educated and very well-read. It was great to spend the day with him. He'd been there only two months but already knew the major problems—the constant pressure from poachers, virtually no finances, equipment in disarray, and flagging morale among the guards and other field staff.

Sharma was beginning to think about solutions. He was very determined and courageous. What

I remember most about him was that he was just over the moon at being posted to Kaziranga, to be working with wildlife instead of in commercial forestry.

In the afternoon Sharma had to go off somewhere for a few hours so he left me at the Gandamari guard outpost in the middle of Kaziranga. I'm sure you remember it. It was the place where we tied our boat to the verandah during the 1976 floods. I sat and talked to the five guards who were there. I asked them about their living conditions, where their families were, and so on.

They told me they had no warm clothes or blankets for the winter; they had no socks or boots when walking out on patrol; they had no flashlight batteries for night patrols; they had little or no ammunition so they could do no target practice; they had no equipment to clean their rifles; they were always getting sick with malaria and other things; they had no mosquito nets; they were charged by rhinos and elephants and shot at by poachers when out on patrol.

I was more than shocked. I was speechless. Things were even worse than I had heard and I couldn't understand how these people kept going. When I asked them about that they said it was their duty, their job. I thought to myself, What in the heck am I doing here? I've come to look at rhinos and elephants and this wonderful remaining piece of terai. I had no right to do that while the very people who are supposed to be keeping it intact are being ignored by the outside world.

The sun was setting and I sat on that verandah for hours gazing out over the bheel where a few rhinos were grazing. It suddenly came to me how a lot of these problems could be solved so simply. There was, of course, nothing we could do about making sure salaries were paid on time and other such big issues. But the smaller, basic problems we could do something about—things like boots, clothing, mosquito nets, and, looking farther ahead, mobile clinics and other medical facilities.

That evening I sat down with Sharma to work out the number of guards and a list of what was needed, from warm jackets to jungle boots. We also discussed things like compensation for villagers when their crops were eaten by rhinos and elephants and the need for radio communications. We tried to think of everything.

I went back to Calcutta where I discussed the whole thing with my mother, Anne. A second official wish list arrived from Assam's chief wildlife warden and in April 1993 we wrote up a proposal. The Rhino Foundation was born. It had occurred to me before this that many tea companies were making substantial profits growing tea in Assam. Some use the rhino as their logo; the rhino is also the state animal. Surely they would contribute to a fund to help protect the rhino.

Anne took over the ideas from here, for she lives in Calcutta—which is much nearer Assam than Delhi—and she has always had a special interest in the northeast. She also knows the key wildlife people and most of the senior executives of the tea companies. Within months the operation was set up and the guards received the first of their warm clothing. The Rhino Foundation is going from strength to strength. It is helping to keep the rhinos alive, and the morale of their guardians high.

Apart from the lack of funds, the main problem in Kaziranga remains the poaching of rhinos for their horns, so when I began undercover work in 1994 I always kept my eyes and ears open for any trade in rhino horns. I finally got a sniff of that in May of 1995. One of my informers in Delhi told me about a Tibetan woman who said she had tiger bones and skins for sale. She let it be known she could also supply rhino horns. She said she acted as an agent for a relative in north Bengal. My informer then told the woman, Rita Yaqub, that a French jewelry designer and manufacturer was interested in buying rhino horns. He suggested to Yaqub that she get her relative to come to Delhi to do business.

Posing as a French jeweler, I met the so-called relative, a Mr. A. P. Lepcha, who was of Chinese origin. I told him I had a lucrative business setting gold-encrusted jewels in rhino horn dagger handles and producing other trinkets for sale in the Middle East. Lepcha was short and potbellied, nervous but very informative and confident about what he could supply. We talked about lots of different products—ivory, musk, tiger claws, and so on. He said he could supply everything, but then they always do.

He was, however, very specific about rhino horns. He told me he had more than fifty horns for sale. The price would be $32,000 per kilogram. He said he would deliver the goods in Siliguri in North Bengal, about a three-hour drive from the Kingdom of Bhutan. We arranged to meet there and I kept in touch by phone.

Rita Yaqub, the Tibetan woman, was going to get a cut from the sale. Being rather greedy, she was keen for the deal to go ahead as soon as possible. I bought her an air ticket to Siliguri and followed a few days later. On the afternoon of the day I arrived, June 10th, Lepcha came to see me at my hotel. He gave me a detailed list of sixty-two horns, some weighing as little as seventy-five grams. The largest horn weighed 1.4 kilograms.

I said to Lepcha that I personally didn't have the funds to buy so many horns and that I would have to bring in my partner from the Middle East. I was then joined by a colleague from Delhi.

We negotiated for four or five days and it became evident that there was a bigger person involved. Lepcha called him his boss. It was absolutely critical that we meet this person. Lepcha also told me that he could only supply fifty-two rhino horns as ten of them had just been sold, in Bhutan, to two Korean buyers. We later got confirmation of this from one of our informers.

Lepcha said that his boss did not want to meet us. We kept stalling, saying that as we had to pay cash, about $183,000, it would take a while to get together. While we were talking about this, the telephone in our hotel room rang. It was the boss wanting to talk to Lepcha. I told Lepcha that if I could not meet the boss I would at least like to speak to him. I spoke to this absolutely charming man. He was very polite, called me "madam." Finally I said, "Listen, we have to meet. I'm delighted with the quantities you can provide. I'm also very impressed with the way our deal is progressing and I hope we'll be able to have a long-term association. It would be a great pity if we didn't meet." He agreed with that. The following morning we went to another hotel and met this charming, "cool" young man. He was thirty-three years old but looked younger than that. But at the same time he was very sophisticated and worldly-wise. He said his name was Wong Kim Quee and that he was Taiwanese.

Wong asked us to meet him again at a restaurant the next day. Lepcha came to pick us up and took us to this sleazy hotel and there was Wong sitting in a corner. We sat down with him and he plied us with beer. He was wearing a navy blue sweatshirt with "Washington D.C. Polo Club" written on it. Again he was most charming, with exquisite manners. He was very sweet to me, positively flirting. It was also the most critical conversation we had with him. He warned me that it was a dangerous

Kaziranga with the Mikir Hills
in the background.

business, and that I really shouldn't be in it. He told us that he'd supplied all of the twenty-two rhino horns the Bhutanese Princess was caught with in Taiwan in September 1993.

He was by far the most intelligent and most sophisticated of all the traders we met. Not even Sansar Chand was in his league of sophistication. Wong was quite curious about how we intended to get the horns out. I told him the "plan" and he thought it was the most brilliant thing he'd ever heard. In conclusion, he said that he would be happy to supply us regularly with rhino horns. He said he would "finish off all supplies in the next one or two years." That is, he would drive the rhino into extinction.

All the time he insisted that we do the deal in Bhutan. He said he was safe there. The Indian police could not enter the country and the Bhutanese, he said, had been "paid off." All his stocks were held in Bhutan. We were adamant we wanted to do the deal in India. In the end we agreed to exchange the nonexistent cash for the rhino horns in a small town on the Bhutanese border.

In the middle of the night, the day before the handover, we had a visitor. It was Lepcha in total hysterics. He said, "A dreadful thing has happened." He put his head in his hands and said, "The whole deal is canceled. I've had a terrible dream. I was sitting in this room with this man [pointing at my colleague] when suddenly all the walls and the ceiling caved in. This is a very bad omen. I'm going to tell Wong that the deal shouldn't go through. I think you're trying to trap us."

I quickly called Rita Yaqup and told her what had happened. She could only only see lots of money slipping through her fingers, and she came rushing over. For about an hour and a half she tried to pacify Lepcha. She massaged his feet and said, "Come on, brother, we stand to make hundreds of thousands of rupees. What are you worried about?"

I tried to remain unflustered and said, "Well, if you don't want to do business we'll go elsewhere."

In the meantime we'd been in touch with the police and they told us that the place where Wong wanted to do the deal was actually in Bhutan. Things began to unravel. We knew they had brought some rhino horns into India. They'd shown us two. We decided to go ahead with the raid immediately.

The police arrested Wong, Lepcha, and Rita Yaqub and recovered two rhino horns which they valued at $32,258. The three were put in jail,

A Kanha meadow ringed by sal trees, with a gular tree in the foreground.

where according to our contacts they would not be given bail for at least three or four months. Under interrogation they gave much valuable information. It was the first time an international gang trading in wildlife parts had been apprehended in India.

But as in the Sansar Chand case, all kinds of funny business went on at the courts and the accused were released on bail within a month and vanished.

I felt very despondent after those two cases. I thought to myself, "There is no hope for Indian wildlife. Under this system the tiger, rhino, elephant, and all the other 'valuable' species are doomed. We're simply wasting our time."

★   ★   ★

But under the hara tree surrounded by birds and langur monkeys, where everything is peaceful, the problems do not seem as stark or overwhelming. In a few days we will travel to Kaziranga again and talk to Pankaj Sharma and some other range officers. Perhaps they are more optimistic.

★   ★   ★

Leaving Kanha for me is like leaving home. This time I do not know when or even if I will be back here. Other jungles in India have given us great spectacle and great experiences, but none is like Kanha and its forests. We had many extraordinary and happy times here; it has been a most important place in both our lives.

There is one last surprise as we drive out early on the morning of 2 December. On the road through the forest, only a kilometer or two from Shergarh, a doglike animal lies in the middle of the road. When we are near, it stands up and looks at us for a few moments before slowly loping off into the forest. It is a wolf! The first I've ever seen in the wild. It does not go far before lying down and rolling over on its back, paws in the air.

Kanha had always seemed vaguely incomplete to me before, because if these were the forests where Kipling's *Jungle Book* stories were set, where were the wolves? How could Mowgli have been raised here? But here was Akela looking at us through slitted eyes. Kanha is the complete jungle.

How Kaziranga Protects Its Rhinos

**KAZIRANGA—
7 TO 12 DECEMBER 1995**

Since we were last in Kaziranga together, in July 1976, many rumors have come out of Assam about the park, but there has been little reliable information. It has been said that poaching was wiping out the rhinos, that riverine and hill forests were being felled, that encroachment by refugee farmers continued to eat into the park, that political dissidents were killing the animals, that the staff was corrupt. Was all this true? Could there be some basis to Wong Kim Quee's boast that the source of rhino horns would be finished off in a few years? We decide to go and see for ourselves what is happening.

★ ★ ★

Kaziranga is divided into four compartments called Ranges. Each is under the control of a range officer who lives in or near his compartment. All four of Kaziranga's current range officers are outstanding men. Their main management concern is to control poaching and all four are implacable in their pursuit of poachers and the traders in rhino horns.

The confrontation between poachers and the range officers and their staff is a shooting war. Many poachers are shot and killed, others are arrested and imprisoned. No forest guards have been killed by poachers in recent years. Ironically, two forest guards were badly mauled by rhinos not long ago.

Parties of poachers can be in the park at any time, day or night. They shoot their rhino, cut off the horn in a matter of seconds, and melt away into the tall grass. There are so many guard outposts that no shooting can go undetected. Minutes after hearing the shots, patrols close in on the suspected place. When these, or routine, patrols meet a company of poachers, the poachers are shot without warning.

The Kaziranga "army" that wages war against the poachers has greatly increased since we were here in 1976. Then there was a field staff of 168 guards living in 20 outposts. Now there are 435 guards living in 115 camps.

The increase in personnel became necessary in the 1980s and 1990s when there was a great upsurge in poaching. This was a direct

response to the high prices paid for rhino horns—from $2,000 per kilogram in 1976 to $32,000 in 1995.

However, during this same time, from 1976 to 1993, the numbers of rhinos in Kaziranga increased from 846 to 1,164. Elephant numbers rose from 349 to 1,094 and tigers from an estimated 20 to 72. It is not only the rhino that benefits from the increased protection.

There is no chance for Wong Kim Quee and his cohorts to "finish off the source" of rhino horns in Kaziranga. The Assamese people, who see the rhino as a symbol of their culture, will never allow that to happen.

Madhya Pradesh, in central India, is officially designated the Tiger State. But no such pride and passion is evident in the protection of *their* symbol, the tiger.

★   ★   ★

Kaziranga is safe for the moment and once again provides us a great experience. It is a wilderness in the sense that its habitat is intact and its animals abound. To purists, the many roads, the constant patrolling by forest guards, and the war with poachers may disqualify it from being a true wilderness.

But there are still some true and great wilderness areas in other parts of India. Between December 1995 and February 1996 we visit three of those wild places. First we go from Kaziranga to that virtually unknown land of mystery called Balpakram, about a day's drive from Kaziranga. After that we travel to Corbett National Park in the Himalayan foothills, where we follow the footsteps of Jim Corbett, the legendary hunter of man-eating tigers, and visit our friend Brijendra Singh. Finally, we travel to south India, to Nagarahole, one of the few areas of optimum tiger habitat—with tigers—remaining in the world.

PART VI

THE LAST GRE
JUNGLES

My ambition when I was very young wa

tiger, just that, and no more. Later my

was to shoot a tiger, and this I accom

foot with an old army rifle which I boug

rupees from a seafaring man...Later s

my ambition to photograph a tiger...It

trying to photograph tigers that I learn

I know about them.

Jim Corbett in *The Temple Tiger d*
More Man-eaters of Kumaon, 19

Balpakram—Home of Departed Souls

BALPAKRAM—
17 TO 22 DECEMBER 1995

Balpakram National Park is so remote we could not find it on any map nor in any guidebook. Its tropical rain forests lie in the folds of the Garo Hills in the state of Meghalaya and overlook the plains of Bangladesh to the south. These are the westernmost of the great Indo-Malayan forests and among the richest in terms of plant and animal species. According to the Garo people, when a person dies, his or her soul must travel to Balpakram to be judged.

While we wander the park's forests ("It is like stepping into another world," Belinda says),

we experience similar feelings to those we had in Manas: that this is an exceptional, perhaps unparalleled area of biodiversity. The trees, the orchids, the birds, and above all the mammals, have a species richness we have not encountered anywhere else. For example, the park harbors eight species of cat, seven of which are endangered. They range from the tiger to the jungle cat and include that most enigmatic of all cats, the clouded leopard.

Above: limestone formations in the rain forest near Siju Cave.

Left: the endangered clouded leopard hunts mainly in the trees. Its name is derived from the cloudlike markings along its body.

Preceding pages: leopard, Tiger Haven, near Dudhwa National Park.

Above, left to right: a bamboo viper; a lady slipper orchid; a cave frog from Siju Cave.

Adjoining the National Park is Siju Cave, at 1,156 meters long the longest and largest cave in Asia. It, too, is home to unique and endangered species.

As recently as a decade ago, far eastern India contained vast tracts of tropical rain forest. Most of these have now been denuded. Balpakram's 450 square kilometers is one of the last significant tracts left. Thirty-nine species of endangered mammals and numerous rare species of medicinal plants live and grow within its boundaries. All this is about to be devastated by the construction of a huge cement plant and a limestone mine directly above Siju Cave.

Left: a lookout on the edge of slash-and-burn cultivation, with the tropical rain forest of the national park in the background.

Above: the authors in a dugout canoe near Siju Cave.

[CHAPTER 27]

MAN-EATING TIGERS AND JIM CORBETT'S LEGACY

Under normal circumstances tigers kill quickly and cleanly and will strike down no more than they need to survive. Yet the tiger more than any other animal has become the embodiment of wanton savagery. To humanity, which has a fascination for predators, the tiger is the ultimate predator. It is large and powerful, solitary, secretive, flamboyantly beautiful in pattern and form, yet invisible in even a small patch of grass or bamboo—all attributes that have imbued it with almost supernatural powers in the eyes of humans. As a consequence the tiger has become the ultimate prey for man the hunter; his ultimate trophy.

Since time immemorial people have hunted the tiger—first with nets and spears, then with swords, bows and arrows, and latterly with sophisticated firearms. Sometimes the tiger hunt was to protect livestock or to eliminate a man-eater—but mostly, right from earliest times, it was to satisfy some deep desire to prove mastery over the most powerful animal in the jungle. To kill a tiger was to prove one's manhood. This primitive desire to kill the ultimate killer is never far beneath the surface, even now in supposedly more enlightened times.

In the days before firearms and motor vehicles, when the hunters had to outwit the tiger on its own terms and in its own territory with nothing more lethal than a spear or bow and arrow, it undoubtedly was an heroic feat to kill a tiger. The tiger not infrequently managed to turn the tables on its attackers and killed them. But with the advent of guns and rifles of increasing power and accuracy, strong spotlights, the method of shooting from an elephant or a *machan,* and drawing tigers to a predetermined spot by baiting or beating, it became less and less a case of hunting and more and more plain killing. The so-called hunters were seldom at risk, the elephants and the unarmed beaters on foot bore the brunt of the attacks by enraged tigers wounded by inexpert shots. Robert H. Elliot, a coffee planter in south India writing in the 1880s,

said boastingly, "I suppose upwards of forty tigers have been killed in the neighborhood of my plantation, but only two natives have been killed [by tigers] when out shooting." His method of shooting was to have the local villagers beat tigers towards him while he sat in a *machan.*

When the British with their preoccupation with sport came to India, they made hunting one of their most popular "sports." The Indian aristocracy readily joined in and animal killing in the Indian jungles became highly organized, lavish social occasions. The ultimate occasions were, of course, the tiger shoots and tiger killing became the foremost "sport" of India's elite. Scores of elephants, as many as a thousand beaters, and innumerable baits were deployed to ensure a bag of as many tigers as possible.

In 1861 such a shoot was organized by Captain James Forsyth in the Kanha region. He wrote:

"A good many persons will remember a hunt in the month of January, 1861, when we secured a royal tiger for the Governor-General of India, on his first visit to the center of his dominion….I mounted sentry over that beast for nearly a week, girding him in a little hill with a belt of fires, and feeding him with nightly kine [cow], till half a hundred elephants, carrying the cream of a vice-regal camp, swept him out into the plain, where he fell riddled by a storm of bullets from several hundred virgin rifles. He had the honour of being painted by a Landseer, by the blaze of torchlight, under the shadow of the British standard; and my howdah bore witness for many a day, in a bullet hole through both sides of it, to the accuracy of aim of some gallant member of the staff!"

By the late nineteenth century an attitude developed that the more tigers you killed, the bigger man you were. Some of the scores were monstrous. The Maharaja of Surguja killed 1,157 tigers in his lifetime.

Robert Elliot reported that in 1834, 118 tigers were

killed in a "short time" in his district by luring them into pit-fall traps with sharp spikes at the bottom. During one day four tigers were killed in a single trap. In the same book he asks rhetorically: "Is not the intelligent preservation of game one of the most prominent signs of advancing civilization?"

An excuse often put forward for tiger hunting was that it eliminated man-eaters. The truth was less noble; "sportsmen" created as many if not more man-eaters than they destroyed. Except in the Sunderbans, man-eating tigers are nearly always disabled in some way—by old age perhaps, or by wounds inflicted by sambar or buffalo horns or, more often, by porcupine quills. But another common cause was the inept shot of a "sportsman" or poacher. The injury prevented the tiger from bringing down its natural prey and it turned to the only creature it could catch, even when three-legged or with half its face shot away.

Few of the people who went armed into the jungles, either British or Indian, were true hunters who went on foot, or even on elephant, but otherwise alone and pitted their skills and intelligence against those of the animals, especially the tiger. But there were some, and for them hunting was supremely exciting. Two of the best-known were James Forsyth and Jim Corbett, and of those Corbett was probably the most skillful hunter India has known. Not only did he hunt alone and on foot but he hunted man-eating tigers, animals that often stalked him. In those hunts he never failed. He out-tigered the tiger on the predators' own terrain.

But the depredation on tigers was not an entirely one-way affair. A few of the cats became man-eaters, nearly always out of necessity and never for "sport." The most notorious man-eater was known as the man-eating tigress of Champawat, who had killed 438 people over an eight-year period when Corbett shot her in 1909. The next year Corbett killed

the man-eating leopard of Panar who had claimed 400 human lives. Mrs. Alida Sverdsten, an American, shot the infamous man-eating tiger of Ramgiri-Udaygiri in Orissa in 1966. It had eaten an estimated 500 people, though this figure is said, by some, to be exaggerated.

Delivering people of these predators—hunting down and killing the man-eating tigers—was what Corbett called "a new kind of sport." The regular "sportsmen" who hunted tigers with baits, from *machans* or from elephant back when

A man-eating tigress that was trapped in July 1991 after killing fourteen people in Madhya Pradesh.

the animals were pushed in their direction by unarmed beaters, had no taste for this "new kind of sport." When four hunters had been surprised and killed on their respective *machans* by a man-eating leopard in south India, the other hunters gave up all pretense of even trying.

Hunting man-eaters is hunting in its purest form. "Sportsmen" hunters proved inept and were only rarely successful. Only hunters possessing outstanding junglecraft, great personal courage, and an intimate knowledge of the wild animals could hope to succeed. People of that stamp were individualists and all hunted the man-eaters in their own particular way. Captain James Forsyth preferred "quiet hunting which was far more successful than the bustle of many elephants and rabble of men that usually accompany a tiger hunt." When tracking a man-eater he would go on elephant back. A tracker walked practically under the elephant's trunk while Forsyth stood in the *howdah*, rifle cocked. This is reasonably safe if everyone can trust the others' courage and steadiness, including those of the elephant. In the case of Forsyth it worked; the man-eaters were tracked down and killed. Forsyth swore by his favorite elephant and would not dream of going after tigers, least of all man-eaters, on foot. His assessment was that: "A man on foot has no chance whatever in thick jungle with a tiger that is bent on killing him." That kind of man, he said, is "seldom very successful, and sooner or later gets killed, or has such narrow escapes as to cure him of such silly folly." An accurate summing-up for ordinary "sportsmen." but it does not apply to that extraordinary man Jim Corbett.

What made Corbett so uniquely successful in hunting down man-eaters? The reasons are complex and make an odd mixture. First of all there were the man's innate sensitivities—his natural predilection to be in the jungle and to want to know exactly how it worked. Throughout his life he said it was "unalloyed joy" to go into the forests; often to hunt but more frequently just to listen and to watch.

But equally important was the fact that he was what was termed a "domiciled Englishman," that is, he and his family were born in and lived in India and had adopted it as their country. There were no estates or wealth "back home" in England. There was no senior government post with all the trappings of the raj for his family. There was no barrier of privilege between him and his becoming a barefoot child of the jungle.

Edward James Corbett was born in Naini Tal in the sub-Himalayan Kumaon Hills in 1875. His father, who was the postmaster, died when Jim was only four years old and from then on the family lived mostly at their farm at Kaladhungi,

twenty-five kilometers down the mountains from Naini Tal. It was in the forests of Kaladhungi, near what is now Corbett National Park, that Jim learned his jungle skills.

He got his first rifle when he was eight years old and not many years after that shot his first big cat—a leopard—while out on his own. He shot his last tiger, a notorious cattle-lifter, when he was seventy and somewhat unsteady from malaria attacks.

But these junglecrafts, in themselves impressive and seldom surpassed, are not enough to be successful in bringing man-eaters to book. This "new kind of sport" needed a toughness, resourcefulness, and singlemindedness no other hunting required. As well as physical endurance, a certain mental steadiness is needed to follow a man-eater. Often Corbett, on the trail of one of the cats when it had just made a human kill, would find a leg, a hand, a head. Other times he would sit in a tree over the remains of a human kill.

Tigers attacked and killed humans from the time, in prehistoric days, they first ventured into the predators' domain and even today there are still sporadic reports of man-eaters, though more often of man-killers. A fine distinction perhaps if you are the victim, but an important difference nonetheless. Man-killers usually attack someone who accidentally stumbles on the animal while it is on its prey or, if it is a female, with cubs. It is an isolated incident. Man-eaters, on the other hand, systematically hunt, kill, and eat people and terrorize whole districts.

Forsyth stated that 400 to 500 people were killed by "wild beasts" every year in the Central Provinces alone from 1860 till he left the district about eight years later. Nearly all of the "beasts" were tigers with lesser numbers of leopards, bears, and wolves. Most of the offending tigers, however, came into the category of man-killers, each of them claiming no more than one or two victims. Despite the large population of tigers in those days confirmed man-eaters were few.

Corbett claimed that no man-eaters were recorded in the sub-Himalayan hills of the Garhwal-Kumaon region until 1905 when the dreaded Champawat tigress, named after the village close to which she was finally killed, crossed the border from Nepal into India. From what can be gathered from the literature, man-eating tigers were comparatively rare throughout India until about that time, even in the more densely settled forest regions. From then on a combination of rapidly shrinking habitat and badly directed bullets from

Along the Ramganga River in Corbett National Park.

"sportsmen" and poachers converted more and more of the predators to hunters of humanity.

As already mentioned, tigers, with one or two notable exceptions, become man-eaters only when some disability prevents them from bringing down their natural prey. The Champawat tigress, the most terrible man-eater of all, was disabled by a gunshot that knocked out her canine teeth. The Chowgarh tigress was so old that her claws were broken and her teeth worn to the bone. Charges of buckshot, one in the right shoulder and another in the left, turned the tigress later known as the Thak man-eater into a hunter of people. While trying to kill a porcupine, a tigress who became the Muktesar man-eater lost an eye, and some fifty quills were embedded in her arms and the pads of her front feet. A male tiger known as the Chuka man-eater had been riddled with buckshot and had lost one canine tooth. A porcupine was responsible for incapacitating the Talla-Des man-eater.

Man-eating tigers usually attack in daylight; they have no fear whatever of humans and make their kills boldly in the villages, in the fields, or along forest foot trails. Poor people armed only with sticks and sickles are powerless against them. When such a tiger concentrates its attacks on one small area, the place is under siege. No one moves from their house; fields are left untended, crops unharvested, domestic animals ungrazed. Sanitation becomes a problem, for there is no indoor plumbing, and food runs out. One village in Kumaon was under siege for five days from the Champawat tigress who rampaged roaring through neighboring forests at night and paced the fields during the day. Many a time Corbett was asked to stand guard with his rifle in man-eater country while the people hastily gathered their crops or cut fodder for their animals. Sometimes entire villages were deserted and at one time 5,000 timber cutters walked off the job because a man-eater patrolled the forests in which they were to work. When not laying siege, the tiger may strike anywhere in its range of up to 3,000 square kilometers.

Man-eating and man-killing tigers, leopards, lions, wolves, and even hyenas have continued their depredations into the 1980s and 1990s. Three confirmed man-eaters were shot or trapped in the area around Dudhwa in that time.

★ ★ ★

About 300 kilometers east of Delhi in the sub-Himalayan Shiwalik Hills lies India's first national park. It was declared in 1936 and called Hailey National Park after Sir Malcolm Hailey, governor of the then–United Provinces. In 1952, after the

United Provinces became the state of Uttar Pradesh in the Indian Union, the park was renamed Ramganga National Park. In 1957, it became Corbett National Park.

What is left of the jungles around Kaladhungi and Naini Tal where Corbett grew up are just a few kilometers away. Corbett knew the park area well. He tramped its forests, fished its river, and pursued man-eaters through it.

The pristine hills and river flats remain as they were in Corbett's day: real jungles full of tigers, leopards, bears, elephants, deer, monkeys, peafowl, and a diversity of other birds that bedazzle the senses.

Corbett National Park is also India's favorite jungle, often overrun with noisy crowds, we have been told by friends. That is why I had never visited it. Belinda had been there briefly many years ago. We thought we would see wild elephants better in Kaziranga and south India and tigers more easily in Kanha and Ranthambhore. This proved to be true. But nobody had told us about the Ramganga River and the vistas of snow-covered hills in winter.

Our friend Brijendra Singh is an honorary warden in Corbett. He spends many months a year there and is actively involved in protecting the park from poachers and other intruders. Brij is the scion of a princely family, Sikhs from the Punjab on his mother's side, and still has the manner and style of an Indian noble. That is not to say that he is arrogant and overbearing; quite the contrary, he is courteous, considerate, and approachable. Friends, partly teasing him about his origins and partly about his deep commitment to the park, call him the rajah, the king, of Corbett.

Brij could never understand our reluctance to visit what is clearly his favorite place. He said, at the Tiger Link conference, that this time we must come. He would organize our visit and guarantee we would meet no pressing and noisy crowds of people. It is not until nearly a year after the conference that we take up Brij's invitation.

Corbett National Park and Tiger Reserve— 7 January 1996

After a long, tiring, and unpleasant drive from New Delhi we stop at a friend's house set among trees in gardens that sweep down to the Kosi River. The river divides farmland and forest. Our friend points to a small patch of forest on the other side of the wide, swift-flowing stream and says a man-eating tiger was shot there in 1981. He adds that man-eating and man-killing is still going on. A boy was recently killed by a leopard downstream from where we are sitting. Just a week ago a village woman was trampled to death by a wild elephant when she was collecting firewood close to the park. The elephant, our friend says, is a huge male with one of his tusks broken. Both leopard and elephant are still in the jungle.

It is almost dark when we arrive at the Sarapduli rest house deep inside the national park. Apart from the rest house staff we have seen no people. We can hear the Ramganga River in the valley below but it is too dark to investigate. The rooms have thick stone walls and high ceilings. The wooden furniture is sturdy and old-fashioned. It is cold and dark inside and there is no electricity.

The caretaker and the cook come to greet us. Within minutes the rooms are lit with oil lamps and candles, a fire burns in the grate, and hot tea arrives. After the tenseness of the drive we feel wonderfully relaxed and our spirits lift in the middle of this unpolluted jungle where the only sounds are the rush of the river and the chatter of an owlet.

Brij arrives full of bonhomie and energy. We make plans for the next few days. Brij invites us for lunch at the rest house he is staying at called Khinnanauli, which is even farther into the jungle.

8 January

At sunrise I walk down to the river. Its cold meltwater from Himalayan glaciers rushes over boulders through a shallow but steep ravine. On the opposite bank, mixed forest, which includes sal as well as several kinds of conifers, struggles to grow on a rocky slope. The early sun illuminates patches of russet grass. Through binoculars I search for and eventually find several goral, a small species of goat-antelope, grazing. Above them sit a score of rhesus macaques, their red faces turned toward the warming sun. A Himalayan pied kingfisher, a large species finely barred in black and white and with an unruly bushy crest, studies the foaming water from a prominent boulder. Farther downstream a Himalayan grayheaded fishing eagle, perched on a tree branch overhanging the stream, preens its already immaculate plumage. The fresh dung and footprints of elephants, visitors during the night, lie on the wet sand at the river's edge. In the bushes stir bright blue thrushes, scarlet minivets, and tiny crimson and yellow sunbirds.

A male gharial, an endangered species of crocodile that survives in Corbett.

Driving slowly over meandering forest trails we make our way to Brij's rest house. We stop on a high bluff and look down on a sandbank where three gharial lie basking in the sun. These giant, fish-eating crocodiles have heavyset bodies but surprisingly long and slender snouts lined with sharp fine teeth. One is a male, recognizable by the large fleshy protuberance on the tip of his snout.

Khinnanauli rest house stands on a grassy flat bordering the river, which here runs over a wide, but equally bouldery bed. Tall silk cotton trees rise out of the grass. Brij walks up to welcome us and we join him and his wife, Dawn, on the spacious terrace. The talk over lunch is full of banter and good humor but also about the issue foremost on the minds of all of us—what will be the fate of the tiger.

Ever since we arrived I have looked longingly at the wide river, keen to explore it for the variety of birds I know live there. But walking is not allowed in Corbett National Park as tigers and elephants pose a real danger. After lunch I ask Brij if it would be all right to walk just down to the river. "Yes, yes," he says, "but do be careful. Someone was taken by a tiger at that little bridge just near the river, and not far downstream the British bird-watcher David Hunt was killed by a tiger when he rushed into the forest following some special owl."

I remember the incident well. We had met Hunt and his party of bird-watchers at Keoladeo in February 1985, the day before he traveled to Corbett. We were at Keoladeo to show "Land of the Tiger" to our friends there and Hunt and his party sat in on the screening. At the end he strode up to Belinda and, shaking an admonishing finger in her face, said, "It is all the fault of you tiger people. It is because of you that we can't walk in the forest to look at birds." Never having expressed an opinion on the matter Belinda was rather taken aback by the vehement accusation.

A few days later Hunt was killed by a tiger in Corbett's forest. The offending tiger had been observed by a large number of park visitors over many years. He was subsequently caught alive in a cage trap and incarcerated first in the Kanpur zoo and later in the Lucknow zoo. He has since died.

I am not as foolhardy as David Hunt when I walk down to the river. The path and the river are wide with clear views without thickets where a tiger could lie in ambush or where I could accidentally stumble on one.

The bed of the river is several hundred meters wide but the stream flows in only about twenty meters of it. The entire width is covered in pale-colored, rounded boulders. Some are larger than an elephant's head, others smaller than my fist. A sprinkling of the stones are a beautiful pale purple in color. Among them are others with a faint green, yellow, or pink tinge. I jump from boulder to boulder to the center of the river. The water, cold and clear, is pale green. Small fish flash and wink their silver undersides. All manner of colorful birds skip and run among the stones.

On the far bank, hills are forested with sal trees whose leaves have turned bright yellow and are ready to fall. Beyond are snow-covered hills. The wildness, grandeur, and spacious-ness, and the hint of danger from tigers and elephants for a moment literally take my breath away.

From the bank a forest guard waves, without urgency, for me to return. Rock-hopping leisurely I make my way back. Pointing back over his shoulder the guard says, "*Burra hathi are-ha hai*"—a big elephant is coming. I reach the rest house just in time to see the rump of a huge male elephant disappear into the grass on the riverbank. It is heading for the exact spot where I was looking at the river birds. Brij, Belinda, and I walk to a raised part of the riverbank, too high and steep for the elephant to climb. We watch him push out of the grass several hundred meters upstream and amble closer and closer. He is muscular with a large domed head and exudes vigor and power. One of his tusks is broken off leaving a splintered stump. Not far from us he finds a pool and decides to bathe. In one quick, lithe movement he sits down, the icy water reaching up to his neck. He thrashes about, flapping his huge pink ears and with his mouth wide open shakes his head from side to side. He blows bubbles in the water through his trunk, then raises it and showers his head. He lies right down in the water and rolls on his back so that only the soles of his feet stick out of the water. In another agile movement he stands up and walks to the shallows where, black and glistening, he glowers at us. On the edge of the bathing pool about thirty black cormorants stand in a row on boulders, intently watch-ing the elephant. We half expect them to burst into applause.

Scattering the cormorants the elephant walks directly to-ward us, his head held high, looking menacing. He is ready to charge, so we move quietly out of view behind some grass. The elephant walks slowly on, crosses the river, and enters the forest. He is almost certainly the same tusker that killed a woman outside the park about a week ago. Echoing the feel-ings of all of us, Brij says—"Outside the park these chaps are harassed by the villagers with a lot of noise and with fire. The elephants get very angry. We should not provoke him here. He will soon learn that the park is a sanctuary in which he is safe. Just like we do. When we first arrive from Delhi we're very tense and all, but after a few days we calm down."

Twilight is cool on the terrace. A tiger roars in the forest. Someone appears with drinks. Brij is usually reticent about his life at Corbett National Park and his early years in the jun-gle, parrying questions with a joke and a laugh. Tonight, per-haps because he is among family and friends in the jungle, we talk for hours about Jim Corbett, hunting, the jungle, man-eating tigers, and the present poaching crisis.

I ask Brij how he first became interested in wildlife.

"That goes a long way back, in the sense that the whole family was always involved with hunting," he says. "My grand-father on my mother's side looked after large estates of forest which until independence belonged to our family. While there was some hunting, including tigers, the estates were all looked after and there were lots of tigers back then in the 1930s and 1940s. They had these massive camps, they really were a laugh, for about a month at Christmas time. Those were the sur-roundings I grew up in.

"But then we shifted to the hills, to Mussoorie just to the northwest of here. I went to school there. I was raised on some very good books. Jim Corbett's *Man-eaters of Kumaon,* was a particular favorite, but I read all of his books. Corbett was a very important influence, someone I could identify with for in some ways I had a similar kind of life. I too was a loner and used to go out hunting carrying the bare essentials. One would take just two or three cartridges and shoot a pheasant, a goral, or a barking deer.

"I only shot proven cattle-lifting leopards and they were really smart; it was a challenge to hunt them on foot. There was no question of using spotlights or Jeeps.

"That is how I got to know and love the jungle. School had a great influence too because we had many tutors who believed that to form one's character and one's mind we had to be exposed to the outdoors—fishing, shooting, and trekking. That was just my cup of tea of course. I think I got a bit too interested in all that, that's why I haven't graduated to anything else," Brij adds with a laugh.

"My guru when I was learning to shoot and track leop-ards was Ian W. Powell, Colonel Powell. He wrote a book *The Call of the Tiger.* Now he was an *incredible* chap. He was a con-temporary of Jim Corbett's though I think he was a bit younger. Colonel Powell taught me how to call up tigers and how to make sprays to lure tigers into certain areas. He helped me skin my first leopard when I was eleven.

"When I came to live in Mussoorie I found that these leopards that regularly killed cattle were pretty abundant. The villagers used to come and see me and ask me to shoot the leopard. I did enjoy doing that because it required some kind of skill to sit very quietly and it also required some guts to sit on the ground waiting for the leopard. I didn't like to sit in a tree because in the hills the trees are very strangely placed, of-ten with the branches hanging out over a cliff. So I preferred to sit on the ground. If you sit quietly the leopard soon comes and I would shoot it. Usually it took very little time.

"Then one day only a short time after Dawn and I were married in 1964, some villagers came and asked me to shoot a big leopard that had killed a buffalo. We'd just had a car accident and both of us had stitches—Dawn in her head and I in my leg. So I said to the villagers that I would come, only I couldn't walk. 'Don't worry, Sahib,' they said, 'we'll get a horse for you.' So I told Dawn I would go out and try for the leopard till midnight and then come back.

"The leopard did not show up so just before twelve o'clock I started back. It was the monsoon time and raining heavily. The path was very narrow. Somebody carrying a torch was leading the horse, and behind walked another man carrying my guns. Suddenly the horse's legs went over the side of the path. We hung in space for a little while and then fell down the steep slope. Sometimes the horse fell on top of me, sometimes I fell on top of the horse. We fell quite a long way but eventually landed on a wide ledge. I was totally smashed up—my back, my pelvis, and my ribs. I could not even get up. The pain was terrible. Luckily, the villagers had some country brew and I had some rum—which saved my life, probably.

"The villagers went to look for something to carry me out on. First they returned with a bathtub, a tin tub with two handles on each side. The problem was that my back was smashed so badly I could not bend enough to get into the tub. So I said go back again and get something else. Luckily they had brought another bottle of booze. I was in no pain by the time they returned with a charpoy. They carried me out and some time later I arrived home in a taxi, feeling no pain and probably singing. Dawn and my mother were horrified.

"They took me to hospital and that was a nightmare for I almost died. You know when your life is hanging by a thread it makes you think about all sorts of things including hunting and killing. I said to Dawn that if I had to die I'd go to Corbett National Park and die there. I said to her, Let's pack up and go. That's how we came here. I still couldn't walk, but slowly, slowly, with Dawn's help I learned to walk again.

"As a schoolboy I had come here often to camp and to fish and the man who then ran the park, N. S. Negi, had become

Subidar Ali, a *mahout*, survived an attack by a tiger.

my mentor. He said, when I arrived after my fall, Come with me and we'll fish. That was some incentive, but I couldn't hop across the boulders—it jarred my whole spine and gave me great pain. Then he said, Let us take photographs of the animals. I went with him and we started to take pictures, on foot, of tigers and elephants.

"It was scary because a big tusker would suddenly arrive in the middle of the track in front of you when you were on foot, and I knew I couldn't run. I was amazed at what a damned coward I was. All the time, I had a hand on my gun. I said to myself, Oh God, what a useless guy. But I persisted and slowly I began to understand what it really was all about. You need some kind of guts to be there on foot. You need a lot of junglecraft to see a big tusker on foot—it means something, you know. I started to understand it all a bit better and I realized how foolish I'd been all along to be so preoccupied with hunting. This was much more fun. That was my conversion," Brij concludes with another laugh.

Belinda asks if he ever shot a tiger.

"Only once," Brij replies thoughtfully, "a tigress which I had to shoot in this park after she had carried off two people in the night, one after the other.

"That was an unfortunate thing. It happened back in 1988. This tigress had killed a porcupine about a year or so before and we'd noticed she was limping. I suggested that we tranquilize her and treat her as soon as possible, but one way and another the opportunity was lost and the tigress disappeared. When she finally returned it was in the middle of the night, in May—a very hot month—at the Dhikala tourist complex. Ambika, my daughter, and I were staying there at the time. There was no electricity because a storm a few days earlier had knocked down many of the power poles. The *mahouts* and grass cutters were sleeping with their doors open for they have only poky little quarters with no fans.

"At about one o'clock in the morning we heard these tremendous screams coming from the *mahouts'* quarters. We rushed to the Land Rover and Ambika, she's smart, she grabbed my camera bag because she thought it might be necessary to take some pictures. In that bag I also carry a revolver, to fire in the air to scare elephants and poachers and so on. We drove fast towards the commotion. We'd hardly gone any distance when we saw a forest guard running towards us to say that the *mahout* Sher Bahadur had been attacked by an animal. He was lying there in a pool of blood, a very tough Nepali guy, with a strong will to live. He'd been badly mauled.

"He was still conscious. I asked him, 'What happened, what animal did this?'

"'I don't know what it was,' he said, 'it was a big animal. I was sleeping near the door with the children in the middle and my wife on the other side. I felt something standing over the youngest child. I sat up and I was grabbed by the head, and then the neck, my back, and by the buttocks and pulled out.' Then he fainted. Luckily I had a first-aid kit in the car and we dressed his worst wounds. I noticed some deep puncture marks which were obviously made by a large carnivore.

Brijendra Singh and his daughter Ambika. Brij, an honorary warden at Corbett, had to kill a dangerous tiger there in the 1980s.

"We put the injured man in a Jeep and sent him off to hospital. In the meantime the field director had arrived. He said, 'What is it?' 'I don't know,' I said, 'but it is probably a leopard.' I mean I'd never known tigers to go into rooms and lift chaps out of their beds. I suggested we look around because if it were a leopard, it could be anywhere, on the roof, under bushes, in the trees behind the quarters, anywhere. We told everyone to go back inside and close their doors.

"We got into the field director's vehicle. He drove and Ambika sat in the middle. We had a forest guard in the back with a spotlight.

"While we were arranging all this, Shafi, another *mahout*, was sitting at the door of his quarters with his small son in his lap. The boy was crying and he was trying to comfort him. As we drove off and our lights faded Shafi got up, handed the boy to his wife, and turned to close the door. As he did so, an animal grabbed him by the neck and pulled him away. Someone shouted at us, 'Come back, the tiger is taking him away,

come back.' When we reversed the vehicle and drove up again we saw the tiger in our headlights, standing over the man. Shafi began to crawl towards his house. Can you imagine? It was very frightening, bloodcurdling, especially the screams. Ambika was in shock. She couldn't speak for twenty-four hours.

"But she had enough presence of mind to get my revolver out of the camera bag and to give it to me. The tigress began to limp off, so I thought, 'It is the lame one'. I also thought she had to be shot. So I turned to the field director and said, 'Ashok, what do you want me to do?' 'Shoot her,' he said. So I got out of the car and shot her in the head. She fell down. I thought to myself, 'If she gets up and mauls somebody my name will be mud.' So I ran up and shot her in the head again.

"We then ran back to Shafi. He had shocking head injuries, his cheek had been slit open from his chin to his ear, you could see his teeth. We stemmed the flow of blood and got him to hospital. Luckily he too survived.

"The next day there was a postmortem on the tigress. She was just skin and bones, there was hardly anything of her. She weighed only about sixty-eight or sixty-nine kilograms I think, poor thing. She was full of worms and had problems with her lungs. She only had a little vegetable matter in her stomach. It was very sad, pathetic really. She should have been dealt with long before that."

We fall silent, watching the stars overhead and fireflies flickering through the grass and listening to the sounds of the jungle. Eventually Brij continues:

"I love coming to Corbett. This place really fascinates me. There's constant change, not just in the seasons; every day there is a change, you see something different. Also it is so exciting, for nothing is controlled or predictable here. Everything happens just all of a sudden. You might see an elephant, or a tiger making a kill; *anything* can happen. It is the wilderness, the wildness, that attracts me to Corbett, it fascinates me more than anything else. Other reserves somehow seem more organized, or had at some stage been interfered with by people—they had been logged, or villages built within them. But this is an absolutely intact wilderness."

9 January

The dew is still dripping from the trees and the mist is just lifting from the valleys when we set out on elephant back across the river from the rest house. Our *mahout* is Subidar Ali. He wears a scarf over his scalp and has grown a beard to hide the terrible scars left by a tiger's mauling in 1984. Otherwise you would not know about his ordeal. Subidar guides his elephant toward a spit of sand at the base of a range of forested hills. Large tiger pug marks march in a straight line downstream. We conclude the tracks are not worth following—the tiger will be miles away by now. Instead we go in the opposite direction to explore an area of tall grass. After a few minutes rhesus macaques and chital give urgent alarm calls low on the hill slopes. We search and search but cannot locate the tiger or leopard.

Belinda and Subidar chat away in Hindi. Subidar says he has no problems about seeing tigers again. He says: "I'm careful and don't take any risks. I will go near them on the elephant as before. All the tigers are now straight and good."

Belinda is enraptured—in her element. Just being in the wilds, hearing if not seeing tigers, and conversing with the *mahout* as in the old days has, for a few days at least, banished the horror of the poachers and traders from the forefront of her mind. The jungle still has the power to do that.

It is not only the jungle but a uniquely Indian combination of things—the warmth of friends, the rest house in the wilderness, the elephant riding. The whole ambience makes it possible not merely to be in the jungle but of the jungle.

For me these few days engender feelings of elation and hope. I feel something here of what Jim Corbett must have felt when he spoke of the "unalloyed joy" of being in the forest but also something of what Belinda read in Lalit Thapar's eyes back in New Delhi.

Postscript

On the evening of 23 July 1996, Brij contacted Belinda with a message from the field director of Corbett Tiger Reserve to say they had information that someone was trying to sell tiger skins in the area. The next day Belinda and her WPSI colleague Ashok Kumar began a five day undercover operation. They booked into a hotel in Ramnagar, a town close to Corbett. The hotel is right next door to the Project Tiger office. Posing as buyers, Belinda and Ashok persuaded several traders, including the man who is believed to be the leading tiger poacher and trader in the area, Deen Dayal Belwal, to show their hand. Belwal and his gang offered, but did not produce, three tiger skeletons and seven tiger skins. After much negotiating, a deal was made to "buy" one tiger skin and one tiger skeleton. To be supplied with more, Belinda and Ashok would have had to give a cash advance. Late in the night of Sunday 28 July, Belwal and an associate, Bhagat Singh Negi, brought the skin and skeleton, neatly packed in three bags, to the hotel. The skin had a bullet hole in the shoulder and Belwal bragged about how he had shot the animal. The two poachers and traders were swiftly arrested by the forest department authorities who were lying in wait. A third poacher escaped into the darkness, but surrendered to the authorities three days later. The forest department "assault" on the hotel involved thirty-five armed personnel.

The Corbett authorities are now following up the enormous amount of information that was revealed during the operation. Belwal turned out to be an even bigger fish than was first thought and his arrest has sent ripples of alarm among traders far beyond the Corbett region. WPSI has hired a lawyer to assist the prosecution and to petition the courts on just how serious the threat is to the survival of India's national animal.

[CHAPTER 28]

THE LAST GREAT TIGER JUNGLE?

The writings of the British so-called sportsmen-hunters, right up to the early years of the twentieth century, frequently described the jungles as containing vast numbers of large mammals. Tigers were so numerous that as many as fifty were shot in a month's shoot. In one case 120 were killed in a three-month shoot. The thousands of chital that used to congregate on Kanha's meadows during the 1980s were the only herds we saw on such a grand scale. In Kaziranga, with elephants, rhinos, and wild water buffalo increasing and well-protected, something of the prolificness of life of a hundred years ago can still be seen. But even here the swamp deer, gaur, and also the tiger are not present in the numbers of old.

There is one place which has the reputation of still having huge numbers of large mammals, and that is Nagarahole National Park in southern India. Even tigers and two other predators of large mammals—leopards and red dogs—live in the teak and rosewood forests and on the river flats in healthy stable populations.

As the scientist Ullas Karanth, who studies tigers at Nagarahole, told us at the Tiger Link conference, the number of tigers and other predators in a given area is largely dependent on the abundance of prey animals such as deer, wild pigs, gaur, antelope, and monkeys. It has been established that in places where prey is plentiful, a female tiger's range is about ten square kilometers, whereas in places where prey is scarce, in Siberia for example, a tigress' range is of necessity several hundred square kilometers. A male tiger's range in an area with abundant prey overlaps that of about three females. Besides these resident adult tigers there are transients consisting of adults who have lost their territory but mostly of young ones who have not yet established their own range. As tigers can raise two or more cubs per litter every three years or so these transients can be plentiful. It was most likely the transients that swelled the bags of last century's hunters.

We travel to Nagarahole to talk with Ullas Karanth in his study area and in the hope of experiencing one of India's last optimum jungles, to feel something of what the first British explorers must have felt when they entered the pristine forests.

Nagarahole National Park— 13 January 1996

Nagarahole in the 1990s has become one of the most important reserves in the world for saving the tiger. Unlike Kaziranga, another crucial national park, it is not the uncompromising armed protection that projects its significance beyond that of other places. Nagarahole's transcendent importance is the combination of it being one of the last of India's great jungles and the work done there by the wildlife biologist Ullas Karanth on tigers and their prey. It is a combination that in many ways holds the key to the tiger's survival. The results of the scientific work carried out at Nagarahole by Ullas, and increasingly in other parts of India, can be applied throughout the country.

Ullas is one of only two scientists studying tigers full-time in India. His ongoing project is also the only long-term study of this carnivore ever undertaken here. The American George Schaller's pioneering study in Kanha in the 1960s was of just two years duration. The only other long-term study on tigers is carried out by the Smithsonian Institution of the U.S.A. and the Wildlife Conservation Department of Nepal in Nepal's Chitwan National Park.

This afternoon we visit Ullas at his field station. We sit and talk about tigers, tiger conservation, and Nagarahole in the shade of trees growing on the bank of a small stream.

Ullas is a slender man in his forties. His shock of black hair and his mustache are flecked with gray. His eyes sparkle with intelligence and humor. There is a no-nonsense, businesslike air about him. Every minute of his time is organized, not with any single-minded rigidity; it is just that he has work to do and wants to get on with it. His English is eloquent and accented with the soft rolling sounds of the south rather than the sharp angularities of speech of the Hindi-speaking north. What he says is trenchant and forthright, which sometimes gets him into trouble with bureaucrats and politicians. Belinda and Ullas have known each other for some years. They like each other and each admires what the other is doing.

Belinda asks Ullas how he became a scientist and about his special interest in the tiger. He says:

"My interest in wildlife goes way back to my childhood when I used to watch birds. The tiger always interested me. I get this electric feeling when I see the animal in the jungle—every time, without exception. It is so perfect and a rare combination of beauty and power. For me there is a kind of passion involved in working with the tiger. It can never be cold and clinical like if you were a bacteriologist or a microbiologist. There is also a special fascination about being in the jungle watching all the large animals. It sort of takes you back to the Pleistocene before man arrived and started knocking things around.

"As a scientist, though, I'm not interested in just the tiger but the whole predator/prey relationship. The carnivore fauna in India is so rich and diverse—roughly 25 percent of the world's carnivore species exist in India—that it is a most fascinating place if you're interested in carnivore ecology."

I ask Ullas if science can provide the information to save the tiger.

"I think it is more complex than that," he says. "If you

compare conservation to some kind of enterprise like a factory or a business, then the managers, the protection people, the education people all have a role to play. The role of good science in all this is to set the benchmark standards as to what, potentially, can happen in a given park—what you can achieve if you do a good job. The second role is one of evaluation to see if your management is succeeding or not. If you try to manage a park without scientific input, purely on intuitive natural history, it is like running a corporation without accountants and auditors. You don't know if you're running at a profit or a loss. So our role is to be the accountants and auditors in this big enterprise called conservation. It's an important role but not the end-all. Research alone will not save the tiger, but without it you don't know if you're failing or succeeding.

"In the past little or no heed was paid to scientists in tiger conservation or any other wildlife conservation. Over the last ten years things have improved, but so far only on a policy level. In terms of actually encouraging and supporting research in the field, we still have a long way to go. You could compare the problem with India's wildlife conservation program with running the country's healthcare program without input from doctors. We have park managers, amateur naturalists, photographers, writers, filmmakers, and all sorts of people advising the government on wildlife protection programs. Conspicuously absent are trained field biologists."

We ask if there is still prime unlogged teak and rosewood forest left in Nagarahole.

"No. Nowhere in India," Ullas says, "do you find old-growth forests that have never been touched like you would find in Zaire or parts of Amazonia. Probably nowhere in Asia because man has been around for too long in these forests.

But there are good stands of forest that have only been selectively logged twenty or even thirty years ago. Nagarahole is currently an extremely productive and rich habitat. It is a mixed forest in an area of comparatively high rainfall and some fertile soils. The rich understory has large stands of a very nutritious bamboo. Then there are the areas of swampy ground where all kinds of sedges come up. It is *far* more productive for ungulates than sal forest, for example.

"Only recently has Nagarahole come good. When I first came here as a student in 1967 the place was being hammered. It had more valuable timbers than other forests around here and loggers, poachers, and other pressures were tearing the place apart. It was a bloody mess.

"It was only after 1970 when Mr. Chinappa came here as a range officer that protection began. As early as 1974 you could see the changes for the better and by the mid-1980s it had become what it is now. It's still getting better, it's recovering. It is a success story I have seen unfold over the years. On my first visit I saw two chital and maybe a couple of gaur. Now when you go on one round you see a thousand chital and maybe a hundred gaur.

"The state government made a great sacrifice when it made Nagarahole an effectively protected National Park in the 1970s. The timber revenue alone was worth ten crore rupees [roughly $12,500,000 at the then–exchange rate] a year. For a while they continued harvesting the teak plantations, but three years ago they stopped even that.

"Nagarahole was fortunate, particularly in the early days, that it had some good managers. In the late 1970s they resettled about 2,000 people and removed even more cattle from the swampy areas. Chinappa, of course, also made a big difference—he was the best, the finest, and most incorruptible example of that early crew. And it was not easy. Because of his uncompromising stance he made a tremendous number of enemies. He arrested more than fifty poachers during his twenty-five years here. He had encounters which resulted in exchanges of gunfire in which poachers and members of his staff died.

"Some of his enemies tried to frame him for murder in a case that was not connected with anything inside the park at all. A forest guard went and shot somebody in a private quarrel and they tried to pin it on Chinappa. Not long after that there was a riot in the park in which people burnt my car, Chinappa's house, and thirty square kilometers of the forest. That was only a few years ago, in 1992.

A large tusker bathes in the river shallows.

"This Nagarahole success story and some others around the country were made possible through a kind of chemistry that was abroad in India between 1974 and 1984. There were three things that happened. One was Mrs. Indira Gandhi's leadership. The second was the existence of the much maligned state Forest Departments. With all their faults we have this one bureaucracy in this country which is capable of wielding a big stick and protecting wildlife. If you go to southeast Asia there is no such bureaucracy and reserves exist on paper only. Here in India, especially years ago, there was an arm of the government that stopped poaching, controlled forest fires, evicted illegal squatters, and so on. The third force was a vocal middle class that really fought for wildlife. Not at all like the environmentalist mess that exists now.

Wildlife biologist Ullas Karanth (center, holding photographs) with his researchers and associates looking at tiger identification photographs taken with Dr. Karanth's camera traps.

"My study here is specifically on tiger ecology—what is the density of the tiger population, how do you estimate their numbers, what kind of densities can they attain in good habitats, what is the size of the female range, and so on. Another aspect of my study, and one that really fascinates me, is the relationship between tigers, leopards, and red dogs and their prey. Here is this very complex community of ungulate prey, all packed in at high densities, ranging in size from gaur to barking deer—how do those three predators partition this prey resource?

"We have gained some insights as a result of the reliable methods we developed for estimating prey. So far people have concentrated only on counting tigers, using very dubious methods. They are concerned whether there are three tigers less than last year or perhaps there are four more. But nobody bothered about prey and the prey holds the key for tiger conservation. Tigers can pretty much look after themselves, what you really need to look at and manage is the prey base. This emerged really clearly in Nagarahole where we found astonishing prey densities. We are talking about large,

hoofed animals reaching densities of seventy to eighty per square kilometer. This is just what the tiger requires. Another fascinating thing we discovered was that all three predators—tiger, leopard, and red dog—shared the same habitat and all three attained very high densities. The key, it appears from my studies, is not only the fact that there is a lot of prey, but that it is available in all size classes. The tiger takes mostly the largest species, gaur and sambar, but few chital, even though there are a hell of a lot of chital. The leopard and the red dog focus on the chital. So all three predators coexist. Which is not the case in Kanha for example. There's only one major prey really and that is chital. Everybody's going for it and the leopard is largely excluded from Kanha's central area. They live more around the periphery, around the villages. The same is true of the *terai* country of Chitwan and I imagine Kaziranga.

"It has been known for some time that the more prey there is, the smaller the tiger's range. In effect you can pack more tigers into an area if you have more prey. A female's range in Nagarahole is about ten or eleven square kilometers, which is about as small as it gets. It is roughly the same as what they found in Chitwan in Nepal. But we found that in Nagarahole there is more overlap between the females' ranges, which means that there are even more tigers here. Another thing that is very different from Chitwan is that here there are a lot more transients. Because of the superabundance of prey, Nagarahole has a hell of a lot of both male and female transients—and therefore even more tigers.

"To my knowledge Nagarahole could well have the highest density of tigers anywhere. But I would really like to look at places like Kaziranga and Manas which have not been surveyed and could be in the same league."

"So Nagarahole must be one of the key places in the long-term future of the tiger?" Belinda suggests.

"One of them," Ullas asserts. "I think there are thirty or forty places in India like that, or at least potentially. That should be our goal, to identify and save these places instead of trying to save the tiger everywhere—in degraded forests or tiny pockets and other areas without any future. Focus on the better places, work on them to make them better.

"I'm not as pessimistic as other people about the tiger's survival. I think there'll be some places which will be fairly secure, where the prey is secure and the tigers will keep producing enough of a surplus to keep the populations going. How many of those places will remain depends on how focused we are on keeping tiger habitats free from exploitation.

"This must be possible in the small areas of natural habitat that are left. We're talking about roughly 1 percent of India's land area—it is not as though conservation was claiming huge tracts of land. Even if you didn't preserve this minuscule 1 percent you are not going to solve any problem that you couldn't solve with the 99 percent. It's absurd to say, as some people do, that India is a poor country so let's sacrifice the last 1 percent of the natural environment and solve our problems. We have to take a very hard protectionist view, a view that prevailed in the 1970s when India's wildlife conservation movement began. Then it got diluted with all kinds of social activism and an attitude of having your cake and eating it too. Which you can't."

★   ★   ★

We talk on for hours. When we finally turn in for the night, at the forest rest house close to Ullas' field station, the jungle is alive with sounds—crickets, frogs, owls, a distant elephant.

But here too there is a management malaise, as we saw in so many reserves—absentee range officers, poaching (though, as far as Belinda could establish, not of tigers), wood cutting, increased cattle grazing, illegal fishing, low staff morale, no money for equipment, and so on. Tomorrow there will be a rally of tribals, inside the park, stirred up by local politicians. To gain votes the politicians want to give the tribals title to their village land inside the park, something that would destroy Nagarahole, instead of settling them outside the reserve. Ullas feels confident all these problems will be solved.

★   ★   ★

Despite the creeping dispiritedness of park management, not just in Nagarahole but throughout India, we cannot help but be influenced by Ullas' optimism, especially the next afternoon when we have one of our most exciting wildlife experiences. We walk in tall mixed forest with towering teak and rosewood trees where we are surrounded by brilliant birds from paradise flycatchers to giant woodpeckers. At the Kabini River five otters tease a mugger crocodile basking on a sandbank, while ospreys, storks, and night herons catch fish. At a water hole we are closely surrounded by hundreds of large mammals—elephants, gaur, sambar, chital, wild pigs, bonnet macaques, red dogs. At dusk a leopard walks out of the undergrowth and surveys its domain from a prominent rock. A tiger roars not far away.

It cannot have been very different to the jungles of 150 years ago.

In 1996 there are still great wild places in India, places that have all their wildlife, where the animals and plants reign supreme and where you walk among them on their own terms.

EPILOGUE I

In 1974, when we set out to discover the wonders of the Indian jungles, we were wide-eyed and overawed not just by the splendor of the wildlife but also by the inspiring work done by conservationists. The natural habitat began to flourish.

In the 1980s there was a consolidation, a building on the pioneering work of the previous decade. In the 1990s it all began to fall apart. This fact came to public notice only through the unyielding determination of Belinda, Ashok Kumar, Ullas Karanth, and a shamefully small number of other people. Once incontrovertible evidence of the steep decline of tigers was presented, others took up the running effectively. But there was no groundswell of public opinion to save the tiger as there had been in the 1970s.

Our travels of 1995 and 1996 gave us the opportunity to find out what had happened to the jungles that so inspired us twenty years before. What happened in Kanha, Kaziranga, and Ranthambhore we have already related. But what of the others?

Manas may be on the path to annihilation. All large mammals, but especially elephants and rhinos, are reportedly killed in significant numbers. The place is still in the hands of insurgents and the poaching of animals and trees continues.

In southern India, pressures continue on all reserves, but seem less severe than those in most parts of the country. In the late 1970s and early 1980s, Clifford Rice, an American zoologist, studied the Nilgiri tahr and other mammals at Eravikulam. The mountain goats became so used to him that he could touch them. In the last few years, however, the Indian scientist A. J. T. Johnsingh reported a steep decline in the numbers of large mammals there. Liontailed macaques still live in the Ashambu Hills and a few other patches of primary rain forest in the Western Ghats. There are still elephants and also tigers in Periyar, but nearly all tusk-bearing elephants have been killed for their ivory. The number of gaur fluctuates greatly as the wild bovines are susceptible to rinderpest, a fatal disease periodically brought into this and other parks by domestic cattle.

At Tiger Haven the leopards Juliet and Harriet learned to fend for themselves in the Dudhwa forests, although Harriet never abandoned her links with Billy Arjan Singh. According to Billy they both mated with Prince and produced litters of cubs. Tragically, after a few years both Juliet and Harriet were found dead near Tiger Haven, apparently poisoned by local village people.

In September 1976 Billy brought a tiger cub, whom he called Tara, from an English zoo to Tiger Haven with the view of making her a wild, free-living tigress. On 16 January 1978 Tara departed from Tiger Haven into Dudhwa's jungles in the company of a wild male tiger. Billy saw the two together from time to time for another year. After that, Billy is convinced she lived in Dudhwa for many years, while the park authorities say she died.

At the same time Billy continued to lobby to have Dudhwa upgraded from Sanctuary to National Park—which was accomplished in 1977. In the 1980s, its status was further enhanced when it was made a Project Tiger reserve.

Through his writings, the numerous films and magazine stories about him, and his example as an uncompromising crusader, Billy was enormously influential in furthering the cause of wildlife conservation in India. He stimulated interest and caught the imagination of millions of people both inside and outside India. He was a major catalyst who created the climate in which wildlife conservation thrived. It is something that should be remembered now that Billy is often sidelined as an old and embittered man by the more glib city-based conservationists of the 1990s.

Keoladeo at Bharatpur has actually improved. Cows and buffaloes no longer graze there and village people no longer loot the national park's trees and grasses. But it was touch and go several times. Two ruinous droughts, battles with village people in which five of them were killed in a confrontation with police, and plans to divert its water supply, all seriously threatened the marshes. But even here all is not well. The plans to divert the water have been postponed, not abandoned, and two species of birds have disappeared.

When we first went to Keoladeo in 1974 and 1975, sixty-three Siberian cranes overwintered there. When we made our film in 1979 and 1980, thirty-three of the birds came to the marshes. None were seen between February 1993 and February 1996. The birds migrate from within the Arctic Circle in Siberia, and are sometimes killed as they move across Afghanistan and Pakistan. Another much larger population of Siberian cranes overwinters in China.

Two pairs of ring-tailed fishing eagles nested at Keoladeo for as long as people can remember and others came as occasional visitors. During the 1980s all fishing eagles disappeared from the region. It is speculated that the use of pesticides on the lands around Keoladeo caused their demise.

In Saurashtra wild asses still roam the salt flats of Kutch. Two years after our visit Velvadar was hit by a cyclone. Eight days of rain reduced the plain to a quagmire. Blackbuck, their food trapped under water, shivering and wet, became bogged in the sticky soil. More than 1,000 perished. But they bounced back and recently we saw a photograph of herds of the antelopes in grass so tall they could barely look over it.

The lions in the Gir Forest numbered about 180 in 1974. Over the years their numbers steadily increased till they stabilized at around 300. But there are many problems. As one newspaper

In February 1996, Siberian cranes unexpectedly returned to Keoladeo after it was thought this wintering population had become extinct.

put it, "undercurrents of anxiety are gripping forest officials." The major cause of concern is the steep decline of the lions' natural prey. This has put greater pressure on the herdsmen and

their cattle both inside and outside the reserve. It was reported that in 1989 to 1990 seventy-three people were attacked by lions. Twenty people died from their injuries. Over the same period lions are said to have killed 2,618 head of cattle.

Additional homes for the lions have been sought since the 1920s. It was, and still is, very risky to have all your Asiatic lions in one reserve no matter how well-managed it is. Should a deadly and contagious disease break out among them, they would soon be extinct. In the 1920s, 1930s, and 1950s attempts were made to establish lions in other reserves. All failed. A new, more determined, and better-prepared attempt will soon be made to translocate a pride of Gir lions to Kuno Palpur Reserve in central India.

In 1995 and 1996 the onslaught on reserves and wildlife, especially tigers, continues. In December 1995 three tusker elephants were killed in Rajaji National Park, which is close to Corbett National Park, and a leopard was found in a trap. In the same month tiger and leopard skins were recovered near Kanha. An acquaintance who spends several months each year in Kaladhungi, close to where Jim Corbett used to have his farm, said that the winter of 1995 to 1996 was strangely silent. There were no tiger roars or even alarm calls for the first time ever. Over several months three tigers were found dead in forests close to Corbett National Park. The local people said they had been poisoned; the Forest Department insisted they died of natural causes. Two tigers were found dead inside Ranthambhore. The forest guards told Fateh Singh both tigers had bullet wounds in their heads. The senior staff, after destroying the carcasses, said the tigers had been killed in territorial fights.

But there was good news as well. In Bhitarkanika the destruction of mangroves and the building of roads and bridges inside the sanctuary was stopped. The World Bank–funded shrimp culture projects were put on hold. The move to denotify Bhitarkanika failed. All this resulted from the actions of conservationists. In 1994, 700,000 ridley turtles came to nest on their *arribada* island.

A few days after I returned to Australia in February I received the following letter from Belinda:

On 1 February a miracle happened. After an absence of three years, four Siberian cranes suddenly appeared at Keoladeo—three adults and a chick. The chick has a white band on its leg, which means it was banded by my Russian friend Alexander Sorokin in Siberia in July last year. He has been studying the parents since 1981.

During 1994 and 1995 Belinda and her colleagues made their point—poaching and trading, the negligence of park management, and the failure to enforce the wildlife protection laws were combining to push the tiger over the edge. Now that the point has been made, it is not up to her, nor any other individual or nongovernment organization, to deal with the depredation and neglect. It is only the various governments and their agencies that can actually secure the tiger's future. Only they have the resources, can frame and enforce the laws, and can appoint or dismiss park managers.

The future for the tiger and other wildlife does not look optimistic. The Indian governments of the 1990s do not seem interested in environmental conservation. The best that can be said is that they are indifferent. It is this wall of indifference and willful ignorance that conservationists always come up against, that stops progress being made. Their hope is that if they hammer at this wall long enough it may eventually crumble and fall.

At the end of 1995, for example, the new minister for the environment and forests at the central government, in answer to a question in Parliament, stated that in 1995 only one tiger was killed by poachers. The inference was that tiger poaching is not a problem. Still the authorities do not want to face the destruction of the tiger squarely. Belinda and her team were able to prove conclusively, using police and forest department records, that seventy-three tigers were killed by poachers in 1995 and sixty-three in 1994. The actual total is, of course, far higher, as only an estimated one in ten tigers killed by poachers is ever recovered.

Of the nearly 100 poachers and traders Belinda and her colleagues were instrumental in having arrested only one or two are still behind bars—on firearms charges, not poaching charges. All the others are out on bail and it is unlikely any of them will ever be convicted—the courts are too slow and the laws have too many loopholes. Most of the culprits are back in business.

Sometimes it seems as if India is about to surrender its proud heritage in conservation, and some of its most magnificent plants and animals, including the tiger—its national symbol—to the criminal and corrupt. If the tiger, rhino, elephant, musk deer, lion, and others disappear, if Manas and Ranthambhore are extinguished, it is not for some noble humanitarian cause. They will be sacrificed to the greed of those who flout the law and spit in the face of humanity and nature.

And yet our travels also revealed that not all is lost. We saw all the "great" animals and as wide a diversity of habitats as we did in the 1970s. Even the Siberian cranes returned to Keoladeo. We saw a tiger in Ranthambhore and a wolf, which I had never seen before, in Kanha. Manas and perhaps Ranthambhore, two of the most wonderful places on earth, can still be reclaimed by wildlife under the right management. There were inspiring stories, such as the protection of rhinos in Kaziranga, the work of Ullas Karanth, the self-sacrifice and stoicism of Mohammed Zayeed.

The heartening aspect of our travels and Belinda's work is that the revelations of poaching, corruption, and mismanagement, and the malaise of indifference that holds a pistol at the head of the tiger and other wildlife, were discovered before complete, irrevocable destruction had taken place. There is still a small ray of light. With inspired leadership among both politicians and conservationists and the sagacious and incorruptible management of reserves, the tiger will survive in India, and with the tiger most of the subcontinent's other incomparable wildlife.

It is to that end that Belinda and her fellow conservationists will continue to fight, despite the almost daily setbacks. It is as if the tiger were walking the high-wire without a safety net. One slip and it is doomed. The view through the tiger's eyes is bleak but not yet hopeless.

Stanley Breeden
Malanda, Australia
July 1996

EPILOGUE II

Will a legacy of the twentieth century be the extinction of the tiger in the wild? Of all the leading combatants in the fight to save the tiger in India—Ullas Karanth, Valmik Thapar, Ashok Kumar, Bittu Sahgal, Brijendra Singh, Billy Arjan Singh, and myself—only Ullas steadfastly believes we will succeed. The rest of the "tiger gang" has not given up hope, but we are distraught at the lack of effective action on the part of the government and the shortage of funds to expand our own efforts. On the brighter side, it has been conclusively proven that if poaching is reduced, or better still eliminated, and large tracts of tiger habitat protected, tigers can make a rapid comeback.

Of all the tiger range countries, India holds the best chance for sustaining tigers in the wild, but our efforts alone cannot save the tiger. The problem goes far beyond our borders. It is imperative that the use of all tiger parts is banned worldwide and that the main consumer nations, including Japan, China, South Korea, and Taiwan, strictly enforce the immediate prohibition of their sale or possession. Japan, in particular, still allows a thriving legal trade in tiger products. When WPSI sent its conservation officer to a meeting in Tokyo in November 1995, members of the audience literally wept when they heard firsthand the direct connection between the death of a magnificent tiger in the wild and the use of traditional medicine in their homeland. A massive international effort to educate users of oriental medicines and to promote substitutes is imperative.

In India, the government is empowered to protect the tiger, but of late has shown little political will to do so. This is also the case in trying to curb the burgeoning human population. To deal with either of these crises does not win votes. Extradiligent forest officers are seldom supported and indeed are often penalized for doing their job. Committees are formed, excellent reports written, meetings held, but very little action filters through the system and into the field where it is needed so desperately.

Large conservation organizations continue to raise funds and produce glossy magazines on the plight of the tiger, without committing themselves effectively and wholeheartedly to the problem. Foreign donors, perhaps nervous of India's political structure, prefer to contribute lavishly to tiger projects in zoos in the U.S. and Europe, though clearly breeding tigers in captivity for introduction into the wild is no realistic alternative. Such efforts have a dismal track record. Huge amounts are also spent preaching to the converted. Tiger conservation projects in Siberia, which has a population of perhaps 200 to 250 tigers compared to an estimated 3,750 in India, receive ten times the funds that India does.

Of all the leading players, only I have time and again looked into the cold, ruthless eyes of those who make their living killing and selling tigers. I know how confident and successful these people are at going about their business undetected. And it is this knowledge, however incomplete, that gives me relentless energy and determination borne out of anger, to help secure the future of the tiger.

Without political support and adequate funds the time may be near when we will have no alternative but to identify a few large, viable wild tiger populations in India and concentrate all our combined efforts into protecting just these islands. I hope it will not come to that. But this might be the only way of ensuring that the tiger, the most awe-inspiring animal on earth, will still electrify at least a few of the Indian jungles with its presence.

Belinda Wright
New Delhi
July 1996

WILDLIFE PROTECTION SOCIETY OF INDIA

The Wildlife Protection Society of India (WPSI) was formed in 1994 with the specific aim of averting India's wildlife crisis and in particular to provide the additional support and information required to combat the escalating illegal wildlife trade. It is a registered nonprofit organization that has been endorsed by the Indian government. Society board members include eminent conservationists and some of India's leading industrialists. During its short life WPSI has become one of the most effective conservation organizations in the country.

There is an emphasis on saving the tiger primarily because it is a critically endangered species, but also because it is a symbol of India's rich cultural and biological heritage. The tiger's presence in a region encourages protection of its habitat and therefore of all the other wildlife in its domain. If this revered and magnificent animal disappears the political will to protect the forests will be enormously reduced.

The society's projects include:

- a **network of informers** and **undercover investigations** that continually monitor poaching and the illegal wildlife trade. WPSI has assisted the authorities in numerous arrests of offenders and the seizure of illegal wildlife products throughout India, including tiger and leopard skins and bones, ivory, rhino horn, musk, and bear bile. As a direct result, the wildlife trade has greatly slowed and in some areas stopped.
- detailed **field surveys** conducted in forests with high densities of tigers that are outside the tiger reserve network and considered particularly vulnerable. Improved protection measures are developed and recommended to the authorities.
- a comprehensive **database** on Indian wildlife crimes that is continually updated and analyzed. It has exposed the extent of tiger poaching and is used by the media and conservation agencies working to save critically endangered species in the illegal trade, such as the tiger, Indian rhino, Asian elephant, and musk deer.

- **conservation projects** in which WPSI provides expertise and funding to local NGOs and forest communities to directly reduce poaching or other pressures on protected jungles. An example is a relief scheme for owners of domestic animals that are killed by tigers who might otherwise turn to poachers to compensate for their loss.

- **education programs** to spread awareness of the wildlife crisis—to this end, TV documentaries, posters, training workshops, and handbooks for enforcement agencies have been produced. WPSI has carried out workshops on wildlife laws, species identification, and enforcement with the Indo-Tibetan border police at remote outposts along India's border with Tibet. WPSI's documentary about the tiger bone trade, "Bones of Contention," has been widely shown on Indian television. It is shortly to be telecast again in 17 regional languages to reach an audience of 200 million.

- a **cell of lawyers** who regularly assist in the prosecution of important wildlife cases, review wildlife laws, and campaign for constructive amendments.

WPSI's work has already had significant results. The tiger in India is not beyond recovery. India's wildlife crisis can be averted. And you can help. If you would like more information about sponsoring specific WPSI projects or would like to make a donation, please write to:

Wildlife Protection Society of India

M-52 Greater Kailash Part - 1, New Delhi 110048, India. Email: wpsi@vsnl.com Website: www.wpsi-india.org

INDEX